THE CAMPO INDIAN LANDFILL WAR

THE CAMPO INDIAN LANDFILL WAR

THE FIGHT FOR GOLD IN CALIFORNIA'S GARBAGE

BY DAN McGOVERN

UNIVERSITY OF OKLAHOMA PRESS : NORMAN AND LONDON

Library of Congress Cataloging-in-Publication Data

McGovern, Dan, 1942–
  The Campo Indian landfill war : the fight for gold in California's
garbage / by Dan McGovern.
    p. cm.
    Includes bibliographical references (p.   ) and index.
    ISBN: 0–8061–2755–4 (acid-free paper)
    1. Campo Indians—Government relations. 2. Campo Indians—
Economic conditions. 3. Campo Indians—Legal status, laws, etc. 4.
Refuse and refuse disposal—Law and legislation—California—
Campo Indian Reservation. 5. Sanitary landfills—Law and
legislation—California—Campo Indian Reservation. 6. Economic
development—California—Campo Indian Reservation. 7. En-
vironmental policy—California—Campo Indian Reservation. 8.
Campo Indian Reservation (Calif.)—Economic conditions. I. Title.
E99.C19M33 1995
363.72'85—dc20   95–5857
                                                                    CIP

Book design by Bill Cason

The paper in this book meets the guidelines for permanence and
durability of the Committee on Production Guidelines for Book
Longevity of the Council on Library Resources, Inc. ∞

1   2   3   4   5   6   7   8   9   10

To Carolyn. *For being unfailingly kind and supportive to me for over thirty years. For considering me gainfully employed while I took a year off to write this book. And for being my first editor, proofreader, and indexer.*

CONTENTS

ILLUSTRATIONS

ACKNOWLEDGMENTS

THE DEBTS I ACCUMULATED IN WRITING THIS BOOK ARE OF SEV-
eral sorts. First, I am beholden to my former colleagues in Region 9 of the United States Environmental Protection Agency,
who introduced me to the environmental problems of Indian
reservations. Wendell Smith, whose responsibilities include
grant programs to tribes for water quality protection, became
my chief guide to Indian country, as well as one of my dearest
friends. Roccena LaWatch, the coordinator of Indian affairs
in Region 9, and her colleague, Stephen Etsitty, were also invaluable regional resources.

I am especially indebted to Richard Sanderson, the director of the Office of Federal Activities in EPA headquarters,
whose responsibilities include both the coordination of Indian affairs and the review of environmental impact statements.
Having served for over a decade in the leadership of three
federal agencies, I have been privileged to work with hundreds
of outstanding career government employees. None better than
Dick Sanderson. Martin Topper, Dick's colleague and EPA's national coordinator of Indian programs, was also helpful in providing a national perspective.

Second, I am grateful to those who introduced me to the
concerns of the environmental justice community, especially
Richard Moore of the Southwest Network for Environmental
and Economic Justice. When we met, I was an EPA official
and Richard was a representative for a coalition of grassroots
groups who believe that EPA has not treated the environmen-

tal concerns of minority communities equitably. Nevertheless, because Richard and I were determined to talk *to* one another instead of at one another or past one another to the press, a genuine dialogue developed. I am grateful to Richard for giving me and EPA the opportunity to earn his trust and that of the communities he represents.

I also appreciate the assistance of those I interviewed in the course of doing my research. As the text and notes indicate, my greatest debts are owed to the protagonists who personify this conflict—Michael Connolly, the director of the Campo tribe's Environmental Protection Agency, and Donna Tisdale, the organizer of the grassroots group that opposes the tribe's landfill project. I am very grateful to all of my interviewees, but especially to Bradley Angel, Corey Brown, Tom Goldtooth, John Grattan, Taylor Miller, Robert Mussler, Marina Ortega, Florence Shipek, Ed Tisdale, and Arol Wulf.

Gary C. Epperly, who wrote a law school paper on regulating solid waste projects on reservations, kindly shared his insights with me. When I submitted the manuscript to agents and publishers, my secretary Laure Mandin was very helpful.

As a visiting scholar at the Institute of Urban and Regional Development (IURD) of the University of California, Berkeley, I had access to the university libraries, especially the Bancroft Library. I appreciate the assistance of Judith Innes and Kate Blood of IURD and that of the staff of the Bancroft.

Finally, I am indebted to current or former EPA Region 9 employees who worked on this case or allied issues, including Larry Bowerman, Carol Bussey, Christy Camp, Jeanne Geselbracht, Matthew Hagemann, Tom Hagler, Wendy Pulling, Jeff Scott, Jim Vreeland, Linda Wandres, Deanna Wieman, and Jacqueline Wyland.

When I left office, I told my colleagues that I would miss "the opportunity to do good. To do it well. In the company of friends." I am convinced that their only concern has been and will be doing the right thing. But one of the lessons of this case is how excruciatingly difficult it can be to determine what is right.

DAN McGOVERN

Walnut Creek, California

PROLOGUE

I FOUND MIKE CONNOLLY AND DONNA TISDALE AN ODD COUPLE
initially. Apparent antagonists. Yet apparently inseparable. Two
moons trapped in the gravitational field of an unseen planet.
What drew them together?

I encountered Donna and Mike in San Diego at a community meeting hosted by the Environmental Health Coalition.
I was then the regional administrator of the United States
Environmental Protection Agency—the chief federal environmental official in EPA's Region 9, which includes Arizona,
California, Hawaii, and Nevada, as well as 139 Indian tribes.
(I use the term *Indian*, rather than *Native American*, because
in my experience that is the term they most often use themselves.) The San Diego meeting was one in a series organized
by the Southwest Network for Environmental and Economic
Justice to give me a better appreciation of the problems leading many people of color to conclude that their communities
are victims of *environmental racism*. The nation's environmental problems are too often dumped into the backyards of minority communities, the Southwest Network and likeminded
groups contend, because minorities suffer from the lingering
effects of institutional racism, are poorer, and wield less political power.

ENVIRONMENTAL RACISM

Advocates of minority communities are concerned about a
variety of environmental health risks. In the West, one of the

primary concerns of the Latino community is exposure to agricultural pesticides, because the vast majority of hired farmworkers are Latinos. For inner-city minority communities throughout the nation, lead poisoning is a matter of profound concern. The United States has not traditionally analyzed its health data by race, making it very difficult to assess the relationship between race and diseases known to have environmental causes. The notable exception is lead poisoning. Here the data are unambiguous: a significantly higher percentage of black children than white children have unacceptably high blood lead levels, resulting from ingestion of lead-contaminated dirt and dust, which can lead to permanent intelligence impairment.[1]

The pioneering studies of environmental racism involved the relationship between race and the location of large municipal solid waste landfills, which we used to call garbage dumps, and hazardous waste landfills. In 1983, District of Columbia Delegate Walter Fauntroy, who was then chairman of the Congressional Black Caucus, asked the Government Accounting Office (GAO) to study hazardous waste landfills in the eight southeastern states that make up Region 4 of EPA. Although blacks were only about one-fifth of the population of Region 4, the GAO found that in three of the four counties with hazardous waste landfills, the majority of the people were black.[2] In 1987, the role of race in the siting of commercial waste facilities was studied on a national scale. In *Toxic Wastes and Race*, the United Church of Christ reported that the proportion of racial minorities in communities with the largest commercial landfills or the greatest number of commercial waste facilities was three times greater than in communities without such facilities.[3] The evidence that race plays a role in the siting of waste facilities continues to mount, leading the Clinton Administration to open investigations, under the 1964 Civil Rights Act, of facility permits granted by state officials in Louisiana and Mississippi.[4]

The fact that landfills, for example, tend to be concentrated in minority communities is ultimately attributable, environmental justice advocates contend, to racial discrimination. This is the argument they make: Historically, discrimination in employment and housing relegated people of color to poor, segregated communities—ghettoes. Continued discrimination in housing sales and rentals, as well as in mortgage financing, makes it difficult for even the more affluent people of color to buy their way out of the ghettoes. NIMBYism is an acronym of recent coinage, but landfills have never been popular neighbors. The growing realization that the last generation of landfills has proven to be a threat to public health, as well as a nuisance, has simply stiffened the resolve of residents around proposed sites—Not in My Backyard. The NIMBY revolt has made it virtually impossible to site waste facilities in communities with access to political power. But minority communities, poor and excluded from power, do not fare well in NIMBY competition. Therefore, the waste industry and local land use agencies have followed the path of least resistance to the backyards of people of color, consciously targeting them in at least some cases. Everybody gets their garbage picked up but only minority communities get the landfills and incinerators. EPA, environmental justice advocates charge, has too long deferred to local land use agencies, refusing to recognize that minority communities are being discriminated against in fact, if not intentionally.

I had understood that the meeting in San Diego was to focus on the environmental problems of Barrio Logan, a largely Latino neighborhood of the city, where zoning practices permit facilities storing and using hazardous materials, like metal plating shops, to be located right next to homes. During the briefing and tour of the community, I became increasingly perplexed by the presence of Mike Connolly and Donna Tisdale, because clearly they were as much strangers to Barrio Logan as I was. Their principal concern seemed to be chaperoning me, each making sure that the other didn't have a moment alone with me.

When we returned to the Environmental Health Coalition office to discuss what we had seen, I learned that Mike and Donna were embroiled in a controversy involving a different community—a proposal to develop a large commercial solid waste landfill on the Campo Indian reservation near the town of Boulevard, in southeastern San Diego County. At the time of my visit to Barrio Logan, almost every Indian reservation in the United States had been approached by at least one waste company. In San Diego County, which has more reservations (eighteen) than any other county in the United States, three commercial waste projects were under serious consideration. In addition to the Campo project, there were proposals for a solid waste landfill on the Los Coyotes reservation and a hazardous waste incinerator on the La Posta reservation, which adjoins the Campo reservation.

DONNA AND MIKE: ROLE REVERSAL

The Southwest Network for Environmental and Economic Justice, the Indigenous Environmental Network, and San Diego County's Coalition for Indian Rights and its successor, California Indians for Cultural and Environmental Protection, among other organizations, condemn the targeting of Indian reservations as an especially insidious form of environmental racism. Insidious because tribes are being asked—for a price—to accept waste projects nobody else wants. Why would Indian tribes agree to projects that other poor minority communities reject? The answer lies in the quasi-sovereign character of Indian reservations, and the fact that reservation land is held in common by the members of the tribe.

When a landfill is proposed for a black or Latino community, for example, the community may reasonably anticipate little but grief. Unlike an Indian tribe, a Latino or black community will not own the proposed site of the waste project.

Therefore, the minority community will not share in the proceeds of the sale or lease of the site. Someone may get rich, possibly even a black or Latino someone, but not the minority community as a whole. Admittedly, the county in which the minority community is located will profit from the contribution the proposed facility will make to its tax base, if the project is a private venture. However, the county officials may not—almost assuredly will not, environmental justice advocates would contend—invest the additional tax revenues in the minority community. Finally, the jobs created by the project will not necessarily be filled by members of the minority community. Because they foresee suffering all of the burdens and receiving few of the benefits, black and Latino communities confronting waste projects are increasingly of one mind—Not in Our Backyard.

The situation is different with tribes. Because reservation land is held in common by tribal members, the proceeds derived from the lease of their land for a waste project will accrue to the entire tribe, to be distributed per capita or invested in tribal projects such as subsidized housing or other economic development ventures. The tribe can insist upon preference in hiring, so that jobs created by the project will be available to tribal members.

How powerful the incentives are depends on the size of the pie and the number of slices. If a tribe has thousands of members, the slices may be too thin to provide much of an incentive. For example, the eighteen-thousand-member Rosebud Sioux tribe was guaranteed preference for the sixty to one hundred jobs that the developer claimed would be created by a proposed landfill project on their reservation. "How dumb do they think we are?" commented a tribal member who opposed the project. "They say we have 85 percent unemployment. So we get a mega-dump and what do we have? 84.5 percent."[5] However, if the tribe has three hundred members, like the Campo, or fifteen, like the La Posta, the incentives become proportionately greater.

Although I was familiar with the terms of the debate over reservation waste projects, I was surprised not only by the arguments made that day in San Diego but also by the identity of the advocates. The Southwest Network for Environmental and Economic Justice is a coalition of grassroots groups representing minority communities. Therefore, since the Southwest Network had organized the meeting, I expected the argument against the Campo project to be made by an Indian, perhaps by a Campo. I had attended a meeting in Arizona some weeks earlier where a young Havasupai Indian woman, a member of the Southwest Network, had asked EPA to stop a uranium mining project on the rim of the Grand Canyon that she argued would contaminate the Havasupais' water supply, as well as violate their religious tenets concerning the sacredness of what non-Indians refer to as the environment.

However, Donna Tisdale, who is white, turned out to be the person speaking against the landfill. Moreover, Donna became involved in the Campo controversy not because she had previously been active in the environmental justice movement but because the project would be, almost literally, in her backyard. The reservation boundary and the proposed landfill site are just over the rise from the ranch belonging to Donna and her husband Ed. Donna is convinced that the landfill will inevitably leak and contaminate their water supply. Donna and Backcountry Against Dumps (BAD), the grassroots group she organized among her mostly white neighbors, were in the midst of a legislative battle to kill the Campo project by making it unlawful to deliver waste to a facility not licensed by the state.

Mike Connolly (Misquish) is a member of the Campo tribe. As the chairman of the Campo Environmental Protection Agency, Mike is careful not to become an advocate for the project he is responsible for regulating. However, he vehemently rejects assertions by non-Indians—be they white ranchers, white mainstream environmentalists, or minority environmental justice advocates—that it is "un-Indian" to consider commercial waste facilities as economic development projects. What is at stake, Mike contends, is the very survival of a people. No one wants to live next to a landfill. Neither do the Campos. If they had viable economic development alternatives, they would not have undertaken the project. But they do not have such alternatives, he insists.

After my initial meeting with Mike and Donna in San Diego, I dealt with the Campo project frequently during the remaining months of my tenure as regional administrator. I remain troubled by the case. That is why I have written this book—to try to sort out my thoughts. And perhaps help my friends in the environmental justice movement to sort out their own, for I sense that they don't know what to make of the Campo case. The movement is clearly uncomfortable with a white like Donna who attacks the right of Indians to decide whether to have waste projects on their reservations. But it seems just as uncomfortable with an Indian like Mike who says that a decision in favor of a waste project may be the right choice, under the right conditions.

Mike and Donna have been generous in sharing their files, their thoughts, and their feelings with me. I have come to admire both of them; they are as indefatigable and as effective a pair of advocates as I have ever met. I am in the uncomfortable position of having become a friend to people who are enemies to one another. They have chosen sides, and I have tried not to. I suspect that nothing I say in this book will please both of them. If neither will admit the justice of my portrayal of the other's position, I hope that they will at least find that I have presented their own views honestly and sympathetically.

PART ONE

A THEATER IN A WIDER WAR

CHAPTER ONE

DRAWING THE BATTLE LINES

IN TIP O'NEILL'S PHRASE, ALL POLITICS IS LOCAL. THAT HOLDS true of the politics of environmental justice. Accordingly, our inquiry must begin in the small community of Boulevard, the focus of opposition to the Campo landfill project.

If you were to take Interstate Highway 5 down the coast of megalopolitan southern California, from Los Angeles through Orange County to San Diego, 150 miles or more, you would pass through one vast urban sprawl, unrelieved except for the eighteen miles of coastline below San Clemente belonging to Camp Pendleton, where marines practice amphibious landings and a herd of buffalo roams the coastal mountains running through the 125,000-acre base. However, as has been true since the Spanish established their missions along the coast from San Diego to Sonoma, the population thins out as soon as you move inland. Accordingly, as we drive east from San Diego toward Boulevard for about fifteen miles on Interstate 8, we pass through the high water mark of the population tide that has surged in from the coast, at El Cajon. Until we approach El Cajon, I-8 is ten to twelve lanes wide. In El Cajon the highway drops its load of commuters, like the driftwood line on a beach, and continues diminished, two lanes in each direction.

Instead of strip shopping centers and subdivisions, the highway now passes through barren hills. Mountains appear in the distance and the highway begins to climb, with a sign warning of the possibility of strong winds for the next sixty-five miles. Off the road to the right we see Alpine, the midpoint of our journey. If you lived in Boulevard, or on the Campo reservation, you would have to drive the thirty miles to Alpine, or another fifteen miles to El Cajon, to buy groceries at supermarket prices. Just beyond Alpine a billboard invites us to take a "shortcut to Las Vegas" and play twenty-one at the casino on the Viejas Indian reservation, but we stay on I-8 and enter the Cleveland National Forest, where ninety percent of the vegetation is not broadleaf woodland or conifer forest, but coastal sage scrub, chamise, and other forms of chaparral.

We've been gaining elevation steadily since we left San Diego and sea level some forty miles ago. No hairpin curves. Just interstate highway straightening and flattening everything in its path. At Laguna Summit, elevation 4,055 feet, we see five or six distinct ridge lines of the Peninsular Ranges in the distance, with Mt. Laguna, to the north of the Cuyapaipe Indian reservation, reaching 5,975 feet. In another ten miles we leave the Cleveland National Forest. The adopt-a-highway signs tell us about the interests of the local community groups— the San Diego Trail Riders tidy up this stretch of road, with the Camping Are Us Singles Group maintaining the next couple of miles. About sixty miles into our journey we enter the La Posta reservation, then the Campo reservation, with the Manzanita reservation adjoining it to the north; in two more miles we reach the 4,140-foot Tecate Divide, leave the Campo reservation a mile after that, and take the exit for state highway 94 and Boulevard.

As we leave I-8, we see Boulevard's Buena Vista Motel immediately to our right. Its grounds have served as the site of barbecue fundraisers for Backcountry Against Dumps (BAD). Donna Tisdale says that after one of the barbecues, the woman managing the motel got into an argument with some Indians, including Campos, about the proposed landfill, "and they wound up shooting her car windows out."[1] For whatever reason, the signs—printed and hand lettered—confronting us as we look for the motel office are not welcoming:

NO PUBLIC RESTROOMS
GAS 6 MILES EAST
No
Cigarettes
Matches
Gasoline
Water
Beer
Everything
6 miles east I-8
or
4 miles west I-8
NO PETS ALLOWED

It was not always thus in Boulevard. In 1978, the *San Diego Union* profiled the community of 415 (now 1,330) in an article entitled, "A Right Turn to Contentment." The town, which got its name from settlers who liked to think of it as being on a thoroughfare between San Diego and Imperial County, was described by the writer as "one of the friendliest anywhere." Whenever the Boulevard folks visited a bigger city, they told the reporter, "we can't wait to get home." What made their home sweet, they said, was its "well water, fresh air and slower-paced life." As for excitement, well, a realtor was said to have chased the preacher's AWOL pig down the main street, finally lassoing it. Admittedly, there was some sense of isolation. A popular bumper sticker read, "Where the Hell Is Boulevard?" And a man who had tried to have a phone installed in his office, which was next to the Boulevard post office, complained that the phone company had denied that there was a Boulevard post office. Apparently testing the limits of this rural Twilight Zone, he went to the main post office in San Diego, where "they also denied there was such a thing as a Boulevard Post Office." There was a post office in Boulevard, the reader was assured,

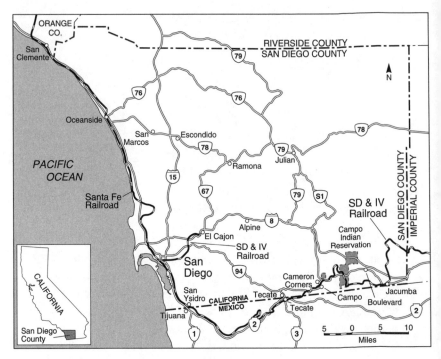

Location of the Campo Indian reservation in San Diego County

though whether the fellow ever got his phone was left hanging.[2]

Boulevard is better known now. It has been the dateline for battle dispatches reporting on the Campo landfill war in national newspapers and television news programs on the networks, even the BBC. However, if Boulevard was ever one of the friendliest places anywhere, that changed in the fall of 1989 when the Campo tribe announced its intention to study the possibility of developing a six-hundred-acre landfill on the reservation for garbage from the cities of San Diego County. The landfill, the citizens of Boulevard and the surrounding area feared, threatened the essential ingredient of the good life they had known—their well water.

NOT IN OUR BACKYARD

The first public meeting to discuss the project was hosted by the Campos in their tribal hall on October 12, 1989. The meeting was a required initial step in the preparation of a federal environmental impact statement (EIS). Under the National Environmental Policy Act (NEPA), any federal agency proposing a major project that may significantly affect the environment must disclose to the public its possible environmental impacts. A large commercial landfill is a major project that may significantly affect the environment. The federal hook here is the fact that reservation land is considered to be held in trust by the Department of Interior for the benefit of a tribe, so that the lease of reservation land by a tribe to a landfill developer requires the approval of the Interior Department. The purpose of the October 12 meeting was, in the parlance of NEPA, *scoping*. Scoping is the process in which the lead agency for NEPA implementation, in this case the Interior Department's Bureau of Indian Affairs, solicits suggestions from citizens and other public agencies regarding the issues that should be examined in the environmental impact statement.

Donna and Ed Tisdale's place, Morningstar Ranch, is southwest of Boulevard. Less than a mile from the Mexican border, the ranch adjoins the Campo reservation near the site of the proposed landfill. The Tisdales' well is about twelve hundred feet from the site, and the announcement of the scoping meeting certainly got their attention. Going door to door, no mean feat in ranch country, Donna tried to make sure that her neighbors were aware of the meeting and of its significance.

As a grassroots organizer, Donna seems to have been cast against type. She grew up in the Imperial Valley—the desert valley east of Boulevard that bloomed when the Colorado River was "regulated" by the Hoover Dam and part of its flow diverted down the All-American Canal. Donna's family moved to town, the outskirts of Brawley, when the children entered school, but she remained "sort of a loner [who] entertained myself." She always had a horse, and she read—mostly horse stories, she confesses. Donna married at the age of eighteen, was widowed young when her husband died in an accident, and then supported herself in a series of jobs, anything she could find, in San Diego. She met her husband Ed while she was working as a secretary in a construction company; she was then in her early twenties.

Ed is older than Donna. He grew up in Tennessee, where his family was flooded out by the Tennessee Valley Authority. That experience made a fighter out of him, Ed says, and he is determined not to be driven from his land again. Ed bought Morningstar Ranch in 1963, while working in construction as an installer of patio room additions and training horses on the side. In 1974, he moved to the ranch, commuting to work in San Diego.

Donna joined Ed in 1977. They worked the land together, without help, clearing the brush and putting in fences. While Ed continued to work in San Diego, Donna did all the chores around the ranch, fed the animals, whatever needed to be done. Around 1985, some health problems made the daily commute to San Diego too much for Ed. Since then the Tisdales have made their living by raising cattle and hay. They have two teenagers and Ed has three children—all in their thirties—and seven grandchildren.

Like many ranchers and farmers, the Tisdales seem to be land-poor. They were offered $750,000 for 60 of their 140 acres before the landfill project was announced, but they live in a double-wide trailer, with the passage of time marked off by the cowboy hats Ed has worn out. Sweat stained, with holes at the peak of the crowns where Ed handled them, the hats hang on the living room wall like the mounted heads of game animals. The Tisdales had hoped to build a house and then rent out the trailer, but that dream, along with a plan to feed organic beef, has had to be deferred because of the expenses of "landfill fightin'," as Ed puts it. The community has spent over a hundred thousand dollars on the campaign to stop the Campo project, and Donna doesn't even want to think about how much the Tisdales have spent themselves. They retained a lawyer and a geologist. Donna and Ed flew to Sacramento once or twice a week while the legislature was considering bills intended to thwart the landfill project. With a copier and a fax machine, the Tisdales' small kitchen became the nerve center of BAD.

The Tisdales have now been fighting the landfill for over four years. Donna searches for the silver lining: "I figure Ed and I must love one another a lot, because we're still married, and if we can make it through this, we'll probably stay married forever." However, she feels that "our whole life has been put on hold." Organizing BAD and managing its campaign against the landfill has been a "financial strain, a strain on family time, emotionally and physically. And it's taken away from the business, because work that I used to do around the ranch . . . it either doesn't get done, or we have to hire someone to do it. We lived close to the bone to begin with." The Tisdales need to put a new roof on the trailer, Donna says, not pay more legal fees. All this was in the future as Donna set out in October of 1989 to encourage her neighbors to show up at the scoping meeting.[3]

One of the neighbors Donna visited became her mentor. While Donna was "kind of a recluse, a quiet country girl," whose community involvement had been pretty much limited to "minimal PTA," Arol Wulf was a lifelong activist. Arol grew up in New York City and traces her roots in activism to SANE, Bertrand Russell's antinuclear campaign. Later, while living in Hollywood, she was active in opposing the Viet Nam war. By coincidence, Arol has long been committed to causes involving Indians; she was a supporter of Leonard Peltier and the American Indian Movement (AIM), as well as of the Navajos who refused to move from Big Mountain, territory disputed by the Hopis and the Navajos.

Arol and her husband had moved to the Boulevard area a few years earlier to establish one of the iterations of their Zendik Farm, an organic farming commune, or "intentional community," as she prefers to call it. The population of the commune fluctuates between twenty and twenty-five, mostly kids who simply show up, having read about the commune in its widely distributed underground magazine. The young people are, Arol says, "in a sense, throw-aways." Not necessarily street kids, they are more likely to be from middle or upper class families. But everybody has given up on them. In the commune they learn arts and crafts, how to cooperate, and how to "activate." In 1990, when her husband's respiratory condition made it impossible for him to remain at the high altitude of the Boulevard region, they moved the commune to Austin, Texas. Before Arol left, though, Donna Tisdale had learned how to "activate" with the best of them.[4]

By all accounts, the scoping meeting at the tribal hall did not go well. The Campos' neighbors may have misunderstood the very limited purpose such a meeting is intended to serve—eliciting concerns that should be explored in subsequent phases of the EIS process. They were expecting—demanding—answers on the spot, and they didn't receive them. Moreover, the battle was joined on one of the implications of Indian sovereignty—the extent to which Indians have the right to make decisions concerning their own land when those decisions will affect their neighbors.

Mike Connolly, who became the chairman of the Campo Environmental Protection Agency when it was subsequently formed, was not at the scoping meeting. However, as he has reconstructed it, there was a failure to communicate. The Campos, Mike says, had *not* decided to develop a landfill at that point. They had merely decided to conduct an EIS to

study the possibility. They recognized that federal law established constraints upon any community's freedom to pursue
such a project, and they had no desire to take unwarranted risks
with their own environment or that of their neighbors. They
invited the participation of their neighbors in the EIS process,
welcomed their comments, and intended to take them seriously. However, *subject to federal law*, they insisted upon their
right to do whatever they ultimately thought best concerning
their own land. At the scoping meeting their neighbors seemed
to be challenging that fundamental right. Stung, the Campos
shot back: We can do whatever we want, and there's nothing
you can do about it.5 This might explain the impression Donna
took away from the meeting—"that it was a done deal, that
they were going to do it regardless of our concerns, and it was
kind of an in-your-face attitude." For Arol it was a disquieting
experience, "to find myself, you know, against the Indians," but
she felt that her non-Indian neighbors were being "railroaded."
As they were walking out of the meeting, people said, well, it
looks like this is going to happen. Arol thought, "Fuck that!"
She and Donna began to organize BAD.6

CRAWLING OUT OF THE HILLS TO SAY:
NO WATER, NO FUTURE

Two weeks later, on October 26, 1989, a crowd of several hundred crammed into the Boulevard fire station's two-engine ga-
rage to protest the landfill project. Donna and Arol, sitting at
the speaker's table with three other members of the nascent
organization, seemed to relish their incongruity. Donna introduced Arol as "our resident hippie"; Arol acknowledged the
introduction by identifying herself as "your local cult leader."
However, as if to compensate for the paisley teardrop tattoo
on her cheek that branded her as an outsider, Arol had chosen to wear a conservative loose-fitting top and skirt that any
countrywoman would have considered appropriate for a dressy
occasion. Donna, on the other hand, was dressed in a bright

red western shirt with silver stars, jeans, and red cowboy boots. Donna's appearance contrasted sharply with her manner, which was brisk, earnest, and, despite the self-deprecating remarks about one's oratorical skills that are obligatory in community meetings, remarkably self-possessed. She had clearly emerged as the leader of the motley crew that was assembling for the first time. "Indians, cowboys, ranchers, rednecks, bikers and . . . hippies. We've crawled out of the hills to have our say: No water, no future."[7]

The two-hour meeting was divided about evenly between scheduled speakers and give-and-take with the audience. The overriding concern expressed by Donna and her neighbors involved groundwater contamination—the possibility that the household hazardous waste routinely deposited in municipal landfills would leach into the aquifer underlying the Campo site and poison the wells upon which the Boulevard area is entirely dependent. After Donna, Arol, and other local people shared their research and misgivings concerning landfills in general and the Campo project in particular, two grassroots organizers spoke. A representative of Greenpeace condemned waste companies for exploiting Indian poverty, reported that Greenpeace had been fighting the Campo developer (then Ogden Martin) at various sites throughout California, and pledged that Greenpeace "will offer its services and its resources to help you fight this company." To Donna's bitter disappointment, Greenpeace would later withdraw its support. Greenpeace's policy is to decline involvement in a campaign against a reservation waste project unless its assistance is solicited by members of the tribe.[8]

The other "outside agitator" invited to address this self-described assemblage of ranchers and rednecks was a representative of the Citizen's Clearinghouse for Hazardous Wastes (CCHW), the organization formed by Lois Gibbs following the Love Canal calamity. CCHW is an invaluable resource for fledgling grassroots groups like BAD, providing them "fact packs" on topics such as landfill liners, dossiers on individual waste companies, and how-to publications on organizing and tactics. Far more accomplished than the Greenpeace organizer at working an angry crowd, the CCHW representative challenged the developer to stand up. There was bound to be a representative of Ogden Martin among them, she told the audience, "because there's always somebody from the opposite side here. If you are here, do you have the guts to point out where you are? [Pause.] I didn't think so." The standard line of waste companies, she continued, was: It's your garbage; it has to go somewhere. "I'd like to tell them where they can stick it, but I won't." These applause lines were balanced by an appeal to members of the audience to take personal responsibility for waste reduction. After offering the support of CCHW, she concluded with an appeal to action: "You have a beautiful backyard here. Do your damnedest to save it!"

The CCHW representative anticipated the charge that much of the opposition to the Campo project is inspired by racism. "Do not let Ogden, do not let the county make you lose your focus. They will try to make it a red man/white man issue. It is not!" Donna echoed her sentiments: "We will have to unite as a community—red and white—to fight this project. If we are divided . . . we will all lose. There is no question about it."

Ironically, the most inflammatory speakers at the rally were two Indian women—Shirley Bautista and Karen Hopkins-Davies—Assiniboine Sioux who lived near the Campo reservation. Bautista complained that "for many, many years my people have been exploited by large corporations such as this. Many of our people have come up with cancer. Children. We have had sterilization among our young people, deformed babies. Just all kinds of things." Bautista's statement—"We as Native People do not believe in the destruction of our Mother Earth"—was greeted with shouts of approval from the almost exclusively white audience.

Karen Hopkins-Davies, Bautista's adult daughter, addressed incendiary rhetorical questions to the Campos, who were not present. "Are you willing to endanger your own future generations for immediate cash rewards? Here are some things that you and they can look forward to: cancer, birth defects, miscarriages, mental retardation, and sterility. In other words, genocide. . . . In the past," Hopkins-Davies continued, "it has been the greed of the white man that has led to the destruction of the Indian people. Now are you . . . going to be the ones selling out your own people?"[9]

Interviewed later, Campo tribal chairman Ralph Goff rejected the idea that the tribe and BAD were necessarily on opposing sides. "I don't feel there are sides to it. If it can't be done right, it won't be done. We're on the same side." What he objected to, Goff said, was the implication that Indians couldn't do things right. The landfill's opponents "just can't believe that we could put a good project together."[10]

However, at the Boulevard rally it was an Indian—Karen Hopkins-Davies—who expressly questioned whether Ralph Goff really understood the potential dangers posed by the project, whether he was sincere in claiming that he retained an open mind on the matter, and whether he was genuinely interested in carrying on a dialogue with the reservation's neighbors. Hopkins-Davies told the audience that she had spent over an hour on the phone that day talking to Goff. "My heart told me that this man is deceived; he does not know what is going to happen." She recounted their conversation: "I said, 'What recourse do we have?' [Goff] said, 'None. It's already been decided.' And I said, 'How can it already be decided?' He said, 'We have already decided that we're going ahead, and we're going to do this.'" Hopkins-Davies rejected sovereignty as a grounds for defending the project. "Now, I realize that they're a sovereign nation. That was my biggest issue, growing up. 'I'm a [member of] a sovereign nation.' But my concern right now is," she continued, that the Campo leaders were "not even trained," but were willing to "take [the project] on, no matter what the consequences are." "I asked [Goff] to come here tonight," she reported, but he had replied, "I don't know if I can fit it in my schedule."[11]

WE ALL DRINK THE SAME WATER

As the landfill war progressed, the Campos continued to decline battle on terrain chosen by their opponents. The chamber of commerce in Campo, a community west of Boulevard and of the Campo reservation, provided the forum for BAD's second public meeting. A plainly anguished chamber official opened the meeting by explaining that Ralph Goff would not be present. "I would be much happier if we had Ralph Goff and the Indians here, and I've got to take part of the blame for that. We contacted Ralph, but we'd already set this thing up. He felt that he should have been in on it from the beginning, and he's right. What we really wanted here tonight was information from both sides." Ralph Goff had decided against attending the meeting, Mike Connolly says, because BAD had sent out a flyer advertising it as a rally against the landfill.[12]

Donna and her neighbors had proven to be quick studies in the activist arts of cultivating the press and convincing politicians that their choice is restricted to leading the parade or being run over by it. The presence at the Boulevard rally of a reporter from the *Los Angeles Times* had been noted and applauded. Two days later a long story on the controversy—featuring interviews with the "Unlikely Allies," Donna and Arol—had appeared on the front page of the local news section of the *Times'* San Diego edition.[13] By the time BAD made its presentation to the chamber of commerce in Campo, less than three months later, the landfill controversy had been the subject of a story in the *New York Times* that was almost fifty column inches long.[14]

At the Boulevard meeting, Arol had complained that BAD was getting the run-around from government: Congressman

Duncan Hunter's office had deflected their entreaties, saying that landfills were a county issue; the county, in turn, had claimed the matter was outside its competence, referring them to state and federal agencies; and EPA officials had completed BAD's frustration by saying that neither the state nor EPA had jurisdiction over a landfill on an Indian reservation. A man standing to the side of the fire station, near the American flag and ladders, reacted by urging everyone in the audience to write a postcard to George Bailey, the county supervisor representing their district, telling him: "I don't want to hear why you can't [do anything]. I want action, and I want an answer." If everyone in the room would do that, the man continued, "I can guarantee you that our supervisor will put it at the head of his agenda." He suggested the same approach with Congressman Hunter, but added: "You have to be tougher with him because he is so firmly entrenched. But you can say: 'I was at a meeting with 250 people. We agreed that if you start doing something and keep us informed, we'll work for you. If you don't, we'll walk the precincts and get you out of there.'"

When Bob Stuart, a representative of Supervisor Bailey, rose to assure the audience that Bailey "is as concerned as you are about possible contamination of your groundwater," the reaction was decidedly hostile. Deftly exploiting the potential good cop/bad cop dynamic, Donna had urged the audience not to repay Stuart's attendance at their meeting by "mugging" him. A doubtlessly grateful Stuart added: "Supervisor Bailey is listening to you." "He's going to have to now," Donna predicted.[15]

When the chamber of commerce met in Campo three months later, BAD was well on its way to making Donna's prediction come true. In addition to a representative of Supervisor Bailey, Donna announced, representatives of the state assemblyman and two congressmen were expected to attend the meeting. Moreover, Donna continued, BAD had in the interim met personally with the elected officials themselves, not just with their staffers. BAD had succeeded, Donna sensed, in convincing the politicians that the proposed landfill would be a "potential disaster" for the area.

The elected officials representing the area surrounding the proposed landfill did come to view the project as a potential disaster, though they may have been more concerned with the political groundswell it had already generated than with the groundwater contamination it might cause in the future. Supervisor Bailey soon came into BAD's camp. Upon his retirement, Bailey was replaced by his chief of staff, Dianne Jacob, who made opposition to the landfill a key plank in her campaign platform. As predicted, enlisting Congressman Duncan Hunter in the cause proved to be more difficult. According to Donna, the turning point came in January 1991, a year after the meeting at the chamber of commerce in Campo, when the *Los Angeles Times* reported that Hunter's constituents had complained bitterly of his failure to attend another large meeting organized by BAD to protest a proposal to build a hazardous waste incinerator on the La Posta reservation, which adjoins the Campo reservation. Hunter made amends by becoming BAD's advocate in Washington, particularly with the Secretary of Interior, who can quash reservation waste projects by refusing to approve the lease of reservation land to the developers of the proposed facilities. However, the politician who climbed onto the bandwagon first, grabbing for the reins, was the state assemblyman who represented the district, Steve Peace. Even before BAD made its case to the chamber of commerce in Campo, Assemblyman Peace had written to Donna that he intended to introduce legislation that would prohibit cities from using landfills that were not subject to state regulation.[16] The Campos, like other tribes, bitterly resist assertions of state jurisdiction. One of the reasons is that state officials, the Campos believe, consistently side with the larger, wealthier off-reservation community. In

Mike Connolly's view, Assemblyman Peace's intervention was calamitous. It encouraged BAD, Mike believes, to focus its efforts on denying the Campos the right to make a decision concerning the landfill, rather than on influencing the decision the Campos would make.

By the time BAD made its presentation to the chamber of commerce in Campo, the issue of racism had been prominently featured in press accounts of the landfill controversy. According to the *New York Times*, Ralph Goff had "suggested that the opposition was rooted in bigotry. 'The issue is simple. They do not want a landfill regardless if it is safe or not. The only reason is they are saying Indians are not able to do it.'"[17] (Mike Connolly insists that Ralph Goff did *not* say or think that everyone who opposed the landfill was a racist. After all, Mike says, the opponents of the project then included members of the Campo tribe.)[18] At the chamber meeting, Donna and Arol rejected the charge of racism. "We would be fighting anybody that was trying to put a dump in our area. This has nothing to do with race," Donna assured the audience. The charge elicited a more personal response from Arol: "I am married to an Indian! My children are quarter-Indian. And they want to call me an Indian-hater!" Actually, she added wryly, "You might call me an Indian-lover."

Of the some half-dozen speakers BAD had invited, three were Indians. One of them, a representative of C.A.R.E. (Citizens Against Ruining our Environment), had to cancel at the last minute because of the flu. (Formed in 1989 by Navajo tribal members, C.A.R.E. had waged a successful campaign against a hazardous waste incinerator and landfill project proposed for their community in Dilkon, Arizona. In June 1990, C.A.R.E. hosted a conference entitled "Protecting Mother Earth: The Toxic Threat to Indian Land" that was attended by over two hundred Indian delegates from thirty tribes.) Lou Grass, a member of the National Congress of American Indians who taught at nearby Imperial Valley College, made a scholarly presentation on soil chemistry and heavy metals. Filling a portable blackboard with chemical symbols, while Donna served as the easel, the earnest professor was not a spellbinder.

But Madonna Thunderhawk was. A member of the Cheyenne River Sioux nation in western South Dakota, Thunderhawk attended the meeting at the invitation of Shirley Bautista. Thunderhawk's credentials as an Indian rights activist seem unimpeachable. A member of WARN (Women of All Red Nations), an organization formed to advocate Indian treaty rights, she had participated in the occupation of the South Dakota hamlet of Wounded Knee by the American Indian Movement in 1973. Middle-aged, slender, with large horn-rim glasses, and her dark hair drawn back severely, Madonna Thunderhawk looked like Lily Tomlin playing the dramatic role of her lifetime. Speaking plainly, slowly, softly, she was the epitome of gravitas.

Her primary interest now, Thunderhawk explained, was organizing communities to resist industrial development that threatens their groundwater, as uranium operations had contaminated wells in her region. She was not, she acknowledged, an expert on landfills, her experience having been limited to the mining industry. She was convinced, however, that BAD could learn a lesson from the battles she and her neighbors had fought against mining pollution in the Dakotas. "So how do we stop Corporate America? . . . We did it by forming what we called the Black Hills Alliance. And probably for the first time in history the cowboys and Indians got together. Because we made groundwater the issue." She was not, she added, suggesting that uniting on that one issue had enabled the cowboys and Indians to overcome everything else that divided them. "We're not that naive. We understand human nature. And we understand racism." However, they had managed to recognize the consequences of a simple fact: "We all drink the same water. Contamination knows no boundaries of any kind. And once you've got cancer, it's all over with. I don't care how much money you have, or what color your skin is. You're the Walking Dead."[19]

Arol concedes that some of the opponents of the landfill are racists. At the first rally, one of the members of Arol's commune heard an old woman say, "Why all this fuss? Just give me a box of bullets, and we'll get rid of those Indians." Indeed, looking back on the experience, Arol stresses: "There are always, always threats of violence up there. People, especially the men, saying, 'Hey, don't even worry about the congressman or all that. We'll just blow it up. A couple of people die, they won't put it in.'" It was very tempting, Arol admits, to "get into 'monkey wrenching' and all the rest of it." However, she and Donna decided from the outset to "go the legislative way." They were determined "to work it through the system," Arol recalls, "even though I don't believe in the system. I really don't."[20]

Arol is not alone is sensing that violence is always an alternative in the backcountry. Around Boulevard, Donna says, not having gunfights is a major accomplishment. "I am really concerned that this thing may end up in bloodshed. I seriously am. That's why I'm fighting so hard," she explains. "Every time we have some kind of function, or we send out a mailer, and we don't try to inflame people, but we try to get them interested, I always get comments like, 'Well, you know, little lady, you're doing a good job, but when you lose, we're going to do it our way.' The looks of these people, and the reputations and stuff, I take them seriously," she reveals. "And there's people on the other side that are just as capable of committing acts of violence. This is still the Wild West; we don't have a lot of law enforcement. People tend to take things into their own hands, and I don't want to see that," Donna insists.[21]

Ed Tisdale is a tall man with pairs of tattoos—sentimental references to his parents and sisters acquired when he joined the navy right out of high school—running up his long arms onto his shoulders. He says he has had to "smack" some would-be supporters who were undermining BAD's cause by threatening violence. However, it appears that Donna must have to "smack" Ed, too, upon occasion. In a television interview, Ed said, "I've got to think that my government is going to protect me because I've paid my taxes. And I'd like to think that if my government don't do that, somewhere in the Constitution, I do believe it's written somewhere that if your government can't protect you, then by God you do it yourself."[22] The Campos would agree. They gave up counting on the government to protect them a long time ago.

BUT WHOSE BACKYARD IS IT?

Before the coming of whites, the territory of the Campos and other bands of Kumeyaay Indians extended from the Colorado River to the Pacific Ocean, for fifty miles north and south of what became the U.S.–Mexico border. Shortly after it entered the Union, the state of California prevailed upon the United States Senate to reject treaties negotiated by federal commissioners that would have reserved a modicum of their land to the Kumeyaays.[23] Following the Civil War, the mountain Kumeyaay, who had successfully defended their territory from Spanish and then Mexican invaders, were overwhelmed by the Americans. By 1875, the Commissioner of Indian Affairs reported that all of the arable land in Kumeyaay territory had been seized by white settlers.[24] In 1893, when the federal government finally established a reservation for the Campos, only about one hundred of the five thousand Kumeyaay who had once lived in the surrounding region survived.[25]

The Campos had ranged from the mountains to the ocean, not merely gathering food but practicing a highly sophisticated plant husbandry. Now they were expected to support themselves on a barren 710-acre reservation—land characterized by the district superintendent of Indian Affairs as "so nearly worthless that a living by farming is out of the question."[26] Predictably, many of them starved to death.[27]

In 1911, the Campos' reservation was enlarged but their living conditions were not much improved. According to testimony before a Senate investigating committee, a boy on the reservation died of starvation in 1932.[28] In 1959, in the first study conducted since the Senate investigation twenty-seven years earlier, the San Diego County welfare department found that the county's Indians were still living under intolerable conditions, partially attributable to discrimination.[29]

Sometimes the discrimination was motivated by undisguised hatred: as recently as the 1920s, the Ku Klux Klan was active in the Campo area.[30] However, misguided paternalism could be even more devastating. Ralph Goff, the Campo chairman, is a member of a generation that was lost to the tribe. Almost all of the reservation children who would now be forty-five to sixty years of age were taken from their "substandard" homes on the reservation and placed with white adoptive parents by county welfare officials. Goff escaped adoption because his white father raised him after his mother died.[31]

The 1959 report of the San Diego County welfare authorities found that the educational opportunities available to the Indian children in the county were also "substandard." Three decades later, the Campo children were still being short-changed. From 1974 to 1989, more than three hundred Campo students went to high school. Seven of them graduated. The fault lay with the school system, the superintendent of the Mountain Empire School District forthrightly admitted.[32] Florence Shipek, the distinguished anthropologist who has studied and befriended the Kumeyaay Indians for forty years, says that as soon as she met Mike Connolly at one of the public hearings on the landfill project she knew that he had not attended the local schools. "His self-assurance, his poise, his use of English—he wouldn't get that out of Mountain Empire [school district]."[33]

Mike Connolly was born in Honolulu, and the family moved frequently because Mike's father was in the air force. After his parents divorced when Mike was eleven, he moved to San Diego with his mother and began to spend school holidays and summer vacations on the Campo reservation with his maternal grandparents. When Mike graduated from high school, his father, who was then working for Boeing in Wichita, got him a job on the production line, drilling holes in aircraft parts. A year later, facing a layoff and lacking seniority, Mike joined the army. He served three years as a medical specialist in a ranger battalion, and then, after a stint as an oilfield roughneck, returned to Boeing, taking a heavy load of classes at Wichita State University as well. At Wichita State he met his wife Peggy.

In 1982, laid off during one of Boeing's periodic contractions, Mike obtained a position with Rockwell in El Segundo, California, as a production planner on the B1B bomber. He worked at Rockwell for four years, moving into manufacturing engineering, while continuing to pursue his bachelor's degree at Long Beach State. In 1986, Mike went to work for Rohr in San Diego as a senior manufacturing engineer. Soon after he joined Rohr, Mike, Peggy and their children moved to the Campo reservation. He commuted to work in San Diego.

Mike was elected to the Campo executive council in 1987. Since the tribe then had next to no income, all of the tribal government officials volunteered their time. As a member of the executive council, Mike directed the search for the chairman of the Campo Environmental Protection Agency (CEPA). Although the eventual goal of the Campo EPA is to exercise broad responsibility for protecting all aspects of the reservation environment, the initial task of the director would be managing the creation of an agency, system of laws, and code of regulations to govern the landfill. Mike felt it was critical that the person representing the tribe with the hostile off-reservation community have a "brown face" and not find it necessary to defer constantly to consultants on technical questions. At the salary the tribe could afford, $40,000 a year, they did not attract such a candidate. Therefore, Mike accepted the job himself, taking a $15,000 pay cut from his position at Rohr. When he became CEPA chairman, Mike had five years of college and more than a decade of engineering experience, but no bachelor's degree. He has since earned his degree at National University in San Diego, which has a program geared to working adults. Mike has also taken extensive training appropriate to his current responsibilities. For example, as a result of our initial meeting in San Diego, EPA funded training for him in dealing with emergencies involving hazardous materials. Mike is now qualified to provide such training himself, and Indian and non-Indian emergency response personnel, including some firefighters from Boulevard, have attended his courses.[34]

In 1987, when the Campo tribe first began considering landfill proposals, the unemployment rate of the tribe was seventy-nine percent; fewer than half of those who did have jobs made more than $7,000 a year; and the annual budget of the tribal government was only $15,000. In 1992, tribal unemployment had been reduced to thirty percent, and annual tribal government revenues had skyrocketed to $700,000, all because of funding provided by the waste company during the development phase of the project. If the project begins operations, the Campo tribal government should earn as much as $3 million per year, and the tribal members should have full employment.[35]

The Campos have lived in dire poverty for more than a century. They believe that the landfill project offers them real hope, the first hope they've had since the coming of whites, that their children's lives can be better than their own. The Campos are not prepared to let others make this decision for them.

Environmental justice advocates, including many Indians, are concerned that the waste industry is trying to exploit the poverty of the Campos and other tribes, making them offers they cannot refuse for projects no one else wants, no one should want. Mike admits the danger of exploitation, but argues that it is paternalistic—indeed, racist—to assume that Indians are not smart enough to protect themselves in dealings with non-Indians, or wise enough to protect their reservation environment and their own long-term interests. An Indian tribe should listen to the arguments made by environmental justice advocates and other environmentalists against waste projects in general, Mike says. And it should obtain the best expert opinion available to assess the merits of specific proposals. But the sovereign right of the tribe, subject to federal law, to make land use decisions concerning its own reservation must be respected. Donna and BAD should have dealt directly with the Campos and tried to influence their decision, instead of asking the state legislature to take away the tribe's right to make the decision, Mike contends.

Donna responds that Mike is advocating a kind of reverse racism by insisting that non-Indians defer to the decisions of tribal governments. The stakes are high for the Tisdales and their neighbors, too. The Campo landfill could contaminate the aquifer that is the sole source of drinking water for four hundred square miles, killing the entire region. They refuse to tie one hand behind their backs. For grassroots environmental groups like BAD, government is all too often part of the problem, not the solution. Indeed, there would be no need for grassroots groups, they argue, if the governmental institutions that are supposed to protect the environment actually fulfilled their responsibilities. Perceived derelictions of duty by government officials force grassroots groups to engage in no-holds-barred, take-no-prisoners campaigns against their decisions. If the executive branch fails to do its job, environmentalists go to court. If the trial court reads the law too narrowly, they appeal. If judicial relief is ultimately denied, they lobby the legislature to make the law so clear that bureaucrats and judges can no longer ignore it. If the reform bill is defeated, they campaign against the legislators who opposed it. Groups like BAD don't trust the local, state, and federal officials who are in theory accountable to them. Why, Donna asks, should they trust tribal governments in which they can have no role?

CHAPTER TWO

RESERVATIONS: THE WASTE INDUSTRY'S LAST FRONTIER

WHY HAS INDIAN COUNTRY BECOME THE LAST FRONTIER OF THE waste industry? The most compelling reason was discussed in chapter one. Waste companies began approaching Indian reservations in the late 1980s because they anticipated a warmer welcome there than they were receiving elsewhere. Waste facilities were being turned away from the backyards of the nation, first in upper and middle class white neighborhoods, and, increasingly, in poor and minority neighborhoods. Projects rejected by other, equally poor communities would be attractive to Indian tribes, some waste companies reasoned, because the tribes as landowners would directly benefit from the taxes, fees, and jobs created by the projects. That, however, is not the reason given by waste company representatives.

A HAPPY COINCIDENCE OF SCIENCE AND MORALS?

In one interview, a spokesman for O&G Industries, a Connecticut firm, explained the company's interest in developing a five-thousand-acre landfill on the Rosebud Sioux reservation in South Dakota, just miles from where *Dancing with Wolves* was filmed, on *humanitarian* grounds. "It was devastating for me to see how poor the people are," Maurice Hoben, an officer of O&G Industries, told one reporter. "I had never seen such poverty, not even in New York City. Putting 10, 20, 30 people to work as [the facility] gets built will give them a feel of capitalism, and a hope for future opportunity where there is no hope now. That's why they have an alcohol problem."[1]

However, in another interview, Hoben said that O&G's search for a *safe* site had led it to the Rosebud reservation. "We looked at sites in South Carolina and in Florida, which from a marketing point of view are much better than South Dakota, but we didn't like the geological characteristics of the land," said Hoben. "We feel that because of the geography and the geology of this particular site in South Dakota, it may well be the safest landfill in North America."[2]

Notwithstanding the explanations given by O&G's Hoben, tribal officials do not attribute the interest of waste companies in Indian country to a happy coincidence of science and morals. "We as a tribe don't have any sort of regulations at all when it comes to the environment," explained Ike Schmidt, vice president of the Rosebud tribal council. "These companies know this, and that's why they're here."[3]

Waste-Tech Services, Inc. reached agreements with tribal leaders, agreements later overthrown by tribal members, to build commercial hazardous waste incinerators on the Kaw reservation in Oklahoma and the Kaibab-Paiute reservation in Arizona. Elliot Cooper, vice president of Waste-Tech's environmental operations, admitted that his company had approached the reservations in order to avoid increasingly restrictive laws being enacted by states. "If we build a 75-ton facility in a state, they can change their mind [and reduce its capacity] in the midst of our project, even though . . . the extra capacity is necessary for us to make a profit." Cooper gave an Arizona case as an example. The state had entered into a contract with a company to build a hazardous waste disposal facility; according to the company's projections, the oversized facility would not earn a profit unless it imported seventy percent of the waste from other states. Subsequently, Arizona passed legislation reducing the amount of waste a facility could import to forty percent.

California would be the principal market for an Arizona hazardous waste facility, as California is a net exporter of hazardous waste. Waste-Tech had originally considered building a facility in California but Cooper says the company was told by state officials, "Don't waste your time here. It's too political." To service the California market from Arizona, while avoiding Arizona's restrictions on the import of hazardous waste, Waste-Tech decided to locate on an Arizona reservation. "The only way to get into business was to use the trust status of Indian lands," Cooper explained. "Utah already had two projects within 10 miles, and Nevada has an indirect law that says no California waste can be imported, and now Arizona is a problem," he said. "Our only option was Indian land."4

During the negotiations with Waste-Tech, Cecil Scott, the business manager of the Kaibab-Paiutes, was under no illusions as to the company's interest in the reservation, which he attributed to the "allure of bypassing city, county and state regulations."5 Though Maurice Hoben apparently neglected to mention it when he listed the reasons for O&G's interest in the Rosebud Sioux reservation, escaping state regulatory jurisdiction does seem to have been a significant factor in that case, too. The proposed agreement between the company and the tribe provided: "The parties understand, contemplate, and agree that in no event shall any environmental regulations or standards of the State of South Dakota be applicable to this project."6 "Worse yet," noted South Dakota Senator Tom Daschle, "the contract forbids the Sioux from enacting new laws to govern the waste project."7

The question of whether a state's authority to regulate commercial waste projects within its borders extends to projects on Indian reservations has never been resolved by the United States Supreme Court. It will be discussed at length in chapter seven. Greatly oversimplified, the argument that states do *not* have regulatory authority over reservation waste projects runs as follows: Before they were conquered by the

United States, Indian tribes were *sovereign* nations, exercising supreme and exclusive authority over their peoples and territories. Even now tribes retain limited sovereignty. They are subordinate to the federal government but not to the states, unless Congress provides otherwise. And Congress has not granted states authority over reservation environmental affairs. To the contrary, it is the policy of the federal government to promote tribal self-regulation in environmental matters, just as it has been federal policy to promote tribal economic development projects, like commercial landfills and hazardous waste incinerators.

Perhaps the most egregious example of a waste company's seeking to exploit Indian country as a haven from state authority involves the Lower Brule reservation of the Teton Lakota in South Dakota. Writing in *Sierra* magazine, Margaret Knox reported that the tribe, whose "only economic assets are a gambling casino of dubious financial health and a tribally owned farm offering seasonal employment," was considering an offer of $4.5 million a year from South Dakota Disposal Systems (SDDS), a Denver-based waste company. What SDDS wanted to buy, Knox asserted, was not Indian land, but Indian sovereignty. The company owned a large tract of land some two hundred miles from the Lower Brule reservation, where it planned a huge landfill that would receive municipal trash by the trainload from markets as far away as Chicago. South Dakota environmentalists, however, had blocked the project in state courts and through referenda, Knox explained. "So SDDS wants to sell the land to Lower Brule for one dollar: presto, instant Indian land. 'If we can't operate in the jurisdiction of the state, we would add it to reservation land and then operate under Indian jurisdiction,' SDDS president Hunter Swanson told reporters last year."[8] Outrageous, yes. But not unprecedented. National Waste Disposal Systems Inc. had made a similar proposal to the Mississippi Choctaws concerning a hazardous waste landfill.[9]

The proposed deal between SDDS and Lower Brule was probably too cute by half. Both the acquisition of the land by Lower Brule and the lease of the landfill site back to SDDS would require the approval of the Secretary of Interior. Given the transparency of the scheme, and the resultant outrage that South Dakota's congressional delegation would express, it is unlikely that such approval would be forthcoming. The Bureau of Indian Affairs has adopted an informal rule preventing tribes from swapping land in order to operate gaming facilities.[10] Moreover, even if administrative approval were granted, the stratagem might well be defeated in court on the ground that the tribe was simply "marketing an exemption" from state laws.[11] In addition, the fact that the proposed landfill would be far removed from the tribe's traditional lands and its people would weigh heavily in determining who—the tribe or the State of South Dakota acting on behalf of its citizens living in the vicinity—has the greater interest in regulating the facility. Finally, even if the courts upheld the ploy, Congress would be free to redress South Dakota's grievances and, as we shall see later in this chapter, very likely would.

IS INDIAN COUNTRY OUTLAW TERRITORY?

The incentives for a waste company to locate on a reservation differ, depending upon whether garbage or hazardous waste is involved. The primary federal law that governs the disposal of waste is the Resource Conservation and Recovery Act, commonly referred to by its acronym—RCRA—pronounced "rickruh." RCRA broadly distinguishes between hazardous waste, on the one hand, and municipal solid waste, what we used to call garbage, on the other. Hazardous waste is material that poses a threat to human health or the environment. Municipal solid waste is the trash and garbage generated at residences, commercial establishments, and institutions; it includes food, yard trimmings, paper, glass, metals, and plastics. Although hazardous and solid waste are subject to different regulatory regimes under RCRA, municipal solid waste does include small quantitities of hazardous ingredients, such as wood preservatives or herbicides. The fact that household waste does have hazardous constituents is one of the reasons that landfills are such unpopular neighbors.

RCRA gives the United States Environmental Protection Agency very different roles in regulating hazardous as opposed to solid waste. EPA is the primary regulatory authority for hazardous waste, although the agency may delegate its authority to a state. That is, EPA issues permits for the design, construction, and operation of hazardous waste facilities, and enforces the conditions of those permits through administrative, civil, and criminal proceedings.

By contrast, the states are the primary regulatory authorities under RCRA for solid waste. Briefly, EPA's role has been limited under the statute to setting minimum standards for solid waste landfills and to establishing guidelines for the development of state programs to manage solid waste. If a state's solid waste management plan satisfied the guidelines, EPA could provide it financial and technical assistance. However, the authority to issue permits for landfills resides in the states, not EPA, as does the authority to enforce the conditions of those permits.

What is the practical significance of this distinction for proposed hazardous or solid waste projects on Indian reservations? For a hazardous waste project, EPA would exercise direct regulatory authority, issuing or denying the necessary permits, conducting inspections to determine whether the permit conditions were being honored, and bringing enforcement actions if they were not.

On the other hand, EPA does *not* have direct regulatory authority over solid waste landfills, regardless of where they are located. Neither do states have regulatory authority over solid waste landfills on reservations, assuming that the sovereignty argument outlined above is valid. That leaves the tribes themselves. However, because of their poverty, most tribes have found it impossible to construct, operate, and regulate modern landfills for their own waste, much less as commercial ventures. Indeed, open dumps are one of the most troubling environmental problems on many reservations. For example, the Oglala Sioux tribe, which had been the subject of at least ten proposals for commercial solid and hazardous waste facilities by 1991, was sued by tribal members for operating open dumps for solid waste generated within the Pine Ridge reservation.[12] In 1989, a representative of the Indian Health Service testified before the Senate Select Committee on Indian Affairs that "only a handful" of the 108 tribally owned landfills complied with then-prevailing EPA regulations, much less the stricter standards EPA had proposed. Mervin Tano of the Council of Energy Resource Tribes added: "There is for most of the tribes an almost total absence of the kind of regulatory infrastructure, technical infrastructure, management infrastructure to handle [solid waste] in a way that is environmentally sound."[13]

One of the incentives for siting a commercial landfill on an Indian reservation, then, would be to exploit the potential regulatory gap. A reservation project might be more profitable because its *costs of regulatory compliance* might be lower. Neither EPA nor the state would have regulatory authority over the project. Assuming that the tribe has full authority to regulate the project, and there is some question concerning tribal authority because RCRA does not expressly address the role of tribes, the tribe would be unlikely to have the *capacity*— the laws, funds, and trained personnel—to regulate the landfill as strictly as the corresponding state would regulate facilities subject to its jurisdiction.

Moreover, some state officials would argue, even if a tribe had the authority and the capacity to regulate a commercial waste project on its reservation, the tribe might be sorely tempted to pull its punches on enforcement because of the overwhelming importance of the facility to its economy. When a company asserts that strict enforcement of environmental regulations will force it to lay off employees or even declare bankruptcy, the governor of a state may find it difficult—no matter how diversified the state's economy—to resist the temptation to pressure regulators to cut the company some slack. This is, of course, especially true in a recession. Without impugning the inherent integrity of tribal officials, the argument continues, is it not likely that the chairman of an impoverished tribe might find it even more difficult to resist such temptation if the regulated facility were the engine driving the reservation economy?

There is another factor that may lead to lower costs of regulatory compliance for a landfill located on a reservation. Some states, most notably California, have adopted standards for the construction and operation of landfills that are stricter than the minimum standards prescribed by EPA. Therefore, even if a landfill on an Indian reservation were operated in full compliance with federal standards, it still might enjoy a significant competitive advantage over landfills located elsewhere in a state.

CAMPOS ASKED TO BE JUDGED ON THEIR OWN MERITS

Mike Connolly contends that, however valid the foregoing arguments may be in the abstract, they are not applicable to the Campo project. In testimony before the United States Senate Select Committee on Indian Affairs, Mike explained how the Campos developed the *capacity* to regulate the proposed landfill. Muht Hei, the tribal corporation the Campos created to manage their business interests in the landfill project, required the landfill developer to agree to underwrite all of the tribe's expenses in developing and implementing its regulatory program. The funding provided by the developer enabled Mike and the Campo EPA to retain law firms with environmental expertise, as well as an environmental engineering firm, to draft the tribe's landfill code and regulations. At the 1991 Senate hearing, Mike estimated that before the landfill ever opens, the tribe's regulatory expenses—for drafting the code and regulations that govern the project, reviewing and commenting upon the federal environmental impact statement, and reviewing the applications for permits to construct and operate the landfill—would "end up costing the developer in the neighborhood of $600,000." (Three years later, the expenses had exceeded $1,000,000 and the landfill had still not received a permit to operate from the Campo EPA.)

The developer, Mike testified, is also required under the contract to underwrite the costs of the tribe's landfill regulatory *enforcement* program. The program will be financed by a tax imposed on waste delivered to the landfill. To promote the use of rail transport, the tribe will tax waste brought in by rail at 25 cents a ton, whereas the tax on waste delivered by truck will be $1.25 a ton. Assuming that 80 percent of the waste is delivered by rail, and that the facility operates at its capacity of 3,000 tons per day, Mike estimated that the tax would yield $50,000 a month, which will be dedicated primarily to the enforcement program. Moreover, the developer has been required to make minimum tax payments of $12,500 per month ever since it entered into a lease for the landfill, the lease being subject to approval by the Bureau of Indian Affairs following the preparation of an environmental impact statement.

The developer has also been required to establish a contingency fund that is to be available to the Campo EPA to cover the costs of remedial actions. The fund is to start at $1 million, and is to be fully funded at $30 million when the landfill closes. "One of the problems you can run into in handling a major solid waste facility is what you do if there is a violation, how can you make sure you have means to take immediate action. What we did was structure within our regulations a unilateral access to the contingency fund by the Campo EPA," Mike informed the committee. "So if there is a violation and we cite the operator and he fails to take action, we can go ahead and access the contingency fund, take immediate action and then settle it with them in court later on."[14]

At the same Senate hearing, Kevin Gover, the tribe's lawyer, spoke to the strictness of the Campos' landfill standards and of their enforcement program. Unlike some other tribes, Gover testified, the Campos had "made no agreements [with the landfill developer] to the effect that we could not be stricter than Federal standards, no agreements that we could not be stricter than State standards. [The developer] will meet whatever standards we determine are appropriate, and whatever that may cost." Indeed, Gover continued, the Campos had "established standards that are stricter than [California] standards."

Moreover, Gover argued, the Campos' enforcement program should be even more effective than California's because it would be focused on a single facility. "Our inspectors, our entire regulatory team, is on site all the time. Whereas the State may have dozens or even hundreds in a State like California that they have to keep track of. So we can really pour the resources into doing one thing and doing it extremely well."[15]

On a subsequent occasion, Gover gave another reason for his belief that the tribe's enforcement program would be more rigorous than the state's—the Campo regulators would be protecting their own home. The Campos "are going to take care of the environment because that's where they're going to live, that's where their kids are going to live. . . . There's no place the Campo Indians can go if they foul the reservation, and so they're going to see that that doesn't happen."[16]

Bradley Angel of Greenpeace enters a dissent. Angel believes that the funding mechanism that made the Campo EPA possible—fees imposed on the developer—fatally undermines the credibility of its enforcement program. *Regulatory capture*, the subservience of an agency to the industry it is supposed to regulate, is always a danger, Angel notes; it is inescapable, he argues, if a regulatory agency is dependent on a single company for its funding.

Angel broke ranks with other environmentalists to support the Campos in their fight against proposed California legislation that asserted state jurisdiction over waste projects on Indian reservations. Condemning such legislation as violative of tribal sovereignty, Angel argued that it would "create a 'white vs. Indian' situation that will set back the efforts of those of us, Indian and non-Indian, who are working together in this struggle" against reservation waste projects.[17] He stresses that he is not questioning the integrity of Campo officials. "I honestly believe that Campo wants to do the right thing," Angel says. "We really support the development of EPAs on reservations. However, we have real concerns with those EPAs that are bought and paid for with money from the waste companies, and that's what Campo primarily is, and that's what we're seeing in a number of other places. . . . If you have a situation where your environmental regulations and your environmental enforcement agency are in existence to regulate a project and are paid for by the owners of that project, it's an absolute on-its-face conflict of interest," Angel asserts. "It's ridiculous. It's insane. And it's going to provide zero environmental enforcement."[18]

In fairness, the Campo EPA is not alone in relying on fees to support its regulatory program. Squeezed between the rising demand for government services and a stagnant or declining tax base, government at all levels has relied increasingly on "user fees" to supplement general revenues. The distinction to be drawn is a matter of degree, not of kind. As Kevin

Gover noted, a state may regulate dozens or even hundreds of landfills. Accordingly, insofar as the state's regulatory program is dependent on user fees, the landfill *industry* may acquire additional leverage with regulators, but individual landfill operators may not. On the other hand, the fees supporting the Campo landfill regulatory program are paid by a single "user." If the developer of the Campo landfill were to abandon the project, all of the employees in the regulatory program would lose their jobs. And the tribe would lose the project it is counting on to deliver it from poverty. It is going too far to say, as Bradley Angel does, that the Campo regulators will therefore inevitably pull their punches. They are, though, faced with a significant conflict of interest.

There is no apparent solution to this dilemma. If a solid waste landfill is not strictly regulated, it poses a significant environmental threat. Few tribes, perhaps none, have the tax base to develop and support an adequate program to regulate a commercial solid waste landfill. The federal government will not subsidize such a program. Therefore, if tribes pursue reservation waste projects, the Campo approach to funding the tribal regulatory program is likely to become the model.

However, assume for the sake of argument that a tribe adopts the same landfill standards as the state in which its reservation is located, and that the tribe enforces its regulations just as rigorously as does the state, so that the costs of regulatory compliance cease to be a factor. Would a company interested in developing a landfill still have an incentive to approach a tribe? Yes. For the simple reason that it may be impossible to do business anywhere else in the state.

The overriding importance of the NIMBY phenomenon is illustrated by the search the United States government is conducting for a community willing to serve as the site for a facility to store nuclear waste until the permanent disposal facility is available. Money seems to be no object. Nevertheless, the search has narrowed down to Indian country.

NUCLEAR WASTE NEGOTIATOR LOOKS FOR MRS RIGHT

Private waste companies are not alone in offering impoverished Indian tribes large sums of money to accept waste projects that are not welcome in other communities. After being turned down by everyone else, the federal government is prepared to pay up to a billion dollars to a tribe willing to store radioactive waste on its reservation until a permanent repository is available some twenty years from now.

The demand for a temporary storage site arises from the fact that spent (used) fuel from nuclear power plants is not being reprocessed and reused, as had been intended, and that a permanent repository for the waste may not be available for decades. Approximately twenty-eight thousand metric tons of spent fuel are currently stored at seventy-two commercial nuclear reactor sites in thirty-five states, and the amount of waste is expected to double by the year 2000. The spent fuel, consisting of solid ceramic uranium pellets about the size of pencil erasers stacked end-to-end inside metal alloy tubes, is removed from the reactors after about three years and stored on-site in deep pools of water. The water serves both to cool the fuel rods and to provide a shield against their radioactivity.

The plan had been to store the spent fuel on-site only temporarily, and then ship it off to a reprocessing plant. However, hoping that other nations using nuclear fuel would follow suit, President Jimmy Carter banned reprocessing in order to prevent the proliferation of plutonium, a by-product of reprocessing and an ingredient of nuclear weapons. President Reagan lifted the ban but reprocessing proved uneconomic in light of abundant supplies and diminished demand for uranium. The Department of Energy now plans to dispose of the spent fuel permanently by burying it one thousand feet or more underground, sealed inside multiple layers of thick steel, in an underground facility designed to contain the radioactivity for up to ten thousand years. Because of technical difficulties and the opposition of state officials, the permanent storage facility the Department of Energy proposes to build at Yucca Mountain, Nevada, will not open until 2010, if then.

Continuing to store the waste where it was produced is not that much of a problem if the plant is still operating. Indeed, the United States General Accounting Office (GAO) has questioned the need for the proposed central temporary storage facility, or MRS (Monitored Retrievable Storage) site. The GAO has concluded that virtually all utilities can store their waste on-site well beyond the scheduled opening of the permanent repository at Yucca Mountain in 2010, and that there is little to choose between on-site and central storage in terms of expense and safety.[19] However, utilities contend, the expense of storing waste on-site becomes prohibitive once a plant is retired. According to the Edison Electric Institute, running the fuel pool in an otherwise inactive plant—keeping the filters, pumps, cooling systems, and water tanks in good repair; maintaining security; and staffing the control room— can cost from $7 million to $21 million a year, and dozens of plants are expected to close in the next two decades.[20]

The nuclear power industry, then, has an enormous incentive to avoid the expense of on-site storage. Moreover, the utilities point out, they have been double-billed for storage. While bearing the expense of on-site storage, they have also been required to contribute to the Nuclear Waste Fund for future federal storage in an MRS facility and eventual disposal in the repository. The federal government is, arguably, legally obligated to provide central storage. Under the Nuclear Waste Policy Act of 1982, the Department of Energy entered into contracts with the nuclear utilities that provide, first, that DOE will take title to their waste after repository operations begin, and, second, that beginning not later than January 31, 1998, DOE will dispose of the waste. On June 21, 1994, twenty states filed suit against DOE, asking a federal court to declare that the agency must take responsibility for the waste by 1998.

Commenting upon the suit, the Michigan attorney general charged the federal government with perpetrating a "$10 billion scam" by requiring that sum from utility ratepayers without making significant progress toward establishing either an interim or permanent storage facility.[21]

Moreover, retaining the radioactive waste on-site may not be a viable solution. The Northern States Power Company in Minnesota proposed to build the sort of dry storage containers at its twin Prairie Island reactors that would be used at the MRS. The utility managed to obtain conditional permission for the project from the state public service commission, only to have to seek special authorization from a state legislature that appeared disinclined to grant it. Without an on-site dry storage facility, the Prairie Island nuclear power plant may have to close in 1995, a little more than halfway through its expected lifetime.[22]

The Department of Energy envisions the Monitored Retrievable Storage facility occupying about five hundred acres and resembling a low rise industrial park. After fuel rods had cooled sufficiently in the wet storage provided at the reactors, they would be shipped by truck or train to the MRS where they would be placed in metal cannisters that would in turn be stored within massive concrete structures—either upright cylinders or modular bunkers. The acronym for the facility derives from the fact that the waste would be continuously *monitored* while stored there, and would be *retrievable* for eventual reshipment to the permanent repository. Pending the availability of the MRS, dry storage facilities of similar design are licensed and operating on-site at three utilities.

The spent fuel is a solid, so it cannot spill, and due to its physical and chemical nature, it cannot explode. However, small amounts of radioactive metallic oxides from the surface of the fuel rods, similar to dust, may be generated in handling. The opponents of the MRS program cite the hazards of handling the spent fuel in the course of packaging and repackaging it for shipment, temporary storage at the MRS, reshipment, and, finally, disposal at the permanent repository. Moreover, the mantra repeated in government publications—that the waste would be shipped in "specially designed and tested casks"—does little to allay the opponents' fears concerning the perils of transportation.[23]

Whatever You Need, You Just Let Us Know

The task of finding a community willing to "host" the MRS was assigned by Congress to the Nuclear Waste Negotiator. The legislation creating the position placed the negotiator in the executive office of the president, but having the president identified with such an unpopular program did not suit the Bush Administration, so the post was not filled and the mission languished for three years, until the law was amended to make the negotiator's office an independent agency. The malicious might suggest that the position has itself been treated ever since as a kind of dumping ground or, more kindly, a consolation prize, for Idaho politicians defeated in tries for higher office. President Bush's appointee, David Leroy, had been Idaho's lieutenant governor and attorney general before losing the race for governor in 1986. (Leroy apparently likes a short commute, for he made Boise the negotiator's official headquarters.) President Clinton appointed Richard Stallings, who was a four-term congressman from Idaho before losing a race for the Senate in 1993.

The Nuclear Waste Fund, which has a balance of $3.8 billion and is growing by hundreds of millions of dollars each year, enables the waste negotiator to hold out enormous incentives to a prospective host community. The incentives include direct financial assistance as well as funds for health care, schools, recreation, environmental cleanups, highway and airport improvements, and general economic development programs.[24] "What is negotiable?" David Leroy, President Bush's negotiator, asked rhetorically. "Virtually anything that a prospective host may wish to discuss is negotiable."[25] At a meeting of the National Conference of American Indians, Leroy made the same point in language intended to resonate with his audience, promising that he could be "as flexible as the wind and the sea" in negotiating the package of benefits to be awarded to a tribe willing to accept the MRS.[26] Robert M. Mussler, who was counsel to Leroy and continues in that position under Stallings, describes Leroy's approach more prosaically. "Would you like new schools? We can give you new schools. You need new roads? You can have new roads. Whatever you need, you just let us know."[27]

Not surprisingly, Leroy raised high expectations. Miller M. Hudson, a negotiator representing the Mescalero Apache tribe, anticipated that the federal government and the nuclear industry would "pour a huge bucket of money over any community" that would take the MRS. Hudson allowed as how $50 million a year would be a reasonable sum. That is steeper than the figure that executives in the nuclear industry are said to have in mind, but it is in the ballpark. Mark D. Luftig, an analyst for Kemper Securities who specializes in utilities, believes that $25 million to $50 million annually "shouldn't be a problem," if a community would accept waste from all the utilities.[28]

Bob Mussler of the nuclear waste negotiator's office characterizes the $50 million sum as a "back-of-the-envelope figure." "We need to do some work to try to understand why [$50 million] and not $500 million," Mussler says. The only guidance offered by Congress is that the figure must be "reasonable," reasonable enough for the agreement to be recast as legislation, passed by Congress and signed by the president.

What would be reasonable compensation for a community's assuming whatever risk to its environment, public health, and image the MRS poses? This question, says Mussler, was "completely ignored" by Leroy, and it is a question that Mussler believes Stallings must address at the outset of his administration. "You can't approach somebody with a black box, and say, wouldn't you like to have what's in the black box?" Sophisticated community officials will not find that approach credible because they realize that "what's behind the curtain is not a cornucopia of whatever you want."[29]

Black box or Pandora's Box, it was sufficiently tempting, at least initially, to lead about thirty counties and Indian tribes to apply for grants of $100,000 to study whether they wished to consider the MRS further. Most of the communities have dropped out. The only remaining applicants seriously considering the project are Indian tribes—the Skull Valley Goshute of Utah, the Fort McDermitt Paiute Shoshone of the Nevada–Oregon border region, the Tonkawa of Oklahoma, and until recently, the Mescalero Apache of New Mexico.

States Veto Participation of Counties

All four counties that received grants to consider hosting the MRS facility ultimately withdrew from consideration because the potential payoff, no matter how large, was insufficient to overcome state and local political opposition. In November 1991, after receiving an MRS study grant, the county commissioners in Grant County, North Dakota, were removed from office, and the project was dropped by their successors. In each of the three other cases, the governor of the state indicated he would exercise his power to veto the county's participation.

In March 1992, referring to the application from Apache County, Arizona, Governor Fife Symington drew a line in the sand: "Let me emphasize that under no circumstances will this administration support a high-level waste storage or disposal site in Arizona, be it temporary or permanent." In August 1992, Wyoming Governor Mike Sullivan halted the efforts of Fremont County, Wyoming, to consider hosting the MRS. In a letter to Fremont County commissioners, Governor Sullivan said: "Are we willing to ignore the experience

history would provide us for the siren song of promised economic benefits . . . [?] As Governor, I say not." Finally, in January 1993, Utah Governor Michael Leavitt vetoed the participation of San Juan County on the ground that Utah would
"suffer significantly from the stigma of being what would be
characterized nationally as a 'nuclear dumping ground.'" He
added: "Anyone who looks realistically at the project agrees
that an MRS site will become a permanent storage site."[30]

Skull Valley Goshutes: Street Smart from Salt Lake City

One of the two tribes to apply for a second-phase grant of $2.8
million to begin environmental studies, conduct consultations
with the off-reservation communities potentially affected, and
enter into preliminary negotiations is the 112-member Skull
Valley band of Goshutes. In the report prepared at the conclusion of the previous study phase, the executive committee of
the Goshutes describe their eighteen-thousand-acre reservation, some eighty miles southwest of Salt Lake City, as being
surrounded by a munitions depot, nerve gas storage facility,
radioactive waste dump, hazardous waste incinerators, and a
magnesium plant "rated by some as the most polluting plant
in the United States."

"Having studied the issue and understanding it, we are
thankful for the media hype and hysteria. If it was not for the
media misinformation and hysteria, the dollar value of this
industrial project would be considerably less," the Goshutes
say. "Let's be serious for a moment and realize that the nerve
gas incinerator and dump out at the Tooele South Area [near
the reservation] is at least 1,000 times more dangerous than
this temporary storage facility could ever hope to be," they
conclude.

When the Goshutes first heard of the MRS program, "we
thought it was a scam, just like all of the numerous other get
rich quick schemes and scams we'd encountered." It sometimes seems to them as if they have been approached by every

"businessman who had failed at anything or simply wanted the Tribe to take the financial risk." The Goshutes include in this category proposals pitched to them to landfill "sludge from New York and New Jersey," and to fund an experimental hazardous waste incinerator.

Having concluded that the MRS project is worthy of further consideration, at least, the Goshutes resent allegations that they are being exploited. "The charges of 'environmental racism' and the need to 'protect' and 'save' us smacks of patronism," they say. "This attitude implies that we are not intelligent enough to make our own business and environmental decisions." Such solicitude is misplaced, asserts tribal attorney Danny Quintana. "We were born at night. But it was not last night. . . . [W]e are street smart from Salt Lake City. If someone can con us let them try."[31]

Mescalero Apaches Make Money, Not Rugs

The first tribe to apply to the nuclear waste negotiator's office for one of the $2.8 million second-phase grants was the Mescalero Apaches. The Mescaleros have a 460,000-acre reservation in south-central New Mexico that they share with the Chiricahua Apaches; the 3,400 members of the two tribes include descendants of Geronimo and Cochise. The Mescaleros have demonstrated considerable initiative in developing the natural resources and recreational attractions of their reservation. The tribe's economic development projects include a lumber company that turns out 16 million board feet a year, a cattle company that raises 7,000 head, a ski resort that draws 250,000 visitors annually, and the 440-room Inn of the Mountain Gods, with a convention center, golf course, and casino. Wendell Chino, who has been president of the tribal council for thirty years, brags: "The Navajos make rugs. The Pueblos make pottery. And the Mescaleros make money." But not enough money. "John Wayne is gone, but the Apache is still here—we are undeveloped, underdeveloped and in desperate need of cash," complains Chino.[32]

The *New York Times* found that "[w]hat little opposition exists within the tribe [to the MRS] is subdued. The tribal council is employer, landlord, local government and family circle, so misgivings are voiced quietly."[33] A member of the the Indigenous Environmental Network (IEN) living on the Mescalero reservation reports that the situation there is "very explosive." Tribal members who oppose the MRS are, the informant tells IEN national spokesman Tom Goldtooth, "threatened with job loss, they lose their house assignments, phones are disconnected," and lives are threatened.[34] Although allegations of intimidation are rejected by tribal officials, President Chino has undeniably discouraged dissenters from discussing the project with outsiders. In a January 1992 letter sent to all tribal members, Chino wrote that "using the white man's influence, T.V. and papers *against your own people* is not the Apache way."[35]

Not all dissent has been stifled, however. At a rally and press conference in Albuquerque sponsored by, among others, the National Environmental Coalition of Native Americans, Mescalero tribal member Tyron Hoahwah complained: "We're living under a dictatorship. We can fight this only if people on the reservation stand up and fight [Chino]."[36] A petition opposing the MRS and calling for a general meeting of the tribe to discuss the pros and cons of the project was reportedly signed by nearly two hundred tribal members.[37]

Rufina Marie Laws, who was defeated by Chino 391 to 176 in the tribe's most recent election, opposes the project on religious grounds. "We were given this land by the Great Spirit. The ground that we walk is the same ground as our forefathers walked upon." Laws says her relatives pleaded with her not to campaign against the waste site, fearing reprisals against the family.[38] The fear of reprisals, Laws charges, proved to be well founded. One evening, her daughter and grandchildren were accosted by three Mescalero women when they stopped at a convenience store. "You're Cindy, aren't you?" one said. "We don't like what your Mom is saying . . . she needs to watch what she's doing about the MRS." Before Laws' daughter could respond, one of the women punched her in the face.[39]

Another outspoken opponent of the MRS, Joseph Geronimo, a teen counselor with the Mescalero Tribal Human Services, also reports retaliation. According to Geronimo, he was attacked at a reservation powwow last year by President Chino's relatives, who threatened to shoot him. Geronimo filed a complaint against his alleged assailants in tribal court, but says that tribal authorities never investigated. Geronimo adds that his brother, Harlan, who had opposed Chino in the previous election, was harassed by unknown "hell raisers," who shot two of his horses and left a bagful of rattlesnakes on his porch. Fred Peso, the director of the Mescalero tribe's MRS project, characterizes the charges as "ludicrous."[40]

Asked about allegations that Mescaleros who oppose the MRS are being intimidated, Bob Mussler of the nuclear waste negotiator's office responds: "This is a sovereign tribe that has a right to govern itself and to elect its representatives. And it is just not our business to get involved in those issues of tribal governance. . . . [I]f there was anything concrete that we had to look at, as opposed to just allegations of people who aren't satisfied," Mussler continues, "then maybe the situation would be different. But right now . . . there ends up being two sides to every story." A federal government agency working with tribes would be in an untenable position, Mussler argues, if it were to say, "we're not going to work with you unless we're satisfied that you govern yourself . . . to our standards. It's a matter of respect [for tribal sovereignty]."[41]

External critics accuse the negotiator of trying to bribe Indian tribes to accept a project that no one else wants. Elmer Savilla, a Quechan writer whose columns appear in tribal newspapers across the country, says of the nuclear waste negotiator: "Mr. Deep Pockets carries a bagful of goodies, including school assistance, health care programs and employment programs. Could this be called bribery?"[42] Bradley Angel of Greenpeace answers Savilla's rhetorical question. "We believe it's unconscionable that desperately needed services, education, roads and money are being used as bribes to put dangerous, high-level nuclear waste on tribal lands."[43]

Vern Nelson, a spokesman for the negotiator, responds that the benefits offered tribes are "entirely appropriate for a host that is voluntarily willing to help solve a national problem. We want to treat everyone fairly and equally—not to do that would be a form of reverse discrimination."[44] Bob Mussler adds that the facts do not support the charge of environmental racism. While solicitations of interest were sent to all federally recognized Indian tribes, the tribes that have expressed serious interest in the MRS are relatively prosperous. "People who make those charges wish they were true," Mussler asserts. "[E]nvironmental racism is something [opponents of the MRS project] have to allege anyhow. Because it's on the checklist." Recalling Wendell Chino's boast that while other tribes make rugs or pottery, the Mescalero Apaches make money, Mussler says that "to suggest that the Mescaleros are desperate is an absolute absurdity. . . . This is the last tribe that you'd expect to be [called] economically depressed, and us preying upon a poor tribe."[45] Perhaps so, but fifty-two percent of Mescalero Apache adults looking for work could not find it in 1989.[46]

Some Mescaleros accuse their white neighbors of condescension in charging that the federal government is exploiting tribal poverty. "The state has always tried to tell the tribe what to do," says Silas Cochise, one of the elders and a great-grandson of the Apache warrior.[47] Senator Ben Nighthorse Campbell of Colorado, the only Indian in the Congress, believes that tribes should have the right to make this decision. However, he, too, is concerned that the waste negotiator may be offering tribes a deal they can't refuse. Drawing a comparison with the treaties Indians signed as the frontier advanced, Campbell observes, "If you're hurting bad enough, you'll sign anything."[48]

States Effectively Veto Tribal Participation

What seemed to make Indian tribes especially promising prospects for the MRS, aside from their dire poverty, was the impression that the participation of a tribe, unlike that of a county, could not be vetoed by the governor. Certainly that is the impression held by tribes. "If the Mescalero Apaches, the Skull Valley Goshutes or the Lower Brule Sioux were to decide to build MRS facilities, New Mexico, Utah and South Dakota could protest. But these states could not, and should never be in a position to legally tell these Reservations what to do," asserts the Goshute executive committee.[49] With regard to nuclear waste, however, state and federal elected officials in New Mexico do not agree with Ben Nighthorse Campbell that tribes should have the opportunity "to make their own mistakes." Senator Jeff Bingaman of New Mexico led a successful effort to amend an energy department appropriations act to bar funding of the grant program that would have provided the Mescaleros $2.8 million to begin environmental studies and negotiations for the MRS.[50]

Senator Bingaman's demonstration that states can, through their congressional delegations, effectively veto the participation of tribes in the MRS program is consistent with the intent of the Nuclear Waste Policy Act, according to the waste negotiator's counsel, Bob Mussler. "The concept of veto is probably already in the legislation, notwithstanding the fact that the tribes would prefer to ignore it." It would be "completely stupid" to ignore the wishes of a governor, Mussler believes. "That just doesn't make sense. It wasn't what was intended [under the statute], and it's going to be a waste of time."[51]

The Mescaleros treated the cutoff of federal funds not as defeat but as an opportunity to cut out the middle man. In April 1994, the tribe announced that it had abandoned the federal program and had instead entered into a partnership with Northern States Power Company of Minnesota and thirty-three other utilities to develop a private interim storage site. The agreement between the Mescaleros and Northern States Power received the blessings of Nuclear Waste Negotiator Richard Stallings. Testifying before a congressional oversight committee, Stallings said, "If the Mescalero-NP consortium can help alleviate some of the need for interim storage . . . I am strongly in favor of it."

The principal casualty of the New Mexico delegation's power play may have been the waste negotiator, not the Mescalero project. Funding for the office is due to expire in January 1995, and Stallings has said there would be "no point" in its reauthorization unless progress is made by then.[52] It remains to be seen whether the negotiator or private utilities will ever find MRS Right. What is clear is that they have confined their search to Indian country.

WHY ARE THE CAMPOS MAKING THEIR STAND ON A LANDFILL?

Indian tribes, we have learned, have an incentive to accept waste facilities that other poor minority communities lack: because the tribes own the proposed sites, they stand to benefit directly from the taxes, fees, and jobs created by the projects. Nevertheless, most of the tribes that have considered commercial waste proposals have ultimately rejected them. More often than not, tribal leaders primarily concerned with economic development initially embrace waste projects, only to be forced to disavow them by grassroots organizations that arise among tribal members.

On the Rosebud Sioux reservation, for example, the Good Road Coalition, named for the Good Road Cemetery located on the proposed site, stopped the landfill project planned by O&G Industries, just as the Native Resource Coalition had earlier defeated a similar proposal by the same company (under a different name) on the neighboring Pine Ridge Sioux reservation.[53] On the Kaibab-Paiute reservation, the successful campaign against Waste-Tech's hazardous waste incinerator project was led by the Paiute Earthkeepers, supported by Native Americans for a Clean Environment. On the Lower Brule reservation, the land swap with South Dakota Disposal Systems advocated by the chairman of the tribe was opposed by tribal members calling themselves the Protectors of the Earth.[54]

The loosely organized grassroots groups took strength from one another. In 1990, a conference entitled "Protecting Mother Earth: The Toxic Threat to Indian Lands" was held in Dilkon, Arizona, and attracted members of thirty tribes. Fifty-seven tribes were represented at the conference the following year, in Black Hills, South Dakota. As a result of the second conference, the Indigenous Environmental Network (IEN) was formed to provide technical support and organizational assistance to tribal members concerned about waste proposals.[55]

Even the nuclear waste negotiator, who would seem to have the wherewithal to make tribes an offer they cannot refuse, has found relatively few takers among them. There are 287 Indian reservations in the nation. Sixteen applied for the first-phase grants to study the MRS program. Only three remain interested. At its third annual conference, on June 6, 1992, at Celilo Village, Oregon, the Indigenous Environmental Network adopted a resolution opposing the storage of nuclear waste on Indian lands and calling upon the tribes participating in the study phase of the MRS program to withdraw from it.[56]

Tom Goldtooth is the environmental director of Minnesota's Red Lake nation, a band of the Ojibways, as well as the chair of the Indigenous Environmental Network. The IEN "would always help a community group if they come and say we need help in stopping a commercial [waste] facility," Goldtooth says. "We would probably be there full force to help them stop [such an] operation." However, "it is a delicate situation because we also support the sovereignty of our tribal leadership," he adds. "These people are our own relatives. So we don't use the militant AIM [American Indian Movement] tactics. We're not into fighting against each other. We're into healing our own community through communication."[57]

Goldtooth admits to being perplexed by the Campo case. "The only thing that I'm always concerned about," he says, "is that the people in the community fully understand all aspects of what they're doing."[58] It has been his experience that tribes considering landfill projects will decide against them, provided they receive information on the "other side." However, the Campos are united in support of the landfill proposal, Goldtooth acknowledges, despite the fact that the arguments against such a project seem to have been given a fair hearing. A scientist who is a technical adviser to IEN went to the Campo reservation and later reported to Goldtooth that the tribal members had been provided information regarding the environmental risks a landfill poses.[59]

Although he is personally opposed to commercial landfill projects, believing them to be inconsistent with the traditional spiritual values of Indian communities, Goldtooth cautions that each case should be considered individually, out of respect for tribal sovereignty. That is what I shall try to do in the remainder of this book—consider the Campo case on its own merits.

The Campo tribe is small, about three hundred persons. Small enough that they can and do make all significant decisions affecting the tribe as a direct democracy, a kind of New England town meeting. After having been consulted at every step of the project, the tribal members have made what they consider to be an informed and responsible decision. They have concluded that the landfill project constitutes the highest economic use of their land, the only viable development opportunity that offers them the promise of economic self-sufficiency. They defend their decision—more fundamentally, their right to make the decision—with the determination of a people who have been pushed to the brink of extermination. How did things come to such a pass? Why are the Campos making their stand on a landfill? Why are they reduced to fighting for the right to dispose of white people's garbage on their land? Why are they so determined to resist assertions of state jurisdiction? Why do they so mistrust the motives of their white neighbors who oppose their project? Why did a grassroots opposition group not arise among the Campos? What combination of external and internal forces united them in support of the project?

To begin to answer these questions, we must inquire into the history of the Campos, their relationship to the land and to the people who took it from them.

PART TWO

THE ORIGINS OF THE WAR

CHAPTER THREE

WHITES AND CALIFORNIA INDIANS

THE FIRST ANGLO-AMERICAN VISITORS TO HISPANIC CALIFOR-
nia—sea otter hunters, beaver trappers, and hide-and-tallow
traders—saw California Indians as an extraordinarily primitive people who posed little threat to them and were of as
little use to them. These visitors from the United States described the Indians as victims of cruelty and exploitation,
which descriptions were part of a larger campaign to under-
mine the moral basis of Mexico's claim to California. If the
Indians themselves were not useful to the visitors, the *image*
of the Indian as victim was very useful as a pretext for sup-
planting the Mexicans and incorporating California into the
United States.[1]

EXPLOITATION

American visitors to California during the Mexican period
were correct in observing that coastal Indians were held in
peonage and that the colony's economy was entirely dependent upon their labor. (Mexico, like Spain, controlled only a
narrow strip of territory along the coast of California; nearly
all of the interior remained under the control of native peoples.) Salvador Vallejo, a ranchero, acknowledged the indis-
pensability of Indian peons: "Our friendly Indians we relied
on very much, for they tilled our soil, pastured our cattle,
sheared our sheep, cut our lumber, built our houses, paddled
our boats, made tiles for our homes, ground our grain, killed

our cattle, dressed their hides for market, and built our unburnt bricks; while the Indian women made excellent servants, took care of our children, made every one of our meals."[2]

Peonage "Makes Slavery Wholly Unnecessary" in Mexican California

Americans muted their criticism of Hispanic exploitation of Indians as they began to settle permanently in California and themselves became dependent upon Indians as their labor supply. Then the practice of peonage came to be seen as fit not for condemnation but for emulation. Although still perceived to be primitive, the Indians were now seen to be useful, even essential, and along with its climate and fertility, one of California's principal attractions.[3]

This attitude is manifested in a letter written by John Marsh which was copied and recopied throughout the United States and is said to have strengthened President James K. Polk's decision to secure California for the United States. Marsh was the first American to establish a medical practice in California; he achieved this distinction by passing himself off as a doctor on the basis of a Harvard bachelor of arts diploma, correctly assuming that he was in the only person in Los Angeles who could read the Latin in which the diploma was written. He later established the first successful rancho in the Central Valley on a huge tract of land he purchased in 1837 at the foot of Mount Diablo, thirty miles east of San Francisco. Marsh responded to American Consul Thomas O. Larkin's call to Anglo settlers to become publicists for California in order to stimulate the immigration that would lead to American annexation. Not incidentally, Marsh sold supplies to settlers at exorbitant profits.[4]

"The Indians of California are easily domesticated, not averse to labor, [and] have a natural aptitude to learn mechanical trades," Marsh wrote Lewis Cass of Michigan, who was the Democratic nominee for the presidency in 1848 and a member of the United States Senate. Marsh told Cass that California Indians were a timid and stupid people who reminded him of Cass's remark that "Indians were only grown up children." Indeed, Marsh said, California Indians were "a real race of infants," who could be taught all the occupations necessary to run a farm, especially "when caught young. . . . Nothing more is necessary for their complete subjugation," Marsh continued, "but kindness in the beginning, and a little well timed severity when manifestly deserved." Moreover, he noted, administering such "well timed severity" was not difficult because the California Indians "submit to flagellation with more humility than the negroes." Concluding his remarks on the "Aborigines of California," Marsh stated: "Throughout all California the Indians are the principal laborers; without them the business of the country could hardly be carried on."[5]

Certainly the business of Johann Augustus Sutter could not have been carried on without Indian serfs. In 1840, Sutter was granted Mexican citizenship and over forty-eight thousand acres of land where Sacramento now stands. Like Marsh, Sutter took the Spanish mission and the Mexican rancho as his models; like Salvador Vallejo, Sutter was entirely dependent upon Indian labor.[6] Indian peonage "make[s] slavery wholly unnecessary here," Sutter commented in a letter.[7] For Sutter's Indian laborers, however, this would seem to have been a distinction with little difference. One pioneer noted that Sutter "had to lock the Indian men and women together in a large room to prevent them from returning to their homes in the mountains at night."[8]

Apprenticeship Makes Peonage Legal in American California

The practices of men like Marsh and Sutter received the support and sanction of the law under legislation enacted by California's first legislature in 1850. Styled an "Act for the Government and Protection of Indians," the law of 1850 prohibited anyone from compelling an Indian to work or to perform any service against his will, "except as provided in this Act." However, under the vagrancy provision, any able-bodied Indian who could not support himself or who was found "loitering and strolling about, or frequenting public places where liquors are sold, begging or leading an immoral or profligate life," was liable to arrest "on the complaint of any resident citizen of the county." Upon conviction of vagrancy, an Indian could be hired out within twenty-four hours to the highest bidder for any term not exceeding four months.[9]

When they needed laborers, ranchers would round up Indians like cattle and have them convicted of vagrancy. If their terms expired while their labor was still required, the Indians would be plied with liquor and then sentenced to another period of forced labor for their profligacy.[10] The impressments generally occurred at harvest time. Consequently, after bringing in the settlers' crops, the Indians faced starvation when they were released, their own harvest season having been lost to them. Out of one band of Indians that were set free after the harvest of 1852, eighteen died of starvation.[11]

Another provision of the law of 1850 established a system of apprenticeship for Indian children. Under the law, to secure the labor of an Indian child, a white person would appear before a justice of the peace with the child's "parents or friends"; upon determining that compulsion was not involved, the justice of the peace would issue a certificate authorizing the white person to have the "care, custody, control, and earnings of such minor, until he or she obtain the age of majority."[12]

Admittedly, the law of 1850 provided that anyone to whom an Indian child was apprenticed or to whom an adult Indian was bailed was required to clothe and feed them properly. However, this requirement was rendered practically unenforceable by the further provision of the law that although Indians could make complaints before a justice of the peace, "in no case shall a white man be convicted of any offence upon the testimony of an Indian."[13] Indeed, in 1851 the *Los*

Angeles Star reported that in Santa Barbara an Indian was murdered in the presence of four or five Indian witnesses, who took the culprit before a magistrate. "Will it be believed that he was almost immediately released from custody, because our laws will not allow an Indian to testify against a white man? The Indians in this part of the State, in the main a harmless race, are left entirely at the mercy of every ruffian in the country," observed the *Star*, "and if something is not done for their protection, the race will shortly become extinct."[14]

As expansive as the apprenticeship provision of the 1850 law was, it did not go far enough for some Californians. In 1856 the *Marysville Herald* recommended that a new law be passed requiring Indian parents "to bind out their children to farmers and others, for a given period, so as to make them useful, and thus conduct them to habits of cleanliness and industry."[15] In 1860, the *Sacramento Standard* urged that the apprenticeship system be enlarged on the ground that the "most humane disposition that could be made of [the Indians], is, probably to reduce them to a mild system of servitude. Call them slaves, coolies or apprentices—it is all the same; supply them with christian masters and make them christian servants."[16]

In 1860 the legislature extended the apprenticeship system to adult Indians by providing that Indians without "settled habitation or means of livelihood" and who had not already "placed themselves under the protection of any white person" could be indentured as apprentices to "any person desirous of obtaining" such Indians. For Indians over the age of twenty, the period of indenture could be as long as ten years, at the discretion of the judge.[17]

Apprenticeship Revealed as Slavery

In 1856, Thomas J. Henley, the superintendent of California Indian affairs, reported that the practice of "kidnapping Indians and selling them into servitude" was being carried on "to an extraordinary extent. I have undoubted evidence that hundreds of Indians have been stolen and carried into settlements and sold; in some instances entire tribes were taken en masse, driven to a convenient point, and such as were suitable for servants, selected from among them, generally the children and young women, while the old men and the infirm were left to starve or make their way back to their mountain homes, as best they could. In many other cases," Henley continued, "it has come to my knowledge that the fathers and mothers have been brutally killed when they refused assistance to the taking away of their children."[18]

Henley's concerns were echoed by George M. Hanson, the superintendent of Indian affairs for the northern district of California. In 1861, Hanson reported that "under the cover" of California's apprenticeship laws, Indians were being kidnapped and sold into slavery by organized gangs. After murdering the Indian men for "alleged offences," the kidnappers "seize the younger Indians and bear them off to the white settlements in every part of the country filling the orders of those who have applied for them at rates, varying from $50 to $200 a piece." This vicious trade was being carried out, Hanson noted, "under the plea of 'Kindness to the poor Indians.'"[19]

Mexican rancheros and early American ranchers like Marsh and Sutter exploited captive Indian labor. What happened in the 1850s was that "the boundary was at last crossed from technical peonage to actual slavery" as Indians were being kidnapped for sale.[20] The prices for Indian slaves depended upon such factors as usefulness, age, sex, and beauty and ranged from thirty to two hundred dollars.[21] An employee of the U.S. Mail Department in northern California testified in 1862: "Indians seven or eight years old are worth $100. It is a d—n poor Indian that's not worth $50."[22]

While kidnapped Indian children were used as servants, the *Marysville Appeal* reported, young Indian women were made to serve both the "purposes of labor and lust." Settlers would pay only sixty dollars for a boy, the *Appeal* observed, but were willing to pay a hundred dollars for "a likely young girl."[23] Among such commodities as tar, acorn, and beads, the *Hiampum Monitor* of February 1, 1855, listed for sale "squaws, fair, middling, inferior, refuse."[24]

EXTERMINATION

The mass migration we call the gold rush placed California Indians at an irretrievable numerical disadvantage. Before the discovery of gold in 1848, Indians outnumbered whites in California by ten to one; by the early 1850s whites outnumbered Indians by two to one.[25] Not only did the white population increase explosively, California's Indians were almost exterminated during the first decade of United States rule. Of the 150,000 Indians living within the present confines of the state in 1845, only 50,000 survived in 1855.[26] (By 1900, there were fewer than 16,000.[27]) Sherburne Cook, who devoted his career to studying this holocaust, observed: "The direct causes of death were disease, the bullet, exposure, and acute starvation. The more remote causes were insane passion for gold, abiding hatred for the Red man, and complete lack of any legal control."[28]

Whites denigrated California's natives as "the poorest sort of Indian." T. Butler King, President Zachary Taylor's personal emissary to California, reported in 1850 that the state's Indians were "the lowest grade of human beings. They live chiefly on acorns, roots, insects, and the kernel of the pine burr; occasionally they catch fish and game. They use the bow and arrow, but are said to be too lazy and effeminate to make successful hunters. They do not appear to have the slightest inclination to cultivate the soil, nor do they attempt it."[29]

To the contrary, prior to the founding of the first Spanish settlement in 1769, California's Indians had adapted to their environment so well that California supported a population of 300,000, much larger than any region of comparable size in

North America north of Mexico. Indeed, California's population density was then about six times the national average.[30] California's Indian population had been cut in half, to about 150,000, by the beginning of the American period. The flood of immigration and the land practices of the immigrants deprived the survivors of the means of sustaining life.

Whites established farms and villages in fertile valleys and rich river bottoms, forcing the Indians to abandon their rancherias and move to less productive areas. Silt from mining operations destroyed fisheries. The whites' cattle ate the native grain grasses and their hogs ate the acorns, the staples in most Indians' diets. White farms and mines destroyed game habitat, and white laws prohibiting Indians from starting brush fires or buying firearms denied Indians both traditional and modern means of competing with whites for the remaining game.[31]

To survive, Indians were forced to raid the livestock and supplies brought in by whites. Retaliation by whites, instead of suppressing the raids, simply forced the Indians further into the mountains where they became even more dependent on raiding for subsistence.[32] Warfare also disrupted the harvest of native plants, preventing the Indians from accumulating enough food for the winter. Moreover, in their retaliatory raids whites would destroy the supplies the Indians had managed to store. The cumulative effect of the conflict was a catastrophic collapse of the Indian population. Actual starvation was less common than chronic malnutrition. The children and the old people, their resistance lowered, were easy prey for the epidemics that swept among the tribes. The birth rate was depressed. An inadequate diet prevented proper development of fetuses, made mothers less able to survive delivery, and reduced their ability to produce enough milk for newborns.[33]

Governor Burnett: Genocide Regrettable, but Inevitable

Cook's account is not the product of 20-20 hindsight. Contemporary statements reveal that unlike the "good Germans" who claimed ignorance of the Jewish holocaust, many white Californians understood perfectly well what was happening to the state's Indians. They had simply hardened their hearts to it, characterizing it as an inevitable consequence of Manifest Destiny.

In his 1851 message to the legislature, Peter H. Burnett, California's first governor, cogently explained the cycle of violence. "We have suddenly spread ourselves over the country in every direction, and appropriated whatever portion of it we pleased to ourselves, without [the Indians'] consent, and without compensation," Burnett noted. "Although these small and scattered tribes have among them no regular government, they have some ideas of existence as a separate and independent people, and some conception of their right to the country, acquired by long, uninterrupted and exclusive possession," he acknowledged. "They have not only seen their country taken from them, but they see their ranks rapidly thinning from the effects of our diseases. They instinctively consider themselves a doomed race; and this leads to despair; and despair prevents them from providing the usual and necessary supply of provisions. This produces starvation, which knows but one law, that of gratification; and the natural result is, that these people kill the first stray animal they find."[34]

With an extraordinary combination of empathy and detachment, Governor Burnett went on to explain that "the white man, to whom time is money, and who labors hard all day to create the comforts of life, cannot sit up all night to watch his property; . . . after being robbed a few times he becomes desperate, and resolves upon a war of extermination." There could be only one outcome, Burnett concluded: "That a war of extermination will continue to be waged between the races, until the Indian race becomes extinct. . . . While we cannot anticipate this result but with painful regret, the inevitable destiny of the race is beyond the power or wisdom of man to avert."[35]

This cycle of violence had always characterized the advancing American frontier. What was unique about the violence triggered by the gold rush was that the traditional response of the federal government—removing Indians from their ancestral lands and resettling them on reservations farther west—would not work in California.[36] When the Pacific Ocean demonstrated the limits of the federal government's temporizing removal policy, the State of California was prepared with a solution of its own—a final one.

It was in this atmosphere of impending genocide that three federal commissioners were sent to California, loosely instructed by the Secretary of Interior to "make such treaties and compacts with the Indians as may seem to be just and proper."[37] One week after Governor Burnett's message to the legislature, the commissioners published their views in the *Alta California*, pointing out the impracticality of removal as a solution. "As there is *no further west*, to which they *can* be removed, the General Government and the people of California appear to have left but one alternative in relation to these remnants of once numerous and powerful tribes, viz: *extermination or domestication*."[38]

Lacking congressional authority to cede land, establish reservations, or make financial commitments,[39] the commissioners nevertheless sought to avoid the threatened bloodbath by negotiating treaties that would have removed Indians from mining districts and other areas of white settlement and concentrated them on large reservations. They ultimately negotiated eighteen treaties with representatives of what the commissioners understood to be tribes.[40] In each of the treaties the Indians acknowledged the jurisdiction of the United States, agreed to refrain from hostilities, and relinquished all claims to the territory they had held. In return the commissioners promised the Indians provisions, livestock, and reservation land totaling 7,488,000 acres, about seven and a half percent of the land area of the state.[41]

Despite the endorsement of President Millard Fillmore, the United States Senate deferred to California's delegation and rejected all of the treaties. In opposing the treaties, California's highest elected officials spoke with one voice and doubtless conveyed the sentiments of the majority of their constituents. Governor John McDougal called for rejection of the treaties and removal of Indians from the state, as did majority reports of the California State Senate and Assembly committees.[42]

The primary ground urged by the California legislature for rejecting the treaties was that the proposed reservations contained valuable agricultural and mineral lands. The federal commissioners, the state senate majority report asserted, had assigned to the state's Indians "no inconsiderable portion" of the comparatively limited quantity of California land "fully adaptable to agricultural purposes," which land the Indians were "wholly incapable, by habit or taste, of appreciating." The state senate, in fact, went so far as to oppose "any and all" treaties that would confer upon the Indians of California an exclusive right to occupy "any of the public lands of the State."[43]

Reserving valuable mineral land to Indians would not be fair to white miners, the assembly report contended. "There is not a mountain stream in California, on which is not to be found some sad memento attesting the blasted hopes and wounded expections of the pioneer miners. They have upheaved the bowels of the earth, diverted the streams from their natural channels, and sent them rushing through the tunnelled mountains," rhapsodized the assembly with praise that sounds more like damns to modern ears. If the proposed reservations were established, "a large proportion of this enterprising population would be totally deprived of their improvements, discoveries and hard earned acquisitions." And for what? To "make room for . . . a few tribes of ignorant barbarians."[44]

Expressing the view shared by most other California newspapers, the *Los Angeles Star* of March 13, 1852, commended the anti-treaty position taken by the legislature, warning that "to place upon our most fertile soil the most degraded race of Aboriginies upon the North American Continent . . . is planting the seeds of future disaster and ruin."[45]

The rejection of the treaties did not, of course, restore the status quo ante. California's Indians did not receive the consideration for which they bargained—reservations, livestock, or provisions. Nevertheless, the land they were prepared to cede under the rejected treaties was surveyed by the United States and homesteaded and patented by whites. The same was true of the land that would have become reservations. California's Indians became homeless in their own land.

Genocide: The Time Has Arrived, the Work Has Commenced

In default of the treaties, California made good on its promise to wage a war of extermination. The war was conducted primarily by volunteer militia. The *Humboldt Times* expressed the hope that the militia companies would "succeed in totally breaking up or exterminating the skulking bands of savages." William Kibbe, the leader of a volunteer company whose work was praised in the *Times*, claimed that his men had killed over two hundred California Indians in the process of opening up new lands for white settlement. "Some twenty-five families of this year's immigration have already taken up claims in these valleys," Kibbe reported. "And this is the country which has been hitherto almost exclusively occupied by Indians."[46]

The position of the *Yreka Herald* was unequivocal: "Now that the general hostilities against the Indians have commenced we hope that the Government will render such aid as will enable the citizens of the north to carry on a war of extermination until the last Redskin of these tribes has been killed. Extermination," the *Herald* declared, "is no longer a question of time—the time has arrived, the work has commenced, and let the first man that says treaty or peace be regarded as a traitor."[47]

J. Ross Browne, who was appointed by the federal government in 1857 to investigate the condition of Indians on the West Coast, described a typical militia expedition against Humboldt Indians. "During the winter of last year a number of them were gathered at Humboldt. The whites thought it was a favorable opportunity to get rid of them altogether. So they went in a body to the Indian camp, during the night when the poor wretches were asleep, shot all the men, women and children at the first onslaught, and cut the throats" of the survivors, Browne reported. "Very few escaped. Next morning sixty bodies lay weltering in their blood—the old and the young, male and female—with every wound gaping a tale of horror to the civilized world. Children climbed upon their mothers' breasts and sought nourishment from the fountains that death had drained; girls and boys lay here and there with their throats cut from ear to ear; men and women, clinging to each other in their terror, were found perforated with bullets or cut to pieces with knives—all were cruelly murdered."[48]

This program of genocide was sanctioned and supported by government at the local, state, and federal levels. Municipal governments offered bounties for Indian heads or scalps. Shasta City, for example, offered five dollars for every Indian head presented at city headquarters. A community near Marysville paid bounties "for every scalp or some other satisfactory evidence" that an Indian had been killed.[49] In addition to the bounties paid by local governments, members of volunteer militias engaged in Indian extermination could submit claims on the state treasury for their expenses.[50] Moreover, while disallowing the most obviously exaggerated claims, the federal government reimbursed the state for the militia expenses. Murdering Indians had become a cornerstone of California public policy.[51]

CHAPTER FOUR

WHITES AND THE CAMPOS

THE CAMPOS ARE A BAND OF THE KUMEYAAY INDIANS, ONE OF several tribes which occupied the territory of what is now San Diego County. The Campos are also known as Mission Indians, specifically Digueños. The term *Mission Indian* refers to Indians whose ancestors were in the Spanish missions from San Diego north to San Francisco, as well as the portions of those tribes whose ancestors remained free of the missions in the mountains and deserts east of the strip of coastal California the Spanish controlled.[1] The Mission Indians of southern California include the Digueños—the Indians associated with the first of the Spanish missions, San Diego de Alcala.[2] Many of the mountain and desert Indians hate the term *Mission Indians* and insist upon use of their band or tribal names.[3] The Bureau of Indian Affairs refers to the Campos as the "Campo Band of Mission Indians," and the Campos' official stationery uses the same phrase. On the other hand, the Campo EPA's stationery is headed: "Campo Band of Kumeyaay Indians." Moreover, Campos, in both informal conversation and official correspondence, refer to themselves interchangeably as a band or a tribe. In later chapters I will refer to the Campos as a tribe because that is how they are treated by the federal government.

When the Spanish entered Alta California, the Kumeyaay occupied the region extending from coastal southern California almost to the Colorado River and for about fifty miles north and south of the border between California and Mexico. Traveling from west to east through Kumeyaay territory, one would leave the coastal plain, pass through the narrow canyons of the Peninsular mountain range, flanked by peaks as high as sixty-five hundred feet, and finally reach the desert west of the Colorado River. The topography of their territory shaped the seasonal journeys of the Kumeyaay as they followed the ripening plants from the canyon floors up the mountain slopes, returning to sheltered foothills or valleys when winter began. Although they have been called hunter-gatherers, the Kumeyaay, as we shall see in the next chapter, had actually developed an intensive and highly sophisticated system of plant husbandry, including the cultivation of plants which bloomed only in droughts. This enabled the Kumeyaay to support a relatively dense population of twenty-five thousand in the portion of their arid homeland that lies north of the California/Mexico border.[4]

Of all the mission tribes in California, the Kumeyaay were the most determined in resisting Franciscan control. Twice within the first six years, attacks on the San Diego mission ended in fatalities. In 1775, about eight hundred people of the Kumeyaay tribe united from some seventy coastal and inland villages to burn the mission; among the dead was a priest, the only martyr in the California missions.[5] In 1787, Pedro Fages, the governor of Alta California, wrote of the Kumeyaay that they were "the most restless, stubborn, haughty, warlike and hostile toward us, absolutely opposed to all rational subjection and full of the spirit of independence."[6]

Unlike the coastal Kumeyaay, mountain bands like the Campos always remained outside the orbit of the mission system. Following the 1775 San Diego mission revolt, the mountain Kumeyaay maintained lookouts above the narrow mountain passes that provided the only access to their territory; whenever Spanish soldiers tried to move inland, the villagers would be summoned and cut off the passes. Unlike some other inland Kumeyaay, the Campos also remained outside Mexican control; grants were made for ranchos at Jamul and Tecate, west of the Campos, but the grantees abandoned these lands after repeated attacks.[7]

Because of the intensive and insightful research of anthropologist Florence Shipek, we know much about the sociopolitical structure of the Kumeyaay. Beginning in 1955, Professor Shipek conducted repeated ethnographic interviews with Kumeyaay elders, five of whom were over ninety-five years of age. She learned that the territory of a Kumeyaay band traditionally extended ten to thirty miles along a drainage and up to the drainage divides. Each band had a central primary village and a number of secondary settlements located at springs or the mouths of creeks.[8]

The leader of a Kumeyaay band, the *kwaaypaay*, usually had no adult male blood relatives in the band. When a kwaaypaay died all the other kwaaypaay would meet for the funeral ceremonies and to select a successor. The new kwaaypaay was generally chosen from among their sons or nephews, and had been trained for the position; he also had to be approved by the band. An outsider was chosen, the elders informed Shipek, because one of the primary duties of a kwaapaay was mediating and judging disputes between band members. An outsider, it was believed, could be expected to be more fair and just, not being influenced by family ties.[9]

Among the kwaaypaay's other duties were ones we would associate with a priest—for example, organizing and directing all of the important ceremonies in the life of an individual, such as naming, marriage, death, and memorials. However, the kwaapaay's duties also included exercising leadership with regard to the important economic and political decisions to be made by the band. With the advice of the band's several shamans who specialized in varieties of ecological knowledge, the kwaaypaay would decide when to make seasonal journeys to the band's mountain territory for acorns or to their section of the coast for seafood. In council with the shamans, the kwaaypaay would also organize defensive strategies and make decisions regarding war, peace, or alliances with other bands.[10]

The nature of the kwaaypaay's role is advisedly characterized as the "exercise of leadership." The Kumeyaay elders all emphasized to Shipek that the kwaaypaay did not give orders but was followed insofar as he had demonstrated greater knowledge or managerial abilities. For example, as the seasons changed, the kwaaypaay would announce that he and his family would be leaving the band's primary village for their lands in the mountains or along the coast. Most of the band members would follow the kwaaypaay because he was thought to know best where to find food—plants and animals—throughout the year. However, band members who thought they knew better would go their own ways. Similarly, while all of the men would rally to the band's defense if it were attacked, each would decide for himself whether to participate in a raid planned by the kwaaypaay. The scope the Kumeyaay allowed for individual decision may be contrasted with the practice of their neighbors to the north, the Luiseño, for example; when a Luiseño band leader made a decision, he was obeyed and followed by all band members.[11]

The leader of a federation of Kumeyaay bands was the *kuchult kwataay*, who apparently acquired this distinction by demonstrating superior ability as a diplomat or war leader. Along with the various kwaaypaay, the kuchult kwataay was responsible for maintaining knowledge of tribal and band boundaries in order to resolve disputes that might arise between members of different bands or between bands directly. The kuchult kwataay would generally select two noninvolved kwaaypaay to assist him in the adjudication.[12]

Each Kumeyaay band maintained an organization of lookouts and runners to serve as an early warning and communication system. Integrated on a tribal basis and operated in relays, the lookout and runner system was highly efficient in expediting the transmission of information from one end of the Kumeyaay territory to the other. For example, the Spanish noted that on the day it occurred in 1781, the Kumeyaay at San Diego presidio and mission knew about the Quechan revolt and destruction of Yuman mission some two hundred miles away.[13]

RESERVATIONS: ONLY LANDS WHITES CONSIDERED NOT WORTH HAVING

Because the gold rush was confined to northern and central California until 1870, the genocidal conflagration it sparked was delayed in San Diego County for almost two decades. Like the Campos, many mountain Kumeyaay lived unmolested on their ancestral lands, maintaining their cultures intact, until after the Civil War. In 1875, Charles A. Wetmore, special United States commissioner of Mission Indians, reported that southern California remained in a "pastoral condition" until the fall of 1867 when settlers began to pour in.[14] Thereafter, the Indians of San Diego County suffered as keenly from violence, racism, and inhumanity as tribes better known to history.[15]

The tragic history of the Indians of San Diego County during the American period is made even more poignant by the fact that if the 1851 treaties had been ratified, there would have been a reservation in the mountains of southern California large enough to permit most of the mountain Indians to remain on their own lands and to allow the surviving coastal Indians to move into the mountains. Moreover, the Indians were not informed that the treaties were not ratified and that they therefore did not have title to their land.[16]

Following the debacle of the rejected treaties, the federal government in the 1850s established a number of smaller reservations in California. The reservations may have been misconceived and corruptly administered; most were dismantled in the 1860s. The Indians of San Diego County, however, were neglected entirely. Finally, in 1870, after almost twenty years of effort by their advocates, the Indians of San Diego County were ceded two small reservations, Pala and San Pasqual, in an executive order signed by President U. S. Grant.[17]

Outraged that the reservations had been established on arable land, whites hired a local lawyer, Charles P. Taggart, in an effort to have the executive order rescinded. Taggart, who had been a part owner of the influential *San Diego Union*, enlisted the *Union* in the cause. The campaign bore fruit within a year. President Grant revoked his executive order on the recommendation of Commissioner of Indian Affairs E. S. Parker, who based his counsel on the grounds, among others, of citizen opposition and the "opinion of the press."[18]

In 1876, one of Commissioner Parker's successors frankly confessed: "Whenever an Indian reservation has on it good land, or timber, or minerals, the cupidity of the white man is excited, and a constant struggle is inaugurated to dispossess the Indian, in which the avarice and determination of the white man usually prevails."[19] Three years later, Secretary of Interior Carl Schurz admitted as much himself:

Many treaty reservations have turned out to be of greater value in agricultural and mineral resources than they were originally thought to be, and are now eagerly coveted by the white population. . . . It is argued that the Indians cannot and will not develop these resources; that the country cannot afford to maintain large and valuable districts in a state of waste. . . . This demand becomes more pressing every year, and although in many cases urged entirely without regard to abstract justice, it is a fact . . . which must be taken into account in shaping an Indian policy.[20]

The *San Diego Union* continued to oppose renewed efforts to establish reservations, editorializing on September 7, 1873: "The land is for the people who can cultivate it and become producers, adding to the prosperity of the commonwealth, and the Indians must go." Not only should Indians be kept off lands currently occupied by whites, the editor concluded, but

Indians should be denied any land "likely to be so occupied by whites within the next twenty years."[21]

Finally, on December 27, 1875, President Grant created several small reservations in San Diego County, totaling 52,400 acres, or about three-fourths the acreage of the reservations he had established in 1870 in the executive order he revoked in 1872. The response of the federal government remained woefully inadequate. The reservations were far too small to support an aboriginal economy, and the land granted was much too poor to support the reservation populations through agriculture. Moreover, the water necessary for agriculture was often diverted upstream by whites.[22]

The problem was that the whites had already taken the best land away from the Kumeyaay. Indian Affairs Commissioner Edward P. Smith recognized this in his annual report for 1875: "[A]ll available agricultural lands have been seized or occupied by individual [white] owners." Smith's statement was supported by a field report prepared in June 1875 by Special Agent D. D. Dryden, who stated that Indian land in Southern California was rapidly falling into the hands of whites. According to Dryden, Indian gardens were "being invaded and their pastures consumed by the stock of white settlers; the water was turned away from their ditches to irrigate the gardens of those trespassing upon their lands; and they have no redress."[23]

Nevertheless, some San Diego County Indians at last had land that they could, with the blessing of the federal government, call their own. The Campos, however, were not among them. Nor would they be for almost two more decades.

CAMPOS, HOMELESS AND STARVING, FINALLY GIVEN A PLACE TO STARVE

In 1866, whites began moving into the Milquatay Valley, in the heart of Campo territory, and establishing ranches. Many of the migrants were southerners displaced by the Civil War;

indeed, so many of the early settlers were from Texas that the Milquatay Valley became known as Little Texas. The migrants were attracted by the fertile valleys and by the fact that unlike much of southern California, title to land in Campo territory was not clouded by Spanish and Mexican grants. The priority of the Kumeyaay's claim was not a matter of concern.[24]

By the mid-1860s, white settlers were well entrenched throughout the entire Campo territory, and by 1867, with the creation of the Milquatay School District, a white community began to take shape. By 1875, the town of Milquatay, soon to be renamed Campo, had emerged as the area's leading commercial center, with stage coaches stopping there on twice-weekly runs between San Diego and Tucson.[25] In 1873, while working for the Mexican government surveying the border area, Jacobo Blanco noted that Milquatay—then a village of a half-dozen houses—was the "most important place in the whole region," being the location of a warehouse "perfectly stocked" to supply the ranches in the region and of the only post office along the road to Fort Yuma.[26]

While the white settlers in and around the community of Campo prospered, the condition of the Indians they dispossessed grew steadily more desperate. With storms bringing as much as three feet of snow to higher elevations in their territory, the winter of 1880 devastated the mountain Kumeyaay. The Campo contributor to the San Diego Union reported: "The Indians all through the mountains are near starving. The failure of their pinon and acorn crops last year left them without any winter store. They have been killing cattle here and there."[27]

The following summer a correspondent for the Union reported that the Indians around Campo were in a "most deplorable state." "Strong men who have visited them at their several rancherias have wept like children on beholding the living skeleton forms of these Indians—about two hundred of them in number. In the mountains there is absolutely nothing for them to live on. Game there is none whatever . . . and these people are actually subsisting on roots, snakes, and a species of large worm now preying upon the vegetation." Making their condition "still more deplorable," the Indian agent denied responsibility for them, claiming that the Indians of the Campo area "belong in Mexico and are not entitled to aid at his hands." "But such is not the case," the *Union* asserted. "These starving people are known by the whites to be native born and raised on American soil."[28]

However, as Meredith Vezina observes, "Indignation by Anglo settlers over the plight of the Indian was generally short-lived, particularly when personal property was involved."[29] In October of 1880, an Indian accused of stealing blankets from a rancher's house was tried by Justice of the Peace Lumen Gaskill, found guilty, and sentenced to one hundred lashes. Two strong men having exhausted themselves in administering the punishment, the "almost dying" man was told that he must leave the country and that he would be hanged if he ever came back. Justice Gaskill drew the following lesson from the incident: "After one of these Indians has been whipped once, he will never steal again; it makes a 'good Indian' of him."[30] As Vezina notes, "the Gaskills did not apply the same standards to their own behavior. When compared to their exploits, stealing blankets seems quite innocent." Lumen Gaskill, the justice of the peace, was convicted of rustling and Lumen and his brother Silas were suspected of having murdered the man whose cattle were stolen.[31]

In 1893, the federal government finally established a reservation for the Campo band. By that time, there were only about one hundred Kumeyaay surviving of the population of five thousand who had once lived in the surrounding region.[32]

In his 1894 annual report, Francis Estudillo, the district Indian agent, observed that the Campos "have good farms, and are industrious," but that the lands "they are farming, and have always farmed, are not included in the reservation as recommended by the commission."[33] In 1896, Agent Estudillo reported that the Campos would be forced off their farms. He noted that the Campo reservation called for "certain lands upon which the Indians do not, never did, and will never be able to live for want of water. Their homes in some instances have been located by whites and eviction must soon follow."[34]

By 1905, the Campos had been moved to the reservation. It was pathetically small—710 acres or about one square mile. However, the reservation's gross acreage does not begin to reveal how inadequate a resource it was for a people who had derived their subsistence from the land. The three reservations in southeastern San Diego County—Campo, La Posta, and Manzanita—had, altogether, no more than 17.5 acres of arable land, and "even this small acreage is made up of dry, sandy land, which is productive only when the rainfall is up to and above the average." Moreover, the growing season was short because of the altitude. This characterization of the southeastern San Diego County reservations appears in a report prepared in 1905 by United States Indian Agent Frank Churchill.

Churchill made his inspection, the commissioner of Indian affairs stated in his annual report, in response to a public outcry resulting from "some magazine articles [that] gave the impression that very many Indians in Southern California were in a starving condition, and anxious appeals [that] came to the Office from various sections of the country that the Indians be given immediate relief."[35] In the January 1905 issue of *Out West*, Charles F. Lummis, whose Sequoya League had organized a private relief effort, wrote of "the plain fact" that the Campos and neighboring tribes "were starving slowly to death." It was a disgrace to the nation, Lummis charged, that there was "no food whatever on these five reservations except acorns, and not many of those," that "these men, women and children had neither clothing nor bedding to withstand the mountain winter," and that, in sum, they "had been left by the government to starve for want of proper lands."[36]

The commissioner read inspector Churchill's report as "confirm[ing] the views of the Office that the destitution among these Indians was not widespread, and that the magazine statements were calculated to mislead the public and were unjust to the Office."[37] Why the commissioner took comfort from their reports is not clear, because both inspector Churchill and the resident Indian agent speak of the "destitution" of the Campo, La Posta, and Manzanita bands. However, the commissioner's critics may well have overstated their case in claiming that "very many" Indians were starving. What the official reports make chillingly clear is that there were not many mountain Kumeyaay left to starve. Of the Campos' reported population of twenty-eight, Churchill could only find fifteen.[38]

The causes of the Campos' destitution are apparent. Their small, barren reservation could not support an agricultural economy, much less an aboriginal economy. At the same time that Churchill was preparing his report, the district superintendent said of the Campos and neighboring bands: "They are not lazy, but the land they have is so nearly worthless that a living by farming is out of the question."[39] Moreover, the Kumeyaay were isolated from the distant San Diego labor market as much by their survival strategy as by the mountain passes; whereas they had successfully repelled the Spaniards and the Mexicans, the Kumeyaay were forced to withdraw ever further into the mountains in the face of the rising tide of Anglo-American immigration.

Area ranchers did provide some employment for the Campos.[40] However, the work was seasonal and the compensation was not money wages but food and old clothing—and these for the ranchhands, not for their families. As a consequence, the families had to shift for themselves and nothing could be saved for the winter.[41] The life of a San Diego

County Indian laborer and his family in the early 1900s is strikingly portrayed in *The Autobiography of Delfina Cuero*, as told to Florence Shipek. Delfina Cuero was born around the turn of the century. Her parents were coastal Kumeyaay who were driven from San Diego's Mission Valley by American and Chinese immigrants who did not recognize their claim to the land their ancestors had always lived upon. Thereafter, Delfina's father became an itinerant ranch hand and the family lived in the brush, wherever they could find work or wild food to gather. The ranchers who employed Delfina's father "gave us some food or sometimes some old clothes for the work. They never gave the Indians money."⁴²

Although they had traditionally practiced a highly advanced plant husbandry, by the time Delfina was born the Kumeyaay "had to move too much to plant anything."

My grandmother used to tell me that when the Indians could live in the same place and could come back to the same place from gathering acorns and things, they would always clear a little place near their house. In it they planted some of the greens and seeds and roots that they liked, just the things that grow wild. That way they had some food close to their house. . . . But when I was young it was no use to plant like that when we couldn't stay to get it. We used to eat rats, mice, lizards, and some snakes. . . . We had to eat whatever we could find to have enough food. We were hungry many times.⁴³

Gradually, Delfina's family had to move farther and farther away from San Diego, "looking for places where nobody chased us away. . . . When the Indians were told to leave a place, they generally just headed farther into the mountains. Pretty soon they would tell us we had to move again. We would pack up everything we had," Delfina recalled, "a few sakay [ollas] and baskets of dried food if we had been lucky and found enough to dry for winter, a few small stone tools, bow and arrows, xampu [a throwing stick for hunting rabbits], and what little clothing we had. We would pack everything on the back of a small burro that my father had and go." Eventually, Delfina's family migrated across the border into Baja California; they "found a place where no one told them to move on, so they just stayed there." And there Delfina lived until old age. "The terrible things I went through trying to keep my children together and fed, I can't begin to tell. Then, I didn't succeed after all. [Unable to feed them, she had to give them up to those who could.] I feel like crying when I think of that time."[44]

Delfina eventually returned to the United States, having managed with Florence Shipek's assistance to prove that she had been born here, and lived out her life on the Campo reservation in the home of the kwaaypaay, Rosalie Robertson.[45]

TWENTIETH CENTURY BRINGS LITTLE HOPE TO CAMPOS

In 1911, the Campo reservation was enlarged with the addition of "new Campo," a separate 14,870-acre parcel of land the federal government purchased from white settlers. Nevertheless, living conditions on the reservation were not much improved. In 1932, a Senate committee investigating the conditions of Indians in San Diego County found on the Campo reservation "Indian families living in hovels built of salvaged packing cases, hammered tin cans or grass. . . . Their water had to be carried a quarter of a mile from a spring of questionable purity." A witness testified that many of the Indians were undernourished and tubercular; he said that a boy on the Campo reservation had died of starvation that year.[46]

When Florence Shipek first visited their reservation in 1955, the Campos had "no indoor toilets, no running water, no electricity, no telephones." Florence could "see daylight" through the walls of some of the houses. Even for Campo men who had attended Sherman Institute, an Indian boarding school in Riverside, and who had served with distinction in the armed forces, the only employment available in the vicinity of the reservation was seasonal farm labor. And that was increasingly hard to come by because migrant Mexican fieldhands were willing to work for even less than were the

Indians. Lacking effective advocates, the Campos were subject to exploitation. For example, two old Campo women lived off the reservation, near a store; the storekeeper received their old age pension checks and doled out just enough food to keep them barely alive. With Shipek's assistance, Rosalie Pinto Robertson, the kwaaypaay, moved the old women to the reservation and managed their pensions, so that they could be fed and cared for properly.[47]

In 1959, in the first study since 1932, the San Diego County welfare department reported that the county's Indians were living "under intolerable conditions because of public discrimination and their own reluctance to accept outside help." The welfare agency concluded, the *Union* reported, that "sanitation facilities on some reservations are 'dangerously inadequate,' housing is poor, medical care rarely accepted, and education and employment opportunities substandard."[48]

Discrimination, which the welfare department report found to be largely responsible for the plight of the county's Indians, can be an abstract and impersonal concept. Ralph Fenner's account of his youth in Campo territory makes it concrete and personal. Fenner's grandmother and great-grandmother were the only survivors of an Indian attack near San Angelo, Texas. Joining the immigrants from that state who gave the Milquatay Valley the nickname "Little Texas," they settled in Campo and raised families of what Fenner called "Texas-trained Indian haters." The Ku Klux Klan met in the Fenner family home; his father and grandfather were the local grand dragons. As recently as the 1920s, the Klan would burn a thirty-foot cross atop a hill overlooking the Campo reservation. His father died when Ralph Fenner was five; the same night, wind blew the cross down. Had the Campos taken this as a sign that an era was ending, they would have been disappointed. "In the late 1920s, my family and the neighbors were still fighting the Indians with 30-30 rifles. There was widespread hatred."[49]

Reporting the Indian Wars

The Campos had reason to fear official violence, too. In 1927, two Indians attending a fiesta on the Campo reservation were shot to death by the Indian agent and sheriff's deputies. The newspaper accounts of the incident deserve close scrutiny because they may reveal as much about the attitudes shared by the *San Diego Union* and some of its readers as they do about the event itself. On July 17, 1927, the *Union* announced on its front page: "Indians Kill White; Fear Campo Riot." The accompanying story is quoted in full to facilitate comparison with followup reports.

> Fearing armed resistance from Indians, following the arrest of a member of their party after the killing of one unidentified white man and the shooting of a government agent believed to be Robinson, six deputy sheriffs late last night were speeding to Campo to reinforce King Powell, deputy sheriff in charge of prohibition enforcement, and a government agent.
>
> The shooting took place when Powell and the government agents attempted to halt an unidentified Indian reported to have been bringing liquor to an Indian fiesta five miles east of Campo.
>
> The Indian was overpowered after the shooting, much to the evident discontent of his companions who became so menacing that Powell sent a hurry call to San Diego for reinforcements. Powell said the Indians were threatening to "kill every white man in the district."
>
> According to word from Campo, where fiesta visitors hurried after the shooting, the Indians showed signs of having been drinking and a serious fight was predicted before morning.[50]

Apparently confirming that prediction, the banner headline across the front page of the *Union* the next day read: "Campo Indians Rebel; Two Die." The gist of the story, which was drawn almost entirely from a statement made by deputy sheriff Powell and confirmed by deputies Charles Murray and Ralph Kennedy, was this: The three deputies attended the fiesta at the request of the Indian agent George Robertson to prevent the sale of liquor and the carrying of firearms. The trouble began when Kennedy attempted to arrest an Indian "for selling canned heat as a beverage." By the time Powell and Murray came to Kennedy's assistance, a gun battle had erupted and the Indians were shouting "in their own language words which have since been interpreted to be 'kill 'em, shoot 'em.'" After warning one of Kennedy's attackers to let go, Powell shot the Indian. In the ensuing melee, another Indian was shot by both Powell and Robertson. "I want to make it clear," Powell said, that "[n]one of us drew a gun until the shooting had begun, and neither Kennedy nor I fired at anyone except men who were shooting at us or at the Indian police."

Although it generally sang the same tune as the official account, the second story had a few discordant notes. A careful reader would have recalled that the *Union* had earlier reported "the killing of one unidentified white man and the shooting of a government agent believed to be Robinson [sic]." Agent Robertson was reported to be in critical condition in the followup story. However, the dead men, and there two of them, turned out to be Indians—Marcus Hilmiup and Frank Cuero. Moreover, two non-Indians had called the *Union* to dispute the story it ran the previous day. One caller said that the only Indian who was armed was Hilmiup, and that as captain of the reservation police he had a right to be armed. The other, confirming that only one Indian was armed, added that she had seen no drunkenness at the fiesta. Noting that neither of the informants claimed to have been present when the shooting actually occurred, the *Union* clearly found Powell more credible. Upon being shown the statements of the witnesses who contradicted him, Powell was quoted as responding: "All I can say is that they were not there and did not know what they were talking about. There were not less than 20 Indians who were armed and they started the shooting."[51]

The investment the *Union* had made in the official version of the killings may explain the fact that, having played the opening acts of this murder mystery on the front page, it buried the climax on the third. After deliberating only twenty minutes, a coroner's jury found that the "deputies exceeded their authority when they entered the Indians' reservation and used poor judgment, when all testimony submitted was to the effect that everyone participating in the festivities on the reservation was peaceful and quiet and no signs of intoxication of any sort had been shown." Eyewitnesses, Indian and non-Indian alike, testified that there had been no liquor or drinking at the fiesta, that the deputies entered the reservation with their guns drawn, and that the officers were the first to open fire. According to one witness, what happened was that the Indian police had arrested an Indian, and when the arrested man resisted, a crowd gathered. When Agent Robertson and the deputies arrived, "they didn't seem to understand the situation." Deputy Kennedy told the crowd to get back, saying, "If you don't get back, I'll shoot you." After two Indians jumped Kennedy, Agent Robertson fired into the crowd, then shot one of the Indians struggling with Kennedy, and finally "started shooting it out with Marcus [Hilmiup], who was killed."[52]

If the *Union* learned anything from the experience of reporting this story, the lesson did not register in the paper's institutional memory. In 1959, the *Union* reported that a fiesta was going to be held on the Campo reservation for the first time in thirty-two years. As to the reason for the lapse, the *Union* said: "The 1927 fiesta was considered clandestine and was stopped by police."[53]

Discrimination in Schooling

The 1959 report of the San Diego County welfare agency, that the educational opportunities available to Indian children in the county were "substandard," should have come as no surprise to the Board of Supervisors. The California public school system had never been hospitable to Indian children. In 1860, the Common School Act excluded Indians from California public schools, along with blacks and Asians; if a school district admitted an Indian, the district's share of state school funds could be withheld. In 1866, the law was relaxed somewhat, giving school districts the power to admit "half-breed" Indian children and Indian children living in white families or under white guardianship; however, segregation was again required in 1870. In 1874, the legislature provided that Indian children were to be admitted to white schools, if separate schools were not available in the district. In 1880, in a "spasm of egalitarianism," the legislature eliminated the separate schools, only to impose segregation again in 1893. In 1935, the statutory basis for segregation was eliminated.[54] It was not until 1940, however, that Indian children attended the public high schools in the vicinity of the Campo reservation.[55]

The debilitating effects of discrimination on the education and self-esteem of Indian children did not end with the dissolution of the segregated school system. In 1965, a report prepared by the California Department of Labor Relations found that five percent of all rural or reservation Indians had received no schooling at all and that fifty-seven percent had completed less than one year of high school; contemporaneously, a national study revealed that Indian students in the twelfth grade had the poorest self-image of all the minority groups examined.[56] Campo students were not reaching the twelfth grade, Florence Shipek believes, because the lesson they were taught in the local public schools was that "Indians live like animals, Indians are worthless, Indians are dumb."[57]

Despite the 1959 report of the welfare agency, the San Diego County public school system was continuing to shortchange Indian children three decades later. During the fifteen years preceding 1989, more than three hundred Campo students went to high school. Seven graduated. "It's not an educational problem," concluded Jerome Miller, superintendent of the Mountain Empire School District where Campo children attend school. "These kids are just as bright as any others. The schools just don't make it for Indian kids; they're not designed to," said Miller, who previously worked with Indian students in Wyoming and New Mexico. "The school programs simply try to make the Indian kids into little white kids with dark skins. They push them into a white middle class mold and try to make them fit. The Indian parents worry about their kids not getting an education," Miller continued, "but they also understand how their children feel. They've been through it. They know the schooling that is offered will only equip their children to take a low-paying job in the non-Indian world. While they grieve for their kids and their future, they understand their pain."[58]

CHAPTER FIVE

INDIANS AND THE ENVIRONMENT

THE CONVENTIONAL WISDOM OF WHITE AMERICANS IS THAT IN-dians did not leave tracks in the wilderness, that they lived in harmony with their environment, without affecting, much less managing it.[1] According to this view, operating a commercial landfill on a reservation is perverse, peculiarly "un-Indian." However, to insist that Indian reservation land be maintained in its "natural state" and restricted to "traditional" uses is effectively to deny Indians economic use of their reservations while their neighbors prosper. This insistence is based on a misunderstanding of how Indians used the land before the Spanish came.

THE CONVENIENT MYTH THAT INDIANS DID NOT MANAGE THEIR ENVIRONMENT

Indians did not leave the land "untouched" or in its "natural state." The Indians of southern California, like those elsewhere, managed the land by the available means to produce the highest economic benefit for their people.[2] "With the emergence of ecology, or at least popularized ecology," writes anthropologist Henry Lewis, "the hunter-gatherer has been seen by some writers to represent a kind of *ecological hero*, a revival of the 'noble savage.' This view is inextricably linked to the idea of a passive relationship to nature."[3]

For Spanish colonists and Anglo-American settlers, however, "noble savage" would have been an oxymoron. The California Indians' perceived passivity in relation to nature was considered proof not only of their savagery but also of their ignobility. Agriculture was considered to be not merely a higher form of economic activity than hunting and gathering, but evidence of higher evolutionary development, social and spiritual.

In 1821, the Franciscan missionary Geronimo Boscana wrote *Chinigchinich*, an account of the Juaneño religion practiced by the Indians living in the vicinity of the San Juan Capistrano mission; in it he characterized native customs and beliefs as "horrible" and "ludicrous," and concluded that the "Indians of California may be compared to a species of monkey."[4] It is not a coincidence that Father Boscana believed that "in no part of the province was to be found aught but the common, spontaneous productions of the earth."[5]

This attitude was not restricted to the Spanish. During the administration of President Thomas Jefferson, who idealized farmers as "the chosen people of God," Governor William Henry Harrison of Indiana Territory asked rhetorically: "Is one of the fairest portions of the globe to remain in a state of nature, the haunt of a few wretched savages, when it seems destined by the Creator to give support to a large population and to be the seat of civilization, of science, and of true religion?"[6]

John Rawls notes that in "assessing the quality of Indian life in California, the standard most often applied by Anglo-Americans was that of diet: societies that cultivated the soil were superior to hunting societies. By this standard the California native ranked as the most primitive of people, for the 'Diggers' often were seen, incorrectly, as neither farmers nor hunters."[7] ("Digger" is a term of opprobrium that was commonly applied to California Indians under the mistaken impression that they lived largely by grubbing up roots.[8]) California Indians, Rawls continues, "were believed to subsist on the crudest and simplest of diets—roots, acorns, berries, nuts, insects. Whites recognized that the Indians did hunt small game and fish, but most descriptions of their diets focused on these more 'primitive' foods."[9]

Anthropologists Lowell Bean and Harry Lawton observe that if "agriculture was a hallmark of civilization to the Spanish, so it was with the later nineteenth century American historians, products of an agrarian society, who viewed farming as the evolutionary goal of human civilization." Indeed, Bean and Lawton conclude, the "romantic myth of the mission fathers tutoring culturally retrograde Indians in crop-growing achieved such popularity in this period that the native cultures of California had little appeal for scholars."[10] Even Hubert Howe Bancroft, the founding father of California historiography, considered it axiomatic that along the shores of the Pacific humankind had "sunk almost to the utter darkness of the brute."[11]

With that gift Texans seem to have for saying aloud what others might only be thinking, Bill Clements, in the course of his successful 1978 campaign to become governor of Texas, asked a rhetorical question echoing that asked by William Henry Harrison almost two hundred years before. "Is this area of Texas more productive, more fulfilling of God's purpose . . . than when there were five thousand Indians here eating insects?" Although Clements was confident that "[t]hese questions sort of answer themselves," we will inquire into one of the assumptions underlying the conventional wisdom that whites were entitled to dispossess the Indians because they could better utilize the land.[12]

JOHN LOCKE: PATRON SAINT OF SETTLERS

The premise that California Indians simply gathered the bounty of the earth, rather than earning it by the sweat of their brows, was central to the conviction held by Anglo Americans that, morally, California was theirs for the taking.

The rationale for the settlers, if they felt the need for one, was provided by the English philosopher John Locke; Locke's writings on government generally and property in particular profoundly influenced the drafters of the United States Constitution. "In the beginning," wrote Locke in *The Second Treatise on Civil Government*, "all the world was America." By this Locke meant that America was in a "state of nature" when the first Europeans arrived; that is, its land belonged to no one.[13]

In *Playing God in Yellowstone: The Destruction of America's First National Park*, Alston Chase demonstrates the falsity of this premise and argues that disastrous consequences, for America and for Native Americans, followed from it. Ignorance of—perhaps deliberate blindness to—the role Indians played in the ecology of their land enabled whites to dispossess them of it with an easy conscience. Chase argues that it also led to mismanagement of the land seized—for example, the area that became Yellowstone National Park.

For Locke, people remove land from the state of nature and earn title to it by working it, mixing their labor with it. There was precedent for invoking Locke to justify seizure of Indian land; the Georgians had done so in dispossessing the Cherokees. Representative Wilde declared that all property was "founded on utility," and that land became individually owned only as labor was incorporated with it.[14] Locke suggested by implication, as Chase points out, that the Indians never worked the land. "Therefore, it was not truly theirs, and the Europeans could make it their own with a free conscience simply by tilling the soil." For this reason, Chase continues, "it was convenient for the first settlers in America to believe that the Indians did not improve upon nature, did not farm, fertilize, or set fires."[15]

Convenient, but false. "It is often assumed," Stephen Pyne observes, "that the American Indian was incapable of greatly modifying his environment and that he would not have been much interested in doing so if he did have the capabilities. In fact, he possessed both the tool and the will to use it. That tool was fire."[16]

FIRE AS A MEANS OF MANAGING THE ENVIRONMENT

The journals and diaries of early Spanish explorers and officials are replete with references to the use of fire by California Indians. In his diaries Father Juan Crespí, who accompanied Portolá in 1769 on the first expedition to establish missions in California, repeatedly mentions the grass having been "burnt off by the heathens."[17] In a journal summarizing his travels from San Gabriel to San Buenaventura, Fernando Rivera y Moncada, the military governor of California from 1774 to 1777, complained of his "horses and mules not having grass, all occasioned by the great fires of the gentiles [unbaptized Indians], who, not having to care for more than their own bellies, burn the fields as soon as they gather up the seeds." Recognizing that they were using fire to enhance their harvest, Rivera y Moncada described the Indians of the Monterey area as burning the grass "so that new weeds may grow to produce more seeds."[18]

Further evidence that California Indians practiced burning as a means of manipulating their environment is supplied in the 1792 journal of the naturalist José Longinos Martínez. "In all of New California from Fronteras northward the gentiles have the custom of burning the brush, for two purposes; one, for hunting rabbits and hares . . .; second, so that with the first light rain or dew the shoots will come up which they call *pelillo* (little hair) and upon which they feed like cattle when the weather does not permit them to seek other food."[19]

The method in what less perceptive observers than Longinos Martínez considered the madness of Indian burning is made clear by Alston Chase: "Fire improves nature in many ways." Among others, it "changes the chemical composition of the soil, promoting more varied vegetation and supporting more diverse wildlife. It releases soluble mineral salts in plant tissue, and increases the nitrogen, calcium, potassium, and phosphorus in the soil as fertilizers."[20]

However, the most important result of burning, Chase emphasizes, "is that it arrests or reverses the normally inexorable seral succession." Yellowstone being Chase's subject, it serves as his example of seral succession. "Left undisturbed, areas such as Yellowstone would progress from grasslands, to shrub, to deciduous stands of aspen, then to lodgepole pine, and finally to spruce and fir, a succession that takes around three hundred years." In the course of succession, Chase explains, "the variety and volume of plant life diminishes, and thus the capacity of the land to support wildlife declines as well. Fire is the only way to interrupt seral succession, and human beings apparently learned this lesson long ago."[21]

It is clear that the Campos and other Kumeyaay well understood the utility of fire in interrupting vegetational succession. They practiced controlled burning of chaparral shrublands, for example, in order to promote the growth of a now-extinct grain grass which provided approximately half their food supply.

Some of the wild grains were impressive, even to Europeans. On September 28, 1542, Juan Rodríguez Cabrillo landed in San Diego, becoming the first European to discover California. The diary of that journey speaks of a seed "the size of maize" used by the natives in making tamales, which were pronounced "good food" by the diarist. Father Francisco Garcés, who accompanied the Anza expedition up the California coast to Monterey in 1774, stated that the San Jacinto plain was thickly grown with grasses, one species of which bore a seed much like rye. Garcés added: "I have no doubt this is the grain which the Gileños [Pima Indians of the Gila River region in Arizona] call wheat, for they told me that near the sea there was wheat which they harvested without planting it."[22]

Like Longinos Martínez, who wrote of the Indians "feed[ing] like cattle" upon the grain grass, the San Francisco Bulletin in

1851 referred to Indians eating "the grasses of the field like beasts."[23] In fact, the Indians harvested the grain, ground it into flour, and then after burning the stubble, broadcast seeds. "Broadcast over fields with the grain seed were the seeds of green leafy foods and other annuals which were ready for harvest at the same time or earlier than the grain," Florence Shipek writes. "This produced an interplanted field not recognized by Europeans accustomed to plough-cleared monocultural fields containing wheat or vegetable row crops."[24]

In the first several years after chaparral is burned, grain and other annuals sprout and grow. Gradually, as the chaparral increases in size, the grain ceases to sprout, even though it is rebroadcast. After several more years the annuals also cease resprouting as the chaparral gets larger. The roots of the chaparral take up all the rainfall and its leaves exude oils and other substances that inhibit the growth of annuals. Deprived of cover, the soil erodes.[25]

The grain grass was not the only "crop" the Kumeyaay managed by controlled burning. Acorns were a staple of California Indians; acorn flour was made into cereal or bread after the tannic acid was painstakingly leached away.[26] Pine trees producing edible nuts were also a valued food source. Each year, after the nut harvest, the fallen leaves or pine needles, broken branches, and low growth in the oak and pine groves were burned, returning the nutrients to the soil. The annual burning also destroyed plant diseases, damaging insects, and parasites such as mistletoe and dodder.[27]

THE KUMEYAAY, HAVING MIXED THEIR LABOR WITH THE LAND, OWNED IT

While burning may have been the most important means California Indians used to manage their environment,[28] it was by no means the only one, certainly not for the Kumeyaay. In the course of becoming the foremost academic authority on the plant husbandry practices of the Kumeyaay, anthropologist and ethnobotanist Florence Shipek collected data between 1959 and 1965, primarily from Kumeyaay elders and plant specialists between eighty and 110 years of age; they had avoided contact with Anglo Americans as much as possible by remaining in the relatively isolated mountains of what is now eastern San Diego County or by fleeing to the northern Baja California Kumeyaay mountain villages. Their information was corroborated by information in accounts written by Spanish, Mexican, and early American settlers.

A native grain about half the size of a grain of wheat once grew throughout the valleys and low slopes in the Kumeyaay area. In 1773, Father Palóu described the Kumeyaay as gathering this grain by cutting it and binding it in "sheaves as is the custom to do with wheat." Although the grain predominated in the valley bottoms and on the low slopes, seeds of leafy green and/or flowering annual plants were broadcast along with the grain, after controlled burns, producing spring greens and vegetables for the Kumeyaay.[29]

Around the edges of the valleys and on low slopes, oak trees were planted, with controlled burns being conducted after the fall acorn harvest. In mountain and desert locations, beneath running springs, beside wet meadows, or in places where summer rainfall would spread through the fields, corn, beans, and squash were grown. In some locations the plants were managed primarily as forage for deer, antelope, mountain sheep, rabbits, and other game. When Kumeyaay animal specialists judged it appropriate, the forage areas were burned to freshen them and maintain them at peak production.[30]

The Kumeyaay had also developed effective techniques of erosion control and water management. They aligned rocks in parallel rows across drainage channels to slow and spread storm runoff, allowing more of the water to enter the ground and catching the fine silt carried by it. The areas behind the rock alignments were used as planting locations. On the mesas, valley flats, and slopes, the soil was further protected from erosion by the covering provided by the grain and other food or medicinal plants broadcast by the Kumeyaay. In the valleys, riparian plants were placed along the stream sides; if a major storm made a new cut in the stream bank, local villagers planted willow branches along the cut.[31]

Shipek's study of Kumeyaay plant husbandry and water management techniques gives the lie to the contention that whites were entitled to seize their land because the Kumeyaay had failed to establish ownership of it by mixing their labor with it. Shipek's study of Kumeyaay land tenure principles also exposes the ignorance underlying the conventional wisdom that Indians did not think of land as property, much less private property. Indeed, if you are going to treat someone inhumanely, it is best not to learn too much about them, lest they turn out to be unnervingly like you. It might have been unsettling for the whites entering the Milquatay Valley, for example, to learn how fundamentally similar the Campos' concept of property, public and private, was to their own.

California was divided into "national" or "ethnic" territories. The Kumeyaay tribe, recall, occupied the region extending from the Pacific Ocean almost to the Colorado River and for about fifty miles north and south of the border between California and Mexico. The territories of some other California tribes were much smaller. For example, the Cupeño, one of the Kumeyaay's neighbors to the north, occupied a somewhat circular area only about ten miles in diameter. Within an ethnic territory, the people spoke related dialects of one language, shared some resources, maintained trails between groups, and had closer ties of various sorts than they had with groups outside their territory. The territory of an ethnic group was divided among the bands that constituted the group. The territory of each band was in turn divided between common areas, such as hunting grounds or religious and ceremonial areas, and private property.[32]

Families and individuals held as private property the areas

in which they invested their labor and upon which they sub-
sisted. These areas "included fields of grain-grass or other annuals, perennials, various shrubs, oak and other trees, cactus
patches, cornfields, and other resources such as clay beds, bas-
ket grass clumps, quarries, and hot and cold springs." That is,
the primary family food resources and some material resources
were considered private property.[33]

(By contrast, the Kumeyaay considered game animals
common property because they were wild. Therefore, when
cattle, which appeared to the Kumeyaay to be an unknown
species of wild game, first began invading their fields and eating the grain grass upon which the Indians were so dependent, the Kumeyaay felt well within their rights in killing and
consuming the cattle. On the other hand, whites, as we have
seen, considered themselves justified in killing Indians who
killed their cattle.[34])

The land use practices of the Kumeyaay that gave rise to
recognized private property rights were straightforward enough.
For example, specific crop areas and stands of cactus were repeatedly cultivated; certain trees were pruned and the debris
around them removed with fire or by grubbing. Property
rights were also acquired by providing water to specific crop
stands by various techniques.[35]

Each family had fields in its home valley, as well as in various locations from the coast through the mountains to the
desert. "Each food, in each area, sprouted and ripened depending upon elevation, distance from the coast, and orientation to sun and wind," Shipek explains. "The time of sprout-
ing each year also depended upon that year's sequence of sun
and rain, as well as on the controlled burning sequence. Thus
some food was always ready to be harvested somewhere."[36]

Such a system required specialized knowledge; the reposi-
tories of such knowledge were shamans. Shamans were of
three types, corresponding to priests, scientists, and doctors.
The scientists who specialized in knowledge about plants were

called *kuseyaay*.[37] Among the Kumeyaay, individual kuseyaay specialized yet further, in particular types of plants and how they are affected by the erratic weather of the region. Working in council, the plant specialists advised the band chief, the kwaaypaay, of what was needful, and the kwaaypaay called upon the band members to do the necessary work.[38]

The plant specialists experimented with all sorts of plants, testing them for their subsistence, medicinal, or technical value, as well as testing whether seeds, cuttings, and transplants would flourish in various locations. Of particular interest were emergency food plants which sprouted only during drought years, perhaps only once in twenty years, when the band's supply of staple vegetables and seeds would be depleted.[39] The plant specialists were enabled to experiment and observe conditions throughout their territory because the band members supported their services by tithes.[40] They passed on their knowledge to their chosen successors in the form of song and dance rituals, which took as long as six days and nights to perform.[41]

SETTLERS, FAILING TO UNDERSTAND
THE ENVIRONMENT, DESTROY IT

Because the Spanish colonists and American settlers did not understand the role California Indians played in the ecosystem, they unwittingly destroyed the natural environment that made California so attractive to them. For example, Spanish and American settlers rhapsodized about the "pastures" that then existed along the California coast. However, the settlers also did their best to suppress the Indians' practice of burning the stubble fields once the grain had been harvested. In 1793, José Joaquín de Arrillaga, governor of Alta California, issued a proclamation prohibiting "all kinds of burning, not only in the vicinity of the towns, but even at the most remote distances" because of the "widespread damage which results to the public from the burning of the fields, customary up to now among both Christian and Gentile Indians in this country, whose childishness has been unduly tolerated."[42] The same position was taken by the newly formed state government. The Act for the Government and Protection of Indians, enacted during the first session of the California State Legislature, forbade setting the prairie on fire.[43]

The settlers did not realize that keeping California open and grass-covered required annual burning. As the Kumeyaay lost control of their land, the native grain grass gradually became extinct and was replaced by European pasture grasses ill-suited to a land where it rarely rains from April to November. Chaparral gradually replaced grasses and annual greens in most areas.[44]

A related problem was overgrazing. Shipek remarks on the irony that an American settler, Major Utt, called the Kumeyaay grain fields the finest "grasslands" west of the Kansas plains and then proceeded, along with other settlers, to destroy them. "The grain was eaten to the roots. The European immigrants, thinking the grain was natural, did not save seed for rebroadcasting, and it thus disappeared; many ground surfaces were left bare." During periods of drought, sheep and cattle were concentrated in the wetter valleys. But without the Kumeyaay to repair the rock alignments that slowed and spread storm runoff, erosional gullies destroyed the wet meadows. Sage and creosote now predominate in locations like the Campo reservation that were once described as excellent pasture with knee-deep grass.[45]

Seemingly not content to ruin the land they had taken from the Campos, whites were responsible for ravaging the pitifully small portion they returned to the tribe. In the early part of the twentieth century, farmers began replacing cattlemen in some valleys. Farmers invariably drained the wet meadows to secure the best soil for their crops. On the advice of a local farmer, the Mission Indians Agency cut and drained the wet meadow on the Campo reservation. "Unfortunately, breaking the surface of the wet meadows opened the extremely fine loam to erosion, which then destroyed the massive loam deposits, leaving only the underlying sand," Shipek writes. "Most valleys, instead of being characterized by the original wet meadows, abundant surface water, and numerous small springs described in early records, now have deep gullies, lack surface water, and have no small side springs at all."[46]

In sum, the Campos successfully managed the land to support their people. They did so with a sophistication that we are just beginning to understand and emulate. Their record as stewards of the land certainly compares very favorably with that of the settlers who took it from them. Now the land remains the tribe's only material community asset, and through no fault of the Campos, a poor asset it is. If the Campos are to prosper materially as a people, rather than as individuals, they must do so by fully exploiting the resources of their reservation. A question we will address later is whether the Campos are continuing to act as good stewards as they seek to realize the very limited economic potential of their land.

PART THREE

THE BATTLEFIELDS OF THE WAR

CHAPTER SIX

MAKING THEIR STAND
ON A LANDFILL

IN 1987, WHEN THE CAMPOS FIRST BEGAN TO CONSIDER DEVELoping a landfill, the tribe's unemployment rate was 79 percent, and fewer than half of those who did have jobs made more than $7,000 a year. The budget of the Campo tribal government was then only $15,000, the income being derived from sand mining and leases for cattle grazing. Six years later, annual tribal government revenues had skyrocketed to $700,000 and tribal unemployment had been reduced to 30 percent. The difference was the funding provided by Mid-American Waste Systems, Inc.—the landfill company selected by the Campos—during the development phase of the project.[1]

In light of the profound and pervasive poverty of the Campos, the economic potential of the project did seem extraordinary. The landfill could receive as much as three thousand tons of waste per day upon reaching full operation and, given its capacity of 28 million tons, could continue at that rate for thirty years.[2] In 1993, the tipping fee—the price paid by a waste transporter to dispose of waste at a landfill—that Mid-American was offering to charge cities using the county landfills was $22 to $26 a ton.[3] Assuming that the contract rate ultimately settled upon were $24 a ton, and further assuming that the rate were *not* adjusted for inflation over the project's thirty-year lifetime, the landfill could gross $672 million. Perhaps much more. In 1993, a management audit recommended that the county raise the tipping fee charged at its landfills from $43 per ton to $65.[4] If the tipping fee charged by Mid-American averaged $65 per ton over thirty years, the Campo landfill would ultimately gross $1.8 billion.

If the tribe's share of the tipping fee were three dollars per ton, the figure used in the environmental impact statement, the Campos could earn as much as $3 million a year in royalties if the landfill were to operate at capacity. The royalty income would be divided equally between the tribe's general fund and Muht-Hei, Inc., the tribal corporation managing its business interests. (*Muht-Hei* means "New Land," the Campos' name for the separate 14,870-acre parcel of land added to their original reservation in 1911.) The royalty income dedicated to the general fund would be used by the tribe to support such programs as housing, education, and health care, whereas Muht-Hei would reinvest its royalties in other economic development projects. Muht-Hei declares per capita dividends to tribal members, and the tribe may decide to make per capita payments out of the general fund as well. Individual tribal members would also benefit insofar as the project fulfilled its promise of providing full employment for reservation residents. The reservation has a potential labor force of seventy-five. The project would create fifty-five permanent jobs, if the proposed recycling and composting facilities were operated. Of the fifty-five permanent jobs, Campos could fill thirty-five, leaving twenty for the off-reservation labor force.[5]

According to Kevin Gover, a Pawnee whose nationally recognized Albuquerque law firm represents the Campos, the tribe plans to use its general revenue income to award full scholarships to every tribal member admitted to college, build new public facilities and refurbish existing facilities, construct new homes for every family living in substandard housing, and provide income supplements to tribal members. The general council of the tribe will determine its budget priorities, and "for the first time, such priority-setting will not be a mere exercise in frustration due to lack of resources; the [tribe] will have the resources to address in earnest the health, educational, and social problems that have plagued it."[6]

Under its agreement with the tribe, Mid-American began making payments to the tribe in September of 1990, when tribal members voted to go forward with the project. The income from Mid-American has already enabled the Campos, for example, to begin making up the educational deficit that is the legacy of generations of discrimination and neglect. One of the tribe's long-term goals is to develop and enhance the technical competence of tribal members so that they can fill positions in the environmental protection agency the tribe has created to regulate the proposed landfill, among other tasks. As a first step toward that goal, Mike Connolly convinced the tribe to underwrite the transportation and tuition expenses of any tribal member who wants to go to junior college. No Campos were attending junior college prior to the inception of this program; a half-dozen were in 1993.[7]

LACK OF ECONOMIC DEVELOPMENT ALTERNATIVES

The potential benefits of the landfill project for the Campos, then, appeared to be very substantial. Indeed, the project appeared to offer the 286 members of the tribe the opportunity to rise in a few years from desperate poverty to a comfortable middle class life, with full employment, a wide range of tribal government services, and a promising future for their children. Aside from environmental concerns, the obvious question is, given the poor quality of their reservation land and its isolated location, do the Campos have other economic development opportunities with similar promise?

The federal environmental impact study prepared by the Bureau of Indian Affairs reviewed the alternatives available to the tribe. First, the Campos considered whether they could reasonably expect to increase substantially the revenue they derive from their two ongoing businesses—sand mining and cattle grazing. The Campos concluded that their sand mining operation has little promise because they are so far from potential markets, making their transportation costs noncompetitive; moreover, at the current removal rate, the reservation has only a ten-year supply of sand remaining. Nor is there much hope of substantially increasing their income from cattle leasing. The reservation does not have prime pasture or grazing land, which as we have seen is not a coincidence. Rather, the reservation has scrub land, which is suitable for only a few head of cattle per acre; actually, much of it is so poor that several acres are required per head. Therefore, the lease rate is very low.[8]

Another alternative, urged by Congressman Duncan Hunter, was establishing a recreational vehicle (RV) park. There are numerous RV parks, trailer resorts, campgrounds and other recreational facilities within a thirty-mile radius of the Campo reservation. However, most of these facilities are closer to or are within public parks or other public lands such as Lake Morena County Park, Anza Borrego Desert State Park, and Cleveland National Forest. The successful facilities are located near natural features attractive to visitors—water, forests, unique terrain, or dramatic vistas. The Campo reservation does not have such natural attractions. Moreover, the low user fees that facilities located on public lands can afford to charge would make it very difficult for the Campos to compete on price. Certainly the Campos could not reasonably anticipate that an RV park would have anything like the income potential of the proposed landfill.[9]

Jim West, a Cheyenne who is a financial advisor to the Campos and other Indian tribes, testified that this project had kindled a "sudden interest" in the Campos by public officials. "Except for one BIA agent referred to in some of the history I've read," West said, "that's the first serious interest in the economic development alternatives of this tribe" in the century since the reservation was established.[10] The Campos may have questioned just how "serious" the interest was after one witness, a candidate for county supervisor, recommended as an alternative to the landfill project that the tribe stage wild west reenactments.[11]

On its face, the most promising economic development alternative available to the Campos would seem to be opening a card and bingo casino on the reservation. Indian gaming has been called a "1990s gold rush." Industry estimates of 1992 gross revenues from gambling on reservations ranged up to $1.3 billion. "Indian gambling is the fastest growing industry in the U.S.," observed I. Nelson Rose, a Whittier College law professor and gaming expert. "It's clearly in the billions of dollars, and probably is doubling every year."[12] By 1994, more than 150 tribes were reported either to have entered the gaming industry or to be poised to do so.[13]

Indeed, the Sycuan, another San Diego County Kume-yaay band, have established a successful casino on their reservation near El Cajon, some forty miles west of the Campo reservation. "The millions have meant the El Cajon tribe hasn't taken a government subsidy in eight years. The Sycuan band has its own fire and police departments, a day care center and a library that recently acquired $350,000 worth of books," the California Lawyer reported. "Last year the $6.5 million casino employed 800 people and grossed an estimated $120 million, all for a tribe numbering just 95."[14]

However, not every tribe can cash in on the apparent bonanza. "It is self-limiting by geography," noted Howard Dickstein, a Sacramento attorney who represents several northern California gaming tribes.[15] A reservation in a remote location would not be able to attract patrons, especially if potential patrons would have to bypass other reservations that offer gaming. This is the case with the Campo reservation, which is about seventy miles east of its potential market, San Diego. A San Diego gambler heading for the Campo reservation would have to bypass the Sycuan reservation, which is about twenty miles from San Diego, and then the Viejas reservation, another gaming reservation that is approximately twenty miles closer to San Diego than is Campo, and much closer to the interstate highway. That casinos are not a sure bet for Indian tribes is demonstrated by the failure of at least five gaming operations on southern California Indian reservations.[16]

Though a gambling casino does not appear to be a viable alternative economic development opportunity for the Campos, gaming does offer an instructive analogy. What gaming and landfills have in common is that both industries are so closely regulated by states that it can be difficult or impossible to secure the necessary permits to engage in business. What Indian reservations have to offer potential investors is a haven from state jurisdiction. (The question of state jurisdiction over reservation businesses will be considered at length in the next chapter.) Having deliberately denied to Indians lands with foreseeable economic potential, the nation now must live with the fact that one of the few competitive advantages Indians have is that they can offer business locations within a state's borders, and therefore accessible to the state's markets, but outside the state's jurisdiction.

WANTED: INVESTMENT PARTNER WITH
DEEP POCKETS AND THICK SKIN

Indians are convinced that they are limited to such "outlaw" business opportunities not only because they were ceded the lands that whites believed to be valueless, but also because their neighbors invariably oppose tribal economic development. Mike Connolly says "the closer you get to the reservation," the greater the "fear of the tribe . . . becoming an economic and political power in this area of the country." The major employers in the region now are government agencies, Mike points out, the U.S. and California forest services, the state highway department, the public school system, the sheriff's department, and the border patrol.[17] Given the economic projections— $3 million a year in tipping fees and more jobs than the

Campos could fill—the proposed landfill would seem to have the potential for, or present the specter of, shifting the economic center of balance of the Campo area to the reservation.

Comments by Backcountry Against Dumps on the final EIS do appear to reflect a grudging attitude toward economic activity on the reservation. "We have heard rumors that the Campo Band is planning to put a cement plant at or near the existing sand mine. How much water will that use and what impacts will it have on the water table along with the loss of groundwater storage due to loss of sand through mining as we noted before?" said BAD in written comments.[18] "We asked for dates that small-scale honey production, orchards and ranching were attempted on the reservation, all [BIA] said was a vague 'from the early 1900's to the present.' Presently, there are bee boxes on the reservations. Every summer we are plagued by bees looking for water at our livestock tanks."[19]

Congressman Duncan Hunter, in addition to proposing the alternative of a recreational vehicle park, suggested that the Campos consider developing a golf resort on the reservation.[20] (One wag, familiar with Congressman Hunter's proposal to resolve the City of San Diego's wastewater crisis by using the sewage effluent to water golf courses, remarked: "Whatever the problem, Duncan's answer is a golf course.") The congressman, apparently, had not discussed his idea with Donna Tisdale, the chair of his task force on waste, because her reaction was: "I would need to have it proven to me that a golf course wouldn't be too water intensive."[21]

It was against this background that Mike Connolly ruefully jested that precisely because their neighbors can be expected to oppose whatever project a tribe chooses, a landfill may be the best choice. The point he is making, Mike explains, is that if the opposition of their neighbors is a given, then tribes must choose projects that satisfy two criteria: the potential return for the developer must be large enough to warrant the expense of protracted litigation; and the industry involved must have a "thick skin"—that is, not be scared off by the adverse publicity generated by project opponents and the elected officials who espouse their cause. The latter criterion would eliminate, for example, motel or restaurant franchises, for whom corporate goodwill is a paramount concern.[22]

A landfill, on the other hand, seems to fill the bill on both counts. Opening new landfills is very difficult, because of both regulatory restrictions and neighborhood opposition. In 1992, the staff of the California waste board estimated that it took about ten years to open a new landfill and from five to eight years to expand an existing facility.[23] The demand for landfill space therefore exceeded the supply, creating the potential of enormous profits, when this project was conceived. Moreover, landfill operators do not expect to be loved by their new neighbors. The residents of the surrounding community invariably fight a proposed landfill, try to rally their local, state, and federal elected officials around their flag, and if all else fails, go to court to stop the project.

Kevin Gover, the Campos' lawyer, explains that the solid waste industry may be a "good match" for Indian tribes on other grounds, too. "The isolation and abundance of reservation land fulfill a primary need of the solid waste industry. Moreover, the industry offers many opportunities for unskilled and semi-skilled workers, as well as opportunities for training in marketable skills." Finally, Gover adds, "developers in the industry are accustomed to capitalizing projects without cash contributions from host communities. Each of these facts made the industry attractive to a community with high unemployment, low educational levels, and absolutely no investment capital."[24]

THE COUNTY CIRCLES
THE WAGONS AROUND ITS MONOPOLY

At one of the public hearings held on the landfill proposal, anthropologist Florence Shipek testified that "over the years there have been any number" of proposals for economic development projects on the Campo reservation that were frustrated by their non-Indian neighbors. "So I'm very sad that about the only thing we've left to them is the trash dumps, because I think it's terrible."[25]

Indeed, the Campos believe that the county is not even willing to give Indians a fair opportunity to compete for trash, but is instead, in an effort to retain its landfill monopoly, trying to prevent the Campos from entering the market. The County of San Diego, along with BAD and the San Diego chapter of the Sierra Club, has been in the forefront of the fight against the Campo project. The special contribution the county made to their allies' case involved the question of whether there was a market in San Diego County for the additional landfill capacity the Campo project would create. The economic viability of the project is a critical issue, its opponents assert, because the environmental safeguards claimed for the project would be very expensive and would not be maintained if the landfill were losing money.

The EIS concluded that the project was viable, relying on information contained in studies published in 1990 by the county's waste department in conjunction with other landfill projects proposed by the county. According to the EIS, the volume of waste generated in the county was rapidly increasing; it was projected to reach 5.8 million tons by the year 2000, as compared with 3.9 million tons in 1990 and 3 million tons in 1985. "Without the development of new landfills or waste-to-energy facilities, the best-case scenario projects depletion of all county landfill capacity by the year 2004." Thus, the EIS concluded, there is likely to be a "substantial demand" for the landfill space provided by this project. Indeed, the EIS continued, if the Campos enter the market, "San Diego County would still need to develop substantial additional landfill capacity within the next 5 to 10 years."[26]

In its comments on the EIS, San Diego County responded

that the county was not running out of landfill space; to the contrary, it had over fifteen years of capacity remaining in its existing landfills. Moreover, the county asserted, none of the three major market sectors on which the Campos were relying—the county itself, cities within the county, or cities outside the county—would in fact be likely to do business with Mid-American. The county would not take its waste to the Campo landfill; the county board of supervisors had voted not to. The cities within the county would continue to take their waste to county landfills because the Campo facility would not be able to offer them lower rates. Finally, the Campos would not be able to import waste from cities outside the county because the county would not issue the necessary permits for transport of out-of-county waste.[27]

It may well be demanding too much of the EIS process to ask that it provide a reliable prediction as to whether a particular new business will succeed, especially in the volatile solid waste industry. Until recently, landfills appeared to be sure things, if—and it was a very big if—the necessary permits could be obtained. The *Decision-Makers Guide to Solid Waste Management*, published by EPA in 1989, noted that the amount of waste the nation generated had risen every year since 1960. In 1987, a report prepared by the California waste board estimated that the state's annual volume of waste would reach 39 million tons by 1991. In fact, the annual volume reached 42.5 million tons by the beginning of 1990. The rising volume of waste, combined with the increasing difficulty of securing permits for new landfills, resulted in what EPA referred as a "capacity crisis," manifested by a sharp rise in tipping fees. "In the not-so-distant past," EPA noted, "tipping fees were in the ballpark of a few dollars a ton. Now the national average is near $26, and in some areas the average tipping fee is more than six times that amount."[28] In its annual survey of tipping fees, the National Solid Wastes Management Association reported in 1989 that "[a]fter hardly budging from the survey's first year, 1982 through 1986, the national sample average has doubled in the past two years!"[29] Because it was next to impossible to obtain one, a permit to open a new landfill then seemed like a license to print money, or at least to turn garbage into gold.

This project was conceived at the height of the capacity crisis, which may account for Mid-American's willingness to spend over $17 million by September of 1993 trying to secure a permit for the facility.[30] Now, however, with the weak economy and statutorily mandated recycling, the landfill boom is beginning to bust in southern California. That, and problems specific to its waste department, may explain why the County of San Diego so vehemently opposes the Campo project.

In 1993, the *Los Angeles Times* reported that the landfill business in southern California had "lost some of its luster." "In Los Angeles County—where state and industry officials not long ago trumpeted the onset of a 'dump crisis' amid a scarcity of landfill space—there is now concern of a landfill surplus in the not too distant future," the *Times* disclosed. "With the possible exception of Ventura County, other Southern California counties also appear to have plenty of landfill space. In Orange County, where all three dumps are county-owned," the *Times* continued, "dumping volume is down so much that landfill officials have suggested taking in trash from Los Angeles and other counties."[31]

The problem became especially acute in San Diego County, where the five county-owned landfills received the waste from the unincorporated area and all of the cities in the county except San Diego. The amount of waste received by the county plummeted by thirty-four percent in three years, from 2.5 million tons in fiscal year 1989–90 to 1.65 tons in 1992–93. The severity of the recession in southern California was one factor. Recycling was another. In a management audit of the county waste department, the Ernst & Young firm remarked on the irony that a successful recycling program can lead to failure in the landfill business. As the recycling rate goes up, landfill tonnage and attendant income go down. Increasing tipping fees in an effort to make up for lost income leads to higher garbage bills and, thus, greater motivation to recycle.[32]

The management audit was prepared because a number of perceived problems, including escalating tipping fees, had caused the cities in the county's landfill system to lose confidence in the county waste department.[33] Compared to the waste department, apparently, the post office is a model of a customer-oriented government agency. When asked about the complaints of the cities that led to the audit, county waste department officials "responded without apparent concern or with a definite lack of concern," according to the report.[34] In a report on "San Diego County's Tra$h Cri$is," the county grand jury echoed this observation when it noted that county employees responded with "impatience, abruptness and occasional rudeness" to expressions of concern voiced by private citizens about the impact the "trash crisis" was having on their lives. "Members of the County government, in casual conversation, have been known to refer to some groups as 'Trash Bags' and 'The Whining Nimbys,'" the grand jury reported. The disaffected were not limited to citizen activists. The grand jury observed that the animosity that "blazed" between the county and the cities that the waste department was supposed to serve was "reminiscent of European city-states of the middle ages defending their battlement with little concern for the needs of private citizens."

Moreover, the grand jury found that the shortcomings of the county waste department were not limited to an attitude problem. In its May 21, 1993, report, the grand jury found that "over the past decade the elected county representatives and the county staff have behaved in a fragmented and irrational manner: arrogant on one hand and then caving in when public outcries become too loud and threatening. Leadership often gave way to political self-interest." Midway through its study it became apparent to the grand jury that "there was no 'process.' Crisis management was the order of the day; new conflicts appeared daily." There was a "general consensus," the grand jury continued, "that the county government, for years, had been guilty of vacillation and short-sighted solutions to long-range problems in the areas of solid waste management." Indeed, "long-range planning," the grand jury concluded, "has been non-existent."[35]

By 1992, according to the audit report, these problems had come home to roost—the county landfill system was about to go broke. The problem was caused by declining revenues and increasing costs, the latter being attributable in large part to debt service on a $139 million recycling facility the county had built near the community of San Marcos. The auditors recommended that the county raise its then-current tipping fee of $28 per ton by 137 percent, to $66.50. The audit report was issued in December of 1992; by the following summer, the county had raised its tipping fee to $43 a ton and was proposing to raise it again, to $65 a ton in the fall. The proposed rate hike sent the county landfill system into a death spiral. The cities that sent their waste to the county's landfills began seriously considering alternatives, including Mid-American's offer to dispose of their trash for about a third of what the county was proposing to charge—$22 to $26 a ton. "It would appear to be a rather viable alternative when and if [the Campo landfill is] completed," the El Cajon city manager observed.[36]

Struggling to hold its waste empire together, the county vacillated between making concessions and threatening retaliation. The proposed rate hike was cut in half—to $55 a ton, and the cities were offered an opportunity to share power through the formation of a joint-powers authority (JPA) to replace the county waste department.[37] However, the county might as well have offered to share authority on the bridge of the *Titanic*. To extend the naval metaphor, the ship of fools described in the grand jury report had run aground on the San Marcos recycling plant. The cost of financing and operating the San Marcos facility is so high—about forty percent of the county's $55-per-ton fee is attributable to it—that shipping their waste to Utah appears to be cheaper for the cities than using the county landfills![38]

Ten of the seventeen cities that had belonged to the county system refused to join the JPA. El Cajon was the first to make a definitive break. Twelve truckloads of El Cajon trash a day, or 75,000 tons a year, are being hauled to a commercial landfill near Lancaster, in the high desert of northern Los Angeles county. The contract price—$40 per ton—is well below the $55 per ton it would have cost El Cajon to continue using the county system. El Cajon's decision was opposed by residents of Lancaster and a ban on the import of out-of-county waste was threatened by the Los Angeles County Board of Supervisors. However, the United States Supreme Court had recently held that a Michigan statute prohibiting private landfills from accepting out-of-county solid waste, unless authorized to do so by the county's solid waste management plan, violated the commerce clause of the United States Constitution.[39] The Board of Supervisors backed off and the El Cajon waste started moving north in July 1994.[40]

In response to El Cajon's defection, the JPA blustered, floating a consultant's proposal to charge nonmember cities five times as much as members—$253 a ton—to use the county's landfills. The predictable reaction was outrage and defiance. A spokeswoman for the cities of Santee, Imperial Beach, and Chula Vista called the proposed rate hike "punitive and vindictive." The mayor of La Mesa agreed, "I call it an extortion rate." An Oceanside councilman noted that his city, along with Carlsbad and Escondido, was negotiating to send its trash by train to a landfill in Utah for $53 a ton. The JPA backed down, offering nonmembers a rate of $65 a ton.

However, Oceanside had by then entered into a tentative agreement to send its waste to a commercial landfill in eastern Los Angeles county for $47 a ton, and Carlsbad and Escondido were still exploring the option of having their waste hauled by rail to Utah.[41] The JPA warned the defectors that they would be held liable for their shares of the San Marcos debt, whether or not they continued to use the county's landfills. County Supervisor Pam Slater admonished the non-member cities that their failure to join in shouldering the San Marcos debt burden would jeopardize the county's general fund and lead to a reduction of such county services as law enforcement, jails, libraries, and parks.

In light of the county landfill system's well-publicized distress, the Campos found it disingenuous of the county to try to squelch their landfill on the ground that it would not be economically viable. They are convinced that the county has opposed their project not out of concern for the environment but because it would compete with the county system. It is difficult enough to assess the motivations of real people, never mind corporate persons like county governments. However, it does appear that the county has been engaged in a high stakes game of monopoly. To pay off the San Marcos debt, Ernst & Young recommended that the county raise its fees to $66.50 a ton. To do that, the county must have known, it had to forestall competition. Competition, the county now asserts, threatens not only its waste system but other essential county services as well. If the competition provided by out-of-county landfills—at $40 to $53 a ton—is proving ruinous to the county, then the competition of the Campos—at $22 to $26 a ton—must have been perceived as a threat.

Because its credibility is undermined by an apparent conflict of interest, the county's opposition to their project has tended to unify the tribe behind it. In the next two chapters we shall see how the opposition of the state has had the same effect.

CHAPTER SEVEN

PEACE DECLARES WAR ON THE CAMPOS

ONE OF THE TWO MAJOR FRONTS IN THE CAMPO LANDFILL WAR was the California legislature, where Steve Peace, a young Democrat who represented the Campo area in the California Assembly, tried to stop the Campo project by introducing legislation to prohibit the disposal of waste in a reservation landfill unless the facility were licensed by the state.

J. Stephen Peace is one of the most controversial members of the legislature. According to the *California Political Almanac*, Peace "was once known for two things: He was the producer of the cult film, 'Attack of the Killer Tomatoes,' and he was [Assembly Speaker] Willie Brown's man to see in San Diego."[1] Although apparently back in the speaker's good graces by the time this legislation was being considered, Peace had turned on his patron a few years earlier, participating in a palace revolution by what the press dubbed the "Gang of Five," and the intriguers themselves called the "Five Amigos." Trying to account for Peace's participation in the doomed revolt, another Democratic member of the Assembly mused that "this is the first time in his Assembly career that Steve Peace has had four friends at the same time."[2] Peace's lack of popularity among his colleagues is attributable, according to the *California Journal*, to the fact that he is given to angry outbursts that go "beyond both legislative protocol and common decency." "'When Peace disagrees with you, he's very unpleasant,' complained a [fellow] Democratic member. 'He doesn't just argue; he questions your intelligence, your judgment and your integrity.'"[3] To demonstrate how inaptly Peace is named, the story most often told involves his attack upon a venerable state senator, whom he called a "senile old pedophile."[4]

The *California Journal* rates state lawmakers, based on a survey of the Sacramento press corps, lobbyists, legislative staff, and the legislators themselves. Among the qualities rated are intelligence and integrity. Peace is consistently rated as being among the lawmakers with the most intelligence and the least integrity.[5] However unpopular and distrusted he may be, Peace is acknowledged by other lawmakers to be a relentless and effective sponsor of legislation. Describing him as "manic and insatiable," one colleague said that Peace has a tendency to "get into your face and stay there until he gets what he wants."[6] Peace's effort to stop the Campo landfill project would demonstrate both his worst and best qualities.

Steve Peace's response to BAD's cry for help was quick and specific. Even before BAD held its second major event, the presentation to the chamber of commerce in Campo, Peace had written to Donna Tisdale that he was preparing legislation that was intended to thwart the Campo project.[7] The task of drafting the bill fell to Peace's chief of staff, David Takashima. Because Indian law is a very specialized field, Takashima consulted Rudy Corona, a personal friend who is a member of the California Attorney General's Office. Characterized by a Campo supporter as a "noted Indian fighter," Corona had participated in a landmark United States Supreme Court case three years earlier in which the California Attorney General's Office had argued, unsuccessfully, that the state had authority to regulate bingo games on Indian reservations.[8]

Convinced that some tribal leaders are "totally willing to desecrate their land in order to make a couple of dollars," Rudy Corona was concerned that "horrendous, cataclysmic" environmental problems might result if the Campos or other California tribes were allowed to develop commercial waste projects that were not subject to the same strict regulations applicable elsewhere in the state. Invoking popularized Indian imagery, Corona points out that "the winds that blow and the waters that run do not stop at reservation border lines."[9] Corona counseled Takashima that any legislation asserting state jurisdiction over reservation waste projects would be challenged and the case would almost certainly wind up in the U.S. Supreme Court. "We knew," Takashima says, "even if we passed this bill the way that we wanted it, that it would fly in the face of Indian sovereignty."[10] Corona's contribution to the cause was crafting the constitutional theory that Peace would invoke in support of his legislation: State regulation of reservation waste projects is consistent with the Supreme Court's decisions concerning tribal sovereignty because California has a legitimate and profound interest in protecting the off-reservation environment from the "spill-over" effects of contamination originating on a reservation.

The legislation—Assembly Bill 3477—that Peace introduced on February 28, 1990, did not directly assert state jurisdiction over reservation waste projects, but rather forbade potential customers from doing business with waste facilities not regulated by the state. "While the state cannot directly overrule the tribe's plan, 'We can make it very difficult for them,' Peace said. The assemblyman crafted the bill to penalize any local agency that attempts to dispose of its waste on a Native American reservation,"[11] During the next three months, AB 3477 sailed through the Assembly, passing the Committee on Environmental Safety by a vote of 13-0, the Committee on Ways and Means by 21-0, and the full Assembly by 68-0. By the time the bill reached the Senate Committee on Toxics and Public Safety, however, a potential roadblock had arisen. The legislature's own lawyer, the legislative counsel, had issued a written opinion advising Senator Art Torres, the committee chairman, that the bill, if enacted, would be struck down in court.

Although Peace had made a transparent effort to sidestep the jurisdictional issue, the question addressed by the legislative counsel was whether California has authority to regulate waste facilities on Indian reservations. Stated differently, the question was whether Indian tribes retain sovereign authority over the subject of waste regulation, to the exclusion of state jurisdiction.

TRIBAL SOVEREIGNTY: THE CASE LAW

In ordinary usage, *sovereignty* refers to the supreme authority an independent nation exercises over both its domestic affairs and its foreign relations. As we shall see, the decisions of the U.S. Supreme Court resolving conflicts in tribal/state jurisdiction tend to be subject-matter specific. An opinion by the Supreme Court upholding a state tax on cigarettes sold in reservation stores to non-Indians, for example, may offer little guidance as to whether the high court will sustain state regulation of hunting and fishing by non-Indians on reservations. Nevertheless, the following fundamental principles underlie the high court decisions analyzing and demarking the limits of tribal sovereignty: Before they were conquered by the Europeans, the Indian tribes of North America were fully sovereign. Conquest, first by European powers and then by the United States, deprived tribes of external sovereignty—that is, their power to enter into treaties with foreign nations— but did not in itself affect tribal authority over their people and their territory. The domestic sovereignty tribes retain, however, is of a "unique and limited character"; it "exists only at the sufferance of Congress and is subject to complete defeasance" or nullification by Congress.[12] On the one hand, "tribal sovereignty is dependent on, and subordinate to, only the Federal Government, not the States."[13] On the other hand, Congress may withdraw sovereign authority over reservation matters from tribes and confer it upon states.

Worcester v. Georgia: The Supreme Court's Gravest Crisis

The reach of state jurisdiction in Indian country was first considered by the U.S. Supreme Court in *Worcester v. Georgia*, 31 U.S. (6 Pet.) 515 (1832), precipitating what one leading historian of the high court called "the most serious crisis" in its history.[14] In 1830, Congress passed the Indian Removal Act, authorizing the president to exchange U.S. territory west of the Mississippi River for the lands of the Cherokees and other eastern tribes. While President Andrew Jackson sought to convince the tribes to move voluntarily, the state of Georgia asserted its jurisdiction over the Cherokees, enacting laws that purported to abolish the Cherokee government, to extend Georgia law to Cherokee country, and to distribute all Cherokee lands among five Georgia counties.[15]

The first case to reach the U.S. Supreme Court testing Georgia's assertion of jurisdiction over the Cherokees involved the conviction in a Georgia court of George Tassel, a Cherokee, for a murder committed on Cherokee land. The Supreme Court granted a writ to review the conviction but Georgia refused to honor the writ, and Tassel was hanged.[16]

Next, the Cherokees filed suit in the Supreme Court seeking to enjoin the execution of Georgia laws in the Cherokee nation. The Supreme Court held that it lacked jurisdiction to hear the merits of the case because the Cherokee nation was not a foreign state within the meaning of the constitutional provision giving the court original jurisdiction over suits between states and foreign nations.[17]

The issue of Georgia's jurisdiction over the Cherokees was finally joined before the Supreme Court in *Worcester v. Georgia*. When missionaries published resolutions in defense of the Cherokees, the Georgia legislature responded by enacting a law that made it a criminal offense for whites to reside in the Cherokee portion of Georgia without taking an oath of allegiance to the state and obtaining a special permit from the governor. A white missionary, Samuel Worcester, was convicted under the law and sentenced to hard labor for four years. Again, the case was appealed to the Supreme Court; again, Georgia refused to appear.

In an opinion by Chief Justice John Marshall, the Supreme Court reversed Worcester's conviction, finding the Georgia law to be "repugnant to the constitution, laws and treaties of the United States." Indian tribes, the Court held, were sovereign nations before being conquered by the United States, and they retained sovereign authority over their territory insofar as the individual states were concerned, unless the federal government provided to the contrary. "The Cherokee nation, then, is a distinct community occupying its own territory . . . in which the laws of Georgia can have no force, and which the citizens of Georgia have no right to enter, but with the assent of the Cherokees themselves, or in conformity with treaties, and with the acts of Congress. The whole intercourse between the United States and this nation, is, by our constitution and laws, vested in the government of the United States."[18]

Though scholars disagree over whether he actually made the statement, President Jackson was quoted as saying of the *Worcester* decision, "John Marshall has made his law; now let him enforce it." In any event, the judgment of the high court was not enforced by the executive branch. The standoff between the Court and Georgia came to an end the following year when the governor pardoned Worcester and another missionary in return for their agreement to leave the state.

Rice v. Rehner: State Authority over Reservation Liquor Sales

One hundred and fifty years after its decision in *Worcester v. Georgia*, the U.S. Supreme Court issued the opinion upon which Peace, Takashima, and Corona principally relied—*Rice v. Rehner*, 463 U.S. 713 (1983). The question presented in *Rice v. Rehner* was whether the state of California could require a federally licensed Indian trader, who operated a general store on the Pala Indian reservation in San Diego County, to obtain a state license in order to sell liquor for off-premises consumption. The high court noted that, despite the emphasis in *Worcester v. Georgia* on the importance of tribal self-government, "'Congress has to a substantial degree opened the doors of reservations to state laws, in marked contrast to what prevailed in the time of Chief Justice Marshall.'"[19]

In order to answer the ultimate question of whether Indian tribes retain sovereign authority over liquor sales on reservations to the exclusion of state jurisdiction, the *Rice* court unbundled the inquiry into three distinct but related questions.

First, did Indian tribes *traditionally* exercise such sovereign authority? The answer to this question, the Court held, was no. The colonists had regulated trading of liquor with Indians before the United States was founded. Consistent with this tradition, Congress had imposed prohibition on reservations early in the nineteenth century. Moreover, the federal government not only permitted the states to regulate liquor sales on reservations, it sometimes required them to do so. For example, as a condition of entry into the Union, Arizona, New Mexico, and Oklahoma were required by Congress to enact prohibitions against the sale of liquor to Indians and the introduction of liquor to Indian country.[20]

Second, does the activity the state seeks to regulate likely have a substantial spill-over effect beyond the reservation? The Court answered this question in the affirmative. "Liquor sold by Rehner to other Pala tribe members or to nonmembers can easily find its way out of the reservation and into the hands of those whom, for whatever reason, the State does not wish to possess alcoholic beverages."[21]

Finally, is state jurisdiction over the subject matter preempted by federal law? The answer, the Court held, was clear. "Our examination of [the pertinent federal statute] leads us to conclude that Congress authorized, rather than pre-empted, state regulation over Indian liquor transactions."[22]

Section 1 of AB 3477, the bill introduced by Peace, sum-marized the three-part test articulated in *Rice v. Rehner* and asserted that state regulation of reservation waste projects was justified under that test.

The Legislature hereby finds and declares that there is no tribal tradition in the handling of solid waste, hazardous waste, asbestos, or other regulated waste material. The health and welfare of the citizens of the state require the proper management and monitoring by local authorities, state authorities, or federal authorities. There is no federal preemption granted the Native American to operate or host solid waste or hazardous waste facilities. Groundwater and air do not stop at the reservations' boundaries. In the interest of pro-tecting the environment and the citizens of the state from solid waste and hazardous waste facilities on reservation land, the Legis-lature enacts this act to clarify that these facilities are required to meet all applicable state and federal statutes, regulations, and standards.

While Peace and his allies relied upon the earlier *Rice v. Rehner* decision involving state jurisdiction over liquor sales on reservations, the opponents of AB 3477 countered that the controlling precedent was the case that Corona and the California Attorney General's Office had lost in the Supreme Court—*California v. Cabazon Band of Mission Indians*, 480 U.S. 202 (1987).

California v. Cabazon: State Authority over Reservation Gambling

The assertion of state authority over reservation gaming in *Cabazon*, like AB 3477's assertion of state authority over res-ervation waste projects, was predicated upon a federal statute known as Public Law 280. Public Law 280 transferred criminal and, to a limited extent, civil jurisdiction over Indian lands from the federal to state governments in several states, includ-ing California. According to the Senate Report, the primary concern of Congress in enacting the statute was lawlessness on the reservations and the accompanying threat to non-

Indians living nearby. Prior to enactment of Public Law 280, law enforcement on reservations was, in the words of one commentator, "irrationally fractionated."

If a non-Indian committed a crime against another non-Indian or a crime without an apparent victim, such as gambling or drunk driving, only state authorities could prosecute him under state law. But if either the offender or victim was Indian, the federal government had exclusive jurisdiction to prosecute. . . . Finally, if offender and victim were both Indians, the federal government had exclusive jurisdiction if the offense was one of the "Ten Major Crimes;" otherwise, tribal courts had exclusive jurisdiction. Since federal law enforcement was typically neither well-financed nor vigorous, and tribal courts often lacked the resources and skills to be effective, the result, described by House Indian Affairs Subcommittee member Wesley D'Ewart, of Montana, was "[t]he complete breakdown of law and order on many of the Indian reservations."[23]

The states covered by Public Law 280 were granted broad *criminal* jurisdiction over offenses committed by or against Indians on reservations within those states. However, the statute's grant of *civil* jurisdiction was more limited. Public Law 280 states were granted jurisdiction over private civil litigation involving Indians, but they were not given "general civil regulatory authority" over tribes.[24] The test for determining whether a law is criminal in nature, and thus within the scope of the jurisdiction granted to the states under Public Law 280, was clarified by the Supreme Court in *California v. Cabazon Band of Mission Indians.*

Having earlier established the nation's first Indian card room on their seventeen-hundred-acre reservation near Palm Springs, the twenty-five-member Cabazon band, along with the Morongo band, brought suit in federal court for a declaratory judgment that California had no authority to regulate bingo played on Indian reservations within the state. The Supreme Court held that if the intent of a state law is generally to *prohibit* certain conduct, it falls within Public Law 280's grant of criminal jurisdiction. However, if the state law generally permits the conduct in question, subject to regulation, the statute must be classified as civil/regulatory, and Public Law 280 does not authorize its enforcement on an Indian reservation. Since California regulated, rather than prohibited, gambling in general and bingo in particular, Public Law 280 provided no basis for the state's asserted jurisdiction over the playing of bingo on reservations.[25]

So far, the lesson of *Cabazon* for AB 3477 would seem to be clear. Since California regulates, rather than prohibits, the disposal of hazardous and solid waste, AB 3477 would not appear to be authorized by Public Law 280. However, the *Cabazon* court indicated that the inquiry should not stop there. "Our cases . . . have not established an inflexible *per se* rule precluding state jurisdiction over tribes and tribal members in the absence of express congressional intent."[26] The ultimate question is whether state authority over reservation activities is preempted by federal law. State jurisdiction is preempted if it interferes with federal and tribal interests, unless those interests are outweighed by the state's interests.[27] There were important federal interests at stake in *Cabazon*, the Court held—"the Congressional goal of Indian self-government, including its 'overriding goal' of encouraging tribal self-sufficiency and economic development."[28] The federal government promoted tribal bingo enterprises, the Court noted, by approving tribal ordinances establishing and regulating gaming activities, and by providing financial assistance to such undertakings.

The Cabazon and Morongo reservations contain no natural resources that can be exploited, the high court noted. The tribal games supplied the sole source of revenue for the operation of the tribal governments and the provision of tribal services. They were also the major sources of employment on the reservations. Self-determination and economic development were not within reach, the Court continued, if the tribes could not raise revenue and provide employment for their members.[29]

The Supreme Court rejected California's contention that the tribes were merely marketing an exemption from state gambling laws. In *Washington v. Confederated Tribes of Colville Indian Reservation*, 447 U.S. 134, (1980), the Court had held that the state of Washington could tax cigarettes sold by tribal smokeshops to non-Indians, even though it would eliminate their competitive advantage and thereby substantially reduce revenue used to provide tribal services, because the tribes had no right to "market an exemption from state taxation to persons who would normally do their business elsewhere." The *Colville* court stated that "[i]t is painfully apparent that the value marketed by the smokeshops to persons coming from outside is not generated on the reservations by activities in which the Tribes have a significant interest."[30]

The *Cabazon* court distinguished *Colville* on the ground that:

> Here . . . the Tribes are not merely importing a product onto the reservations for immediate resale to non-Indians. They have built modern facilities which provide recreational opportunities and ancillary services to their patrons, who do not simply drive onto the reservations, make purchases and depart, but spend extended periods of time there enjoying the services the Tribes provide. The Tribes have a strong incentive to provide comfortable, clean, and attractive facilities and well-run games in order to increase attendance at the games.[31]

The *Cabazon* court found the bingo halls on the Cabazon and Morongo reservations analogous not to the smokeshops in *Colville* but to the hunting and fishing resort that the Mescalero Apache tribe operates on its reservation. In *New Mexico v. Mescalero Apache Tribe*, 462 U.S. 324 (1983), the U.S. Supreme Court had held that New Mexico could not regulate hunting and fishing by non-Indians on the Mescalero reservation. The Mescalero tribe was not merely marketing an exemption from state hunting and fishing regulations, the Court held, but was instead earning revenue for essential tribal services and providing employment for tribal members through the "concerted and sustained" management of reservation land and resources.[32] "Similarly," the *Cabazon* court held, "the Cabazon and Morongo Bands are generating value on the reservations through activities in which they have a substantial interest."[33]

The *Cabazon* court gave short shrift to California's reliance on *Rice v. Rehner*, distinguishing that case on the grounds that "Congress had never recognized any sovereign tribal interest in regulating liquor traffic and that Congress, historically, had plainly anticipated that the states would exercise concurrent authority to regulate the use and distribution of liquor on Indian reservations." By contrast, the *Cabazon* opinion continued, "[t]here is no such traditional federal view governing the outcome of this case, since, as we have explained, the current federal policy is to promote precisely what California seeks to prevent," namely, tribal gaming enterprises.[34] The state's asserted interest in preventing the infiltration of tribal games by organized crime was not sufficient, the Court held, to outweigh the federal and tribal interests in tribal self-government and economic self-sufficiency.[35]

Lower Court Decisions Dealing with Federal Waste Laws

In addition to *Cabazon*, the opponents of AB 3477 relied upon two lower federal court decisions to support their argument that the proposed legislation would be preempted by federal law. In *State of Washington, Dept. of Ecology v. United States Environmental Protection Agency*, 752 F.2d 1465 (9th Cir. 1985), the state of Washington asked EPA to confer upon it primary jurisdiction over the federal hazardous waste program throughout the state, including Indian lands. While otherwise approving Washington's application, EPA retained to itself jurisdiction to manage the federal hazardous waste program on Indian lands in the state. Upon petition for review, the U.S. Court of Appeals for the Ninth Circuit affirmed EPA's decision.

Both the federal hazardous waste law and its legislative history were silent on the issue of state regulatory jurisdiction on reservations. Therefore, under established principles of statutory construction, the court was compelled to defer to the interpretation of the agency responsible for administering the statute, provided that interpretation were reasonable. Buttressing its conclusion that EPA's construction of the statute was reasonable, the court said, was the well-settled principle that states are generally precluded from exercising jurisdiction over reservations unless Congress has clearly expressed an intention to permit it. Moreover, the court noted, excluding state jurisdiction was consistent with the federal government's policy of encouraging tribal self-regulation in environmental matters. The court recognized that the state of Washington has a vital interest in effective hazardous waste management throughout the state, including Indian lands. However, preemption of state regulatory jurisdiction over reservations would not leave a regulatory vacuum, the court held, because EPA would remain "responsible for ensuring that the federal statutes are met on the reservations. Those standards are designed to protect human health and the environment. The state and its citizens will not be without protection."[36]

In determining that it was the policy of the federal government to encourage tribal self-regulation in environmental matters, the court relied upon a 1980 EPA policy. That policy was reaffirmed by Administrator William D. Ruckelshaus in 1984, shortly after argument was heard in *Washington Dept. of Ecology*. The "EPA Policy for the Administration of Environmental Programs on Indian Reservations" is based on, among others, the following principles: EPA recognizes tribal governments as sovereign entities with primary authority and responsibility for their reservations and their peoples, and not as political subdivisions of states. Within the constraints of its authorities and resources, EPA assists interested tribal governments in assuming responsibility on reservation land for the sorts of federal environmental programs that EPA delegates to states for nonreservation lands. Until tribal governments are willing and able to assume full responsibility for delegable programs, EPA retains responsibility for managing federal environmental programs on reservations. As to this last point, the EPA policy recognizes an exception where a state has "express grant of jurisdiction from Congress" to assume responsibility for a delegable federal program on a reservation.[37]

Washington Dept. of Ecology involved the hazardous waste provisions of the federal Resource Conservation and Recovery Act, known by its acronym RCRA. *Blue Legs v. United States Environmental Protection Agency*, 668 F.Supp. 1329 (D.S.D. 1987) involved the solid waste provisions of RCRA. In *Blue Legs*, the Oglala Sioux tribe operated several open dumps on the Pine Ridge Reservation. The plaintiffs, who were members of the tribe, brought suit under RCRA's citizens' suit provisions against the tribe, the Bureau of Indian Affairs, the Indian Health Service, and EPA for violations of RCRA's open dump prohibitions.

The federal district court noted in *Blue Legs* that EPA's authority under RCRA was not the same for hazardous as for solid waste. While the statute gave EPA direct regulatory authority over hazardous waste, it merely authorized the agency to provide technical and management assistance to states for the development of management plans for solid waste. Therefore, the court granted EPA's motion for summary judgment in its favor. On the other hand, the court held that the tribe has the responsibility, stemming from its inherent sovereignty, to regulate, operate, and maintain landfills on the reservation. Accordingly, the tribe was ordered to bring the dumps into compliance with RCRA. The Bureau of Indian Affairs and the Indian Health Service were also made subject to the court's order, because the two agencies were using the tribe's open dumps for solid waste generated by them and their personnel.[38]

What Are the Lessons for This Case?

Read together, *Cabazon*, *Washington Dept. of Ecology*, and *Blue Legs* provided considerable support for the conclusion that AB 3477, if enacted, would be preempted by federal law. State jurisdiction, *Cabazon* held, is preempted if it interferes with federal and tribal interests, unless those interests are outweighed by the state's interests. The same important federal interests were at stake in both the Campo and *Cabazon* cases—"the Congressional goal of Indian self-government, including its 'overriding goal' of encouraging tribal self-sufficiency and economic development."[39] The Cabazon and Morongo tribes, having no natural resources on their reservations, turned to gaming to generate revenue for tribal services and to provide tribal employment. The Campo tribe is more disadvantaged economically than the Cabazon and Morongo tribes, because not only does the Campo reservation lack natural resources, but its remote location precludes even gaming as a source of tribal income and jobs. The landfill project, the tribe contends, is a last resort in its struggle to attain the self-sufficiency and economic development it is the policy of Congress to foster.

Unlike the tribes in *Colville*, the Campos could make a strong argument that they were not merely marketing an exemption from state laws, but would be deriving their income from a project in which they would have a "significant interest." Indeed, the Campo landfill would constitute a much greater capital investment than the gaming halls on the Cabazon and Morongo reservations. Moreover, if the Cabazon and Morongo tribes "have a strong incentive to provide comfortable, clean, and attractive facilities and well-run games in order to increase attendance at the games,"[40] the Campo tribe would seem to have an even stronger incentive to man-age the landfill properly, not only to maximize its income po-tential but also to prevent contamination of the reservation environment.

The state of California has an undeniable interest in pre-venting reservation landfills from contaminating the off-res-ervation environment. However, the opponents of the Peace bill argued, the lesson of *Washington Dept. of Ecology* is that state jurisdiction over reservation waste projects would be in-consistent with the federal government's policy of encourag-ing tribal self-regulation in environmental matters. Moreover, although *Blue Legs* did not consider the question of whether landfills on reservations are subject to state regulation, the district court did hold that tribes have the responsibility—stemming from their inherent sovereignty—to maintain, ope-rate, and regulate reservation landfills. Finally, the opponents of AB 3477 contended, the state's interests would be pro-tected by the federal government, because the Secretary of Interior would have to be satisfied with the safety of a landfill project before approving the lease.

The strongest legal argument available to the proponents of AB 3477 was that *Cabazon* had reiterated that state juris-diction is not preempted if the state's interests at stake out-weigh those of the federal and tribal governments.[41] The state's interest in preventing the contamination of the Campo area's sole source of drinking water was greater than the state's interest in preventing the infiltration of Indian gaming by organized crime, so the argument ran, and outweighed the federal and tribal interests in tribal economic development and environmental self-regulation.

However, in the days preceding the hearing in the Senate Committee on Toxics and Public Safety Management, Steve Peace, rather than relying on this argument, attacked the character, intelligence, and motives of his opponents. "Peace says that arguments that his bill will encroach upon Indian sovereignty are simply political 'cover' for the fact that the tribes are marketing their regulatory independence to East Coast garbage companies—some of them unscrupulous and possibly Mob-connected—as a way to get around stringent state and local controls." The Campos' claim that his bill was an "insult" to their sovereignty, Peace responded, was "ludicrous," intended simply to "deflect attention from the garbage industry guys who want to go around regulations by going on the reservations. They are using the Indians for cover. *That's* what's insulting. They're manipulating them."[42]

In the hearing before the Senate Toxics Committee, the initial questions asked by the committee chairman, Senator Art Torres, seemed to suggest that AB 3477 faced "overwhelming odds" because of the legislative counsel's opinion that it would be preempted by federal law. However, the momentum of the hearing shifted when Peace offered a "parade of sometimes emotional witnesses to buttress his arguments that the Campo case is part of a nationwide strategy by large solid-waste companies to use Indian sovereignty as a way around strict state and local standards for hazardous waste sites and garbage dumps."[43]

AB 3477 SUPPORTED BY ENVIRONMENTALISTS AND SOME INDIAN ACTIVISTS

The credentials of the allies that Peace and Donna Tisdale had enlisted in support of AB 3477 made it difficult to dismiss the proposal as Indian-bashing. The most important institutional advocate was the Planning and Conservation League (PCL). The oldest environmental lobbying group in California, PCL is a nonpartisan alliance of individuals and more than 180 conservation groups, including organizations as diverse as the Wilderness Society, the Society for California Archaeology, the California Native Plant Society, and the Bay Area Chapters of the Audubon Society. The general counsel of PCL, Corey Brown, testified in support of the bill at every legislative hearing, arguing that it would close "a very dangerous loophole in California's toxics and waste laws."[44]

However, given the Campos' claim that the legislation was motivated by anti-Indian bias, the most effective witness testifying in favor of the bill was Katherine Saubel of the Los Coyotes tribe. The Los Coyotes are another small San Diego County tribe. The tribe was deeply divided over a commercial landfill project being championed by the tribal chairman. Katherine Saubel, the spokesperson for the dissidents, supported AB 3477, as well as a bill sponsored by Congressman Duncan Hunter that would have declared a moratorium on commercial waste projects on San Diego County reservations. In chapter eleven, we will compare the two cases in an effort to understand why the Los Coyotes, unlike the Campos, split over their landfill project, the dissenters making common cause with non-Indian opponents of the project.

In an interview, Saubel declared that she was "not educated at all." When she was eight years old a "government man" had told her father that she would have to go away to an Indian school; concerned that she "would lose my language and everything else like a lot of Indians," she talked her father into letting her remain at home. "That is why I have retained my language, fluently. I have written books on a lot of things that pertain to the Indian people. I really understand who I am, what lineage I belong to and what clan I am a member of. I really know myself."[45]

With her short gray hair, large glasses, direct bearing, and natural dignity, Katherine Saubel was "one of the most powerful witnesses" PCL's Corey Brown had seen in twelve years of lobbying.[46] The *Los Angeles Times* agreed.

The most poignant moments [in the hearing before the Senate Toxics Committee] came when 70-year-old [K]atherine Saubel, a Cahuilla Indian from the San Diego-area Los Coyotes reservation, said the bill is necessary to "stop the exploitation" of her tribe, which is also entertaining the idea of leasing its land for a dump.

"They are told by their so-called leaders to accept controversial proposals such as landfills by waving dollar bills in front of their eyes," said Saubel, her testimony creating a hush in the hearing room. "When it is too late, the Indians will realize what they gave up: the land they valued so much before—the clean water, the un-polluted water, even facing the possibility of themselves becoming sick."

The *Times* noted that the "often acerbic [Committee Chair-man] Torres seemed particularly touched by Saubel's com-ments."[47] Steve Banegas, a member of the Barona tribe in San Diego County and a leader of southern California's Co-alition for Indian Rights, also testified in support of AB 3477, saying, "We should not poison ourselves and our families to-morrow for a small profit today."[48]

In the face of these appeals, the Campos' argument, sup-ported by the legislative counsel opinion, that the proposed legislation would be nullified by the courts, was unavailing, as was the Campos' assertion that their landfill regulations would be as strict as or stricter than the state's. AB 3477 passed the Toxics Committee by a vote of 5-1. Kevin Gover, the lawyer who represents the Campo tribe, said that he had expected the committee to vote for the bill all along. "It's clear that the prospect of losing a lawsuit doesn't deter anyone here. . . . This is tough politics for anyone to vote against more regulation of hazardous waste. We're in the ultimate political forum, and it is going to be tough for us to win" in the legisla-ture.[49] Five weeks later, though, AB 3477 was rejected by the Senate Appropriations Committee by a margin of 6-2.

The *Los Angeles* Times reported that there was "more than enough innuendo and allegation" to satisfy devotees of "gossip columns and sensationalistic magazines" at the Ap-propriations Committee hearing on the bill. "The Indians and at least one senator were upset about the 'cheap shot' in-sinuation that the Campos and other tribes were easy dupes for well-heeled and corrupt East Coast garbage companies," the *Times* observed. Peace was even "more vocal than usual," the *Times* continued, in charging that "sleaze merchants" from Chicago and the East Coast were the secret force behind the opposition to his bill. Ralph Goff, the chairman of the Campos, commented: "It was a cheap shot. . . . We aren't going to be taken in by organized crime."

This time Peace's tactics may have backfired, resulting in his defeat in the Appropriations Committee. The mood of the committee appeared to shift after one senator, in announcing his opposition to the bill, commented that Peace had implied that the Indians were being bought off. However, Peace lived to fight another day; after the negative vote, he persuaded the committee to schedule AB 3477 for reconsideration the following week. "Peace was undeterred, saying he will return next week with his own contingent of witnesses. He said he was unable to get them organized in time for Monday's hearing. 'My people don't have a big corporation to pay money to run them up' to Sacramento, said Peace, throwing a last verbal jab at the firms he says are behind the Indians."[50] Later, Donna Tisdale ruefully reflected upon the fact that she and Ed had flown from San Diego to Sacramento to testify at all the hearings except one, the one they lost.[51]

During the recess between hearings, the lobbyists remained in session. Corey Brown of the Planning and Conservation League wrote to members of the Senate Appropriations Committee: "A *vote against AB 3477 is a vote against protecting public health and California's groundwater supplies.*"[52]

Kevin Gover was also writing to members of the committee, exhorting them to "stick with your negative vote" on the bill when it was reconsidered. In his letters, Gover reiterated his contention that the proposed legislation would be struck down by the courts. "It is true, of course, that lawyers may reasonably disagree on the likely outcome of litigation; when, however, the state legislature's own lawyer concludes that the tribes are likely to win, the tribes' case must be unusually strong."

Gover asked that the Campo project be considered on its own merits, and not be lumped in with other cases where tribes might be acting less responsibly. Regarding the allegations that the Campos were unwitting pawns of corrupt landfill developers, Gover said that such allegations were impossible to respond to because "whatever we say, the bill's supporters will claim that we are being duped." However, he pointed out, the landfill companies with which the Campos were negotiating were the largest waste management companies in the nation, many of them already operating waste facilities in California. "If these companies are organized crime fronts, then the state already is overrun with organized crime in the solid waste industry."

Gover argued that AB 3477 was unnecessary because the Campo landfill would be covered by three other layers of regulations. First, in reviewing the federal environmental impact statement that was being prepared on the project, the Interior Department would likely impose "numerous and strict" controls on the proposed facility before giving the Campos approval to lease the site to a developer. Second, the Campo tribe would abide by, and would require a developer to abide by, EPA's criteria and guidelines for the siting and operation of landfills; if the tribe or the developer failed to do so, they would be subject to suit under the citizens' suit provisions of the federal Resource Conservation and Recovery Act (RCRA). Third, the Campos were developing tribal landfill regulations that would be as strict as or stricter than the state's. "We have no interest in fouling the reservation environment; it is the Indians, after all, who will feel the impacts of the landfill most directly."[53]

COMPROMISE PROPOSED BY CAMPOS: VOLUNTARY AGREEMENT WITH STATE

Finally, Gover argued that the jurisdictional dispute was unnecessary. It was the policy of the Campo tribe, he stated, to accommodate the state if we can do so without giving up the fundamental right to decide what will and will not take place on tribal lands. For this reason, we have put a lot of energy into negotiating an agreement with the state by which the state agencies would have free access to the project for inspections and would receive all the information required to allow those agencies to evaluate the environmental quality of the landfill's construction and operation. I would emphasize that we do not have to do this; the Band has determined, however, that it will further the environmental goals of the Band to procure—at considerable expense, I might add—the expertise of these state agencies to support the private sector expertise that we have retained to advise the Band and to assist in the enforcement of tribal laws. We are disappointed and, very frankly, feel a deep sense of betrayal that agencies such as the Attorney General's office, the San Diego County Board of Supervisors, and the Solid Waste Management Board would support this legislation at the same time they pretend to be negotiating with us in good faith. Nevertheless, because we believe that the state agencies have expertise that will further our environmental goals, we will resume negotiations with the state agencies on the final defeat of AB 3477.[54]

This last point is critical because if it is true that the Campos intended to regulate the proposed landfill as strictly as the state would, and were prepared to enter into a voluntary agreement with state agencies to achieve that end, a compromise that respected tribal sovereignty while protecting the off-reservation environment would seem to have been possible.

Mike Connolly recalls that the Campos initiated discussions with county and state officials concerning a voluntary agreement well before AB 3477 was introduced in the legislature. In those discussions, the representatives of the Campos emphasized that they intended to regulate the project as stringently as the state would, and were prepared "to set up a process where the state could come in and make sure that things were being done right." Connolly attended a meeting with the staff of the San Diego Regional Water Quality Control

Board soon after the project was announced, to discuss a cooperative agreement. The Campos offered to reimburse the
regional water board for assistance in establishing the tribal
regulatory program. The idea was scotched, Connolly says,
because Steve Peace, BAD, and the San Diego County Board
of Supervisors convinced the regional water board that a cooperative agreement would give the tribe's environmental
protection program credibility and thereby facilitate the project. Steve Peace also argued that the regional water board
should not work with the Campo Environmental Protection
Agency until the issue of tribal sovereignty was resolved. The
regional water board "was under so much political heat that
they decided to stay out of it," Connolly concluded.⁵⁵

In a letter endorsing the Peace legislation, Art Coe, the
executive director of the regional water board, acknowledged
that the board staff had been negotiating a cooperative agreement with the Campo Environmental Protection Agency to
provide technical assistance on the proposed landfill. The regional water board decided to break off the negotiations, Coe
said, because it believed that "its limited resources will be better utilized addressing those water quality issues and problems
over which the Board has clear regulatory authority."⁵⁶

In an interview conducted after the dust of the legislative
battle had settled, Coe said that the Campos had been "open
to just about anything that we would propose as far as some
kind of cooperative oversight agreement, including their actually reimbursing us for some of the staff costs associated with
that oversight role. . . . Just to editorialize a little bit," Coe
continued, "in this whole proceeding . . . my feeling is, and
the [State Water Resources Control Board] staff working with
us have echoed the same feeling, that there are very few . . .
groups that we have worked with that are as cooperative and
as willing to try to make things work, as the people involved
with the Campo landfill." Mike Connolly, in particular, Coe

observed, had been easy to work with. "I suspect," Coe concluded, "that if it hadn't been for the jurisdictional issue and
the potential problem of butting our heads against a problem
and not having the authority to resolve it, we probably would
have been able to work out a cooperative agreement without
the state legislation."[57]

However, when John Grattan, a lobbyist for the Campos,
had broached the idea of a cooperative agreement between
the tribe and the state as a means of resolving the jurisdictional
conflict raised by AB 3477, the reaction of David Takashima,
Peace's chief of staff, had been an "indulgent chuckle."[58]

It is a tribute to Steve Peace's legislative skills and dogged
tenacity that when the Senate Appropriations Committee reconsidered AB 3477, he not only snatched victory from the
jaws of defeat but did so by a unanimous vote. The *Los Angeles
Times* attributed the turnaround to Peace's having "used testimony from a Riverside County prosecutor and cleverly written amendments to blunt the opposition and resurrect the
bill, sending it to the full Senate for a vote." The testimony of
the Riverside County prosecutor concerned an investigation
of illegal dumping of several hundred truckloads of lead-
contaminated soil in a dry riverbed on the Soboda Indian reservation. The prosecutor told the committee that failure to
enact AB 3477 would leave the policing of Indian landfills to
the Environmental Protection Agency and the Bureau of Indian Affairs, agencies he characterized as quick to claim jurisdiction but slow to respond in the Riverside County case.

One of Peace's amendments limited the reach of the bill
to counties with a population of more than 125,000. This took
the heat off legislators representing twenty-six sparsely populated counties, mostly in northern California, whose relatively large Indian constituencies had been pressuring them
to oppose the bill. One of those legislators, "Sen. James W.
Neilson (R-Rohnert Park) abstained after voting against the

bill last week. The Peace amendments exempted 18 of the 34 reservations in his district."

To placate the central and southern California legislators who represented the other Indian reservations in the state, Peace amended the bill to require a finding that a proposed reservation waste project would adversely affect the environment or public health outside the boundaries of the reservation. "The effect, Peace explained after the hearing, was to make it politically impossible to vote against the bill."

Peace himself, the *Times* reported, "closed the testimony with an impassioned speech that sounded more like a Sunday sermon. . . . 'The only reason these companies are here, arguing, attempting to hide behind . . . the veil of Indian representatives, is they want to build substandard landfills and hazardous waste facilities.'"[59] Following the vote, a lobbyist for the Campo tribe gave Peace a backhanded compliment, saying that he had been "very emotional, very sensational and very effective." Mike Connolly was more direct; asked how Peace had been able to get the committee to reverse itself, Connolly replied, "By lying through his teeth."[60]

Less than two weeks later, Peace parlayed the vote in the Appropriations Committee to resounding victories in the full Senate, as well as the Assembly. Donna Tisdale sensed, however, that the proponents of the bill might have won the battles only to lose the war. After meeting with Pat Kenady, a representative of Governor George Deukmejian, Tisdale expressed concern that the governor might veto the legislation. "'Kenady didn't want to hear anything we had to say,' she said. 'It was very frustrating.'" Showing her frustration, Tisdale said of the Campos, "Unfortunately, they . . . have no love of the land. They just want to make a quick buck off of it."[61] On September 30, 1990, Governor Deukmejian did veto AB 3477, expressing concern that the bill interfered with tribal sovereignty, conflicted with federal law, and was of questionable constitutionality.[62]

LAW OF THE LAND IRRELEVANT FOR LAWMAKERS

It is remarkable how little significance the legislators appear to have attached to the legislative counsel opinion that AB 3477 was preempted by federal law. Indeed, lawyer-lobbyists on both sides of the issue believe that the legislative counsel opinion was completely irrelevant to the legislative battle. It is not that the legislators disagreed with the legislative counsel; they apparently just did not care whether the proposed legislation would be struck down by the courts. "I don't think any legislator voted for or against the bill because of the [legislative counsel] opinion," says Corey Brown, general counsel of PCL. Legislative decisions are "not so much based upon the legal issues, but rather the combination of the policy issues and the political support on one side or the other. . . . [The legislative counsel opinion] was a factor to consider in developing policy arguments, and a tool that can be used in the political process, but I don't think it was a decisive factor in any single vote."[63]

John Grattan, who lobbied for the Campos, agrees with Brown. In particular, Grattan discounts the possibility that the initial vote in the Senate Appropriations Committee, the vote the Campos won, was influenced by the legislative counsel opinion. Indeed, Grattan suspects that the members of the committee may not have known exactly what they were voting against. "There was a fair amount of confusion on the part of committee members as to what the bill did, didn't do." Because a deadline was approaching for getting bills out of the committee, "they were hearing literally hundreds of bills that day. It was a complex legal issue and a complex policy issue; and confusion aids those who want 'no' votes, so confusion aided us. What happened in the meantime was that Steve Peace had access to the members, and he just did a better job of getting votes."[64]

For idealists who want to believe that those who make and

execute the law are guided by it, the action of Governor Deukmejian in vetoing AB 3477 and the grounds stated for the veto seem reassuring. However, the participants on both sides profess to hold no such illusions. An environmental advocate who supported AB 3477 believes the governor vetoed the bill neither out of deference to the highest court in the land nor out of concern for Indian sovereignty, but simply because he was a "complete Neanderthal," who was against anything the environmental community favored. A lobbyist who opposed the bill agrees that the veto may not have been a principled act. Rather, he says, it was an "easy veto" for the governor. Governor Deukmejian was a Republican; Peace was a Democrat, and one not well liked by the Administration. Moreover, Attorney General John Van de Kamp, whose office had supported AB 3477, had campaigned unsuccesfully for the Democratic nomination to succeed Deukmejian. Finally, there was, reportedly, the Armenian connection, which was said to account for many of the governor's actions. The *San Diego Union* quoted "legislative sources" as predicting that Deukmejian would veto the bill because of "his close ties to Armenian-Americans in the waste management industry who helped elect him governor."[65] Of course, this is all speculation, perhaps base speculation, about the governor's motives, but at least it tells one a great deal about the state of mind of those whose business it is to influence legislation.

The veto provided the climax for what turned out to be merely the first act of a legislative cliffhanger. Deukmejian's motivation soon became irrelevant. The role of governor was about to be recast.

CHAPTER EIGHT

AN ARMED TRUCE

TWO MONTHS AFTER GEORGE DEUKMEJIAN VETOED AB 3477,
Pete Wilson was inaugurated as governor of California. Less
than two weeks after that, Steve Peace reintroduced his bill,
which in the new legislative session was assigned the number
AB 240.

Donna Tisdale says that Peace did not have to be persuaded to resume the fight; "he was very gung ho about it."
The last impediment to the enactment of the legislation may
have been removed with Wilson's election, Donna hoped, because he had once been the mayor of San Diego. San Diego,
like other southern California cities, is dependent upon imported water; therefore, Wilson might be more sympathetic to
the argument that the state has an overriding interest in protecting the sole source of drinking water for a substantial number of San Diego County residents.[1]

Corey Brown of the Planning and Conservation League
also saw reason for optimism. As a mayor and as a United
States senator, Wilson had a good record on the environment,
certainly much better than Deukmejian's; he could be expected to give the proponents of AB 240 a fair hearing.[2] David
Takashima thought the personal chemistry would be better,
too. Steve Peace had a personal relationship with the new
governor dating back to the time Wilson had been mayor of
San Diego, and Takashima knew members of the gubernato-
rial staff.[3] With the substitution of Wilson into the cast, there
was reason to hope that the last act of the drama might be

rewritten. The opening scenes were repeated, however, with the familiar lines being delivered with even greater vehemence.

Before AB 240 was first heard in committee, Ralph Goff, chairman of the Campo tribe, wrote to lawmakers in response to the "misrepresentations, half-truths and falsehoods" he reported finding in Peace's recent "dear colleague" letter to them. Denouncing AB 240 as a "groundless, politically opportunistic attempt to gut our efforts to safely achieve economic self-sufficiency," Goff repeated that the tribe had no interest in fouling their reservation environment or that of the surrounding area. Accordingly, Goff said, the tribe had adopted landfill regulations that were at least as strict as the state's. Finally, he reiterated the Campos' willingness to enter into some sort of oversight arrangement with the state, so long as the tribe's sovereignty was respected.

We have initiated negotiations toward an agreement with the state by which state agencies would have free access to the project for inspections and would receive all the information required to allow those agencies to evaluate the environmental quality of the landfill's construction and operation. We have determined that it will further the environmental goals of the Band to procure and utilize the expertise of these state agencies to augment the private sector specialists that we have retained to assist in the enforcement of tribal laws. That policy of openness will continue. Yet we cannot and shall not relinquish the fundamental right to decide what will and will not take place on tribal lands.[4]

In a statement announcing a press conference to be held the day before the first committee hearing, Steve Peace refiled his charges against the tribes and the waste companies. "The garbage gold rush is on targeting Indian Reservations with promises of cash for turning their land heritage into waste dumps." The motivation of waste companies proposing to build facilities on reservations was simple, Peace alleged: "dodging state environmental safeguards and safety standards."[5]

At the news conference itself Katherine Saubel, whose

struggle to stop the landfill project on the Los Coyotes reservation was approaching a climax, was again the legislation's most compelling spokesperson. "Landfill people come in and do as they please on our reservation, and we have nothing to say about it," Saubel complained. "So that's why we want this bill to pass, those of us that are fighting to preserve our land so that it will be pure for our children and our future. Especially the water. We have all these animals that live there, the food that we eat there, that's all going to be destroyed. And that's the [land] that our Creator gave to us so that we could live from it."

Following the press conference, AB 240 sailed through the Assembly Committee on Environmental Safety on a 10-2 vote, and within the month had also passed the Assembly Committee on Natural Resources by an 11-1 margin. Coming out of the Natural Resources Committee, Peace appeared to be driving a juggernaut. The list of organizations supporting and opposing AB 240 suggested that Peace had not only retained his base but had broadened it significantly. As before, the two state agencies primarily interested in the legislation—the state water and waste boards—endorsed it. Peace's campaign to convince legislators that AB 240 was a thoughtful response to an environmental problem of statewide concern, rather than an expression of bias or NIMBYism, received a boost when the Sierra Club joined the Planning and Conservation League in lobbying for the bill. Moreover, the support of environmentalists for the bill was complemented by endorsements from two major waste management firms—Laidlaw Environmental Services and Waste Management of North America—as well as the California Manufacturers Association. The support of the business community appeared to provide the governor ample political cover.

The environmental organizations and the waste companies not operating on Indian reservations had a common interest in keeping the regulatory playing field as level as possible. If waste companies operating on reservations did not have to meet California's strict standards, waste companies operating elsewhere in the state would be at a competitive disadvantage; waste would flow to the less strictly regulated, lower-cost reservation facilities, undermining the effectiveness of the strict state standards. A lawyer for the waste companies stated the argument as follows:

AB 240 is of critical importance to the California waste industry. California facility operators have made enormous capital investments to comply with California's rigorous environmental requirements. If facilities are allowed to operate on Indian lands, meeting only the more lenient federal standards, existing California facilities, which comply with California laws, will be placed at a serious economic disadvantage.

AB 240 is equally important to California environmental groups. Both the Sierra Club and the PCL have worked with industry and state regulatory officials to develop California hazardous waste treatment and disposal standards that, in many cases, are far more stringent than federal requirements. In fact, many wastes deemed "hazardous" under California law may be handled as ordinary, solid wastes under the federal requirements. Absent AB 240, large volumes of "California only" hazardous wastes would flow to Indian lands, where the more lenient federal standards would apply. This would create a huge loophole in California law, effectively destroying the additional health and environmental protection afforded by California law.[6]

Nevertheless, when AB 240 reached the Assembly Committee on Ways and Means, which had passed AB 3477 by a margin of 21-0, it ran into real trouble. What had happened in the interim? For one thing, despite the presence of Katherine Saubel at Steve Peace's side, the Campos had made considerable progress in elevating the issue of tribal sovereignty.

ATTACK ON TRIBAL SOVEREIGNTY LAID TO RACISM

LaDonna Harris has been one of the most influential Indian leaders on the national scene for decades. On behalf of Americans for Indian Opportunity, she wrote to legislators that the effort "to deny the Campo Tribe their right to decide what to do on their own lands is an insult to all Native peoples. We consider this a form of genocide equal to that of California's slaughter of Indians in the 1800's."[7]

Eddie Brown, the assistant secretary of Indian affairs in the Department of Interior and himself an Indian, wrote directly to Governor Wilson. Reminding Wilson that former Governor Deukmejian had vetoed AB 3477 on the ground that regulation of reservation waste projects was preempted by federal law, Brown expressed dismay that the California legislature was considering a bill that failed "to rectify the flaws of its predecessors."[8]

The sovereignty issue also drove at least a thin wedge into the environmental bloc. Writing in opposition to AB 240, Bradley Angel of Greenpeace Action said that he had—at their request—assisted dozens of Indian groups and tribes to organize grassroots tribal opposition to proposed waste projects on reservations. "Indian people have succeeded in defeating dozens of proposals for waste facilities, while at the same time protecting their sovereignty," Angel declared. "Promoting legislation which would apply state law to Indian land will only further polarize the situation, and create a 'white vs. Indian' situation that will set back the efforts of those of us, Indian and non-Indian, who are working together in this struggle," he warned.[9]

Black and Latino members of the legislature who had previously voted for AB 3477 might well have been given pause this time by the Campos' repeated assertions that they were the victims of racial bias and stereotyping. The Campos and their representatives made that case most compellingly in a professionally produced video. In it, Jim West, a Cheyenne who serves as the Campos' financial adviser, protested that the assumption made by the proponents of AB 240 "is that Indian people, as a race, are unable to develop [such a project] responsibly or to regulate it. Therefore, in my mind, AB 240 is clearly a racist piece of legislation."

Mike Connolly also appeared in the video, recounting an experience that seemed to him to confirm Jim West's impression. Mike said that at a public hearing a few months earlier he had been asked by a non-Indian, "Well, who's in control of the regulatory system?" Mike replied, "The tribe is." "Okay, that's fine, but who's really in control?" Mike repeated, "The tribe is." "No, no, no. I mean who's really in control?" The clear implication, Mike concluded, was that "it's not a legitimate regulatory agency if there isn't a white guy standing there that says, 'I'm the final say in this matter.'"

Kevin Gover, the Pawnee who serves as the Campos' lawyer, makes the closing argument in the video.

One of the biggest problems we've had to deal with in this political fight is just overcoming stereotypes and people's predispositions about how smart Indians are. We've had to spend an awful lot of time just convincing people that Indians are smart enough to deal with waste companies, and Indians are smart enough to regulate landfills and manage the environment. And that's the sort of thing you shouldn't have to prove in this day and age.

Indian people have been told all their lives that they're lazy, that they're ignorant, that they don't really want to do anything to improve themselves. And here we are at Campo, we're trying to create jobs, we're trying to create income. We're trying to build houses, we're trying to build clinics, we're trying to get the kids into college. And yet there are still people who want to keep us down.[10]

According to John Grattan, a lobbyist for the Campos, the support for and opposition to AB 240 had come to "cut across all political stripes and cloths." Grattan says one of the leading conservatives in the assembly, Tom McClintock, said, 'It's very simple. Either you believe in sovereignty, or you don't. It's all [the Indians] have left. We've taken everything else away from them.'" Some liberals, with whom McClintock agreed on very little else, joined him in opposing the bill on this ground. However, for those liberals whose defining concern is the environment, the gap in the state's strict environmental laws was the paramount issue. They argued, according to Grattan, that the sovereignty issue was being overblown: "'Come on. Let's not talk about a nation here. There are tribes with as few as twelve members!'"[11]

THE TIDE TURNS

The legislature was called upon to choose between equally legitimate but seemingly incompatible interests. On the one hand was the Campos' interest in regulating the use of their own land, developing their desperately limited economic resources, and exercising responsibility for their reservation environment. On the other hand was the state's interest in preventing reservation projects from jeopardizing the health and endangering the environment of neighboring communities. However, when the Assembly Ways and Means Committee met on May 22, the outcome may have been determined less by a careful balancing of the respective interests than by the fact that the lobbyists for the developer of the proposed Campo landfill, Mid-American, simply had more clout than the lobbyists supporting the bill. The scales may also have been tipped by the fact that Assembly Speaker Willie Brown had not completely forgotten nor forgiven Steve Peace's treachery a few years earlier.

Having passed the Ways and Means Committee unanimously in the previous legislative session, the Peace bill appeared headed for defeat this time, losing a test vote early in the day. Three of Peace's fellow Democrats joined the opposition, including his coauthor on AB 3477. After five hours of what one reporter characterized as "behind the scenes intrigue," the committee ultimately reversed itself and passed AB 240 by a vote of 14 to 8. This time, however, it was not victory that Peace snatched from the jaws of defeat. It was the possibility of compromise. He dissuaded the committee from killing his bill only by pledging to participate in negotiations—which the governor's office had offered to broker—that might lead to legislation authorizing the state to enter into a voluntary agreement with the Campos that would give the state some sort of oversight role in regulating the landfill.

The *San Diego Union* reported that the necessity of compromise became clear after a "fierce daylong lobbying battle in which Assembly Speaker Willie Brown's reported opposition to the bill played a pivotal role." Representatives of the Campo tribe confirmed that Brown had met with them several times in the preceding months and had told them that he opposed AB 240, despite having voted for AB 3477. In addition to the speaker's opposition, Peace attributed his difficulties to heavy lobbying by the politically influential firm of Spencer-Roberts.[12] Karen Spencer represented Mid-American but Peace's allies are convinced that it was her father Stu, a campaign manager for Ronald Reagan, who opened the most important doors for Mid-American.

Trying to put his own spin on the outcome, Peace claimed that he had always preferred a voluntary agreement between the Campos and state regulators, rather than legislation that would wind up in court, but that the Campos had previously refused to bargain seriously. "Without a live bill, Peace questioned whether there would be good-faith negotiations toward a compact that would ensure adequate safeguards against environmental damage to the reservation and surrounding properties." Kevin Gover responded that it was Peace who had refused until then to negotiate. "We forced (Peace) to the table today. That's what happened."[13]

The battle between Steve Peace and the Campos was far from over. While its author now professed to prefer a compromise, AB 240 remained alive and as uncompromising as ever for the time being. And uncompromising was the way the bill's proponents preferred it. The Planning and Conservation League, for example, continued to lobby the full assembly to pass it. And BAD's ultimate objective was to stop the Campo project, not to ensure state oversight of it; regardless of how well constructed and regulated the landfill might be, BAD was convinced, it would eventually rupture and poison their water supply.

The Campos were proceeding on the two tracks laid down by the legislature—trying to kill the bill outright while expressing their willingness to enter into a voluntary agreement providing for a state regulatory role. At the same time, the tribe was trying to arrange a head-on collision by seeking federal legislation that would make it unmistakably clear that the states had no jurisdiction over reservation waste projects. In letters to Assembly members asking them to vote against AB 240 when it reached the floor, and reiterating the tribe's willingness to enter into a cooperative agreement, Campo Chairman Ralph Goff added that "we have asked the United States Congress to examine this issue. Congress, of course, exercises plenary powers in Indian affairs. . . . We are hopeful that the Congress, as a body detached from the local political prejudices that drive AB 240, will see the benefits that both tribes and the states will realize from tribal waste projects.[14]

The Campos lost the vote on the Assembly floor by a better than two-to-one margin. However, their threat of congressional intervention gained credibility when Senator John McCain of Arizona introduced legislation—"The Indian Tribal Government Waste Management Act of 1991"—that was cosponsored by, among others, Senator Daniel K. Inouye of Hawaii, the chairman of the Senate Select Committee on Indian Affairs. The bill declared that the overriding goals of federal Indian policy are tribal economic self-sufficiency and self-government, affirmed the inherent authority of tribal governments to operate waste facilities on their reservations as a means of achieving economic self-sufficiency, and specifically recognized the inherent authority of tribes operating such facilities to accept waste generated off their reservations.[15]

To drive the message home, Senator Inouye attended a conference in Sacramento sponsored by the National Congress of American Indians. Inouye warned that the federal government would step in if the California legislature did not find a means of resolving the dispute without encroaching upon tribal sovereignty. "If matters of this sort are not resolved at this level, then there's an irresistible temptation on the part of the federal government to get involved," he cautioned. Peace was to have addressed the conference, too, but canceled out, saying that he was busy with other matters. United States senators do not customarily pay calls on state legislators, but Senator Inouye went to Peace's office. In their private meeting he presumably delivered much the same message that appeared in the *Los Angeles Times* headline the next day: "U.S. Senator Says Peace Bill on Indian Lands Is Doomed." After his meeting with Inouye, Peace reported that the two sides were still far apart on "fundamental, substantive, serious issues." Crafting a compromise would not be easy, Peace said. "This is as delicate as any international negotiations that take place around the world. It's not any different than trying to negotiate tearing down the Berlin Wall."[16]

TIME TO COMPROMISE

By the time AB 240 reached the California Senate, the tide was clearly running against it. Although the legislative counsel opinion regarding AB 3477 had been, at most, a makeweight in the debate over that bill, the longer, more closely reasoned, and equally negative legislative counsel opinion concerning AB 240 had become, in John Grattan's phrase, "the rhinoceros in the living room that couldn't be ignored." After all, whatever his actual motivation, Governor Deukmejian had relied on the reasoning of the legislative counsel opinion in explaining his decision to veto AB 3477.

Despite his earlier optimism concerning the fate of the legislation under the new governor, PCL's Corey Brown had begun to fear that Governor Wilson would veto AB 240 unless it were amended to incorporate the cooperative agreement approach that the California Environmental Protection Agency (Cal/EPA), headed by a Wilson appointee, was pushing for. Paul Helliker, who was the legislative affairs director for Cal/EPA, confirms that the agency saw "potential constitutional problems" with AB 240, the same problems cited by Governor Deukmejian in vetoing AB 3477.[17] Moreover, there was no guarantee that an uncompromised bill, which Brown still preferred, would pass the Senate. Brown had seen too many environmental bills pass the Assembly, only to die in the upper house. Now, he sensed, the interest goups lobbying against AB 240 simply had more influence in the Senate than did the bill's supporters. Finally, even if AB 240 were passed by the legislature and signed by the governor, it might be nullified by the courts or Congress.[18]

These considerations, especially the growing likelihood of a second veto, cannot have been lost on Peace, whom many regard as unscrupulous but none consider dense. As one of the opponents of AB 240 put it: "For a legislator, especially one playing to the homefolks, one veto is fine; you appear to be principled. But to have your bill vetoed twice makes you seem ineffectual."

In the days leading up to the hearing in the Senate Toxics Committee, representatives of several of the interested parties—Peace, the Campo and La Posta tribes, the Cal/EPA, and the California Attorney General's Office—engaged in negotiations to amend the bill to provide for cooperative agreements.[19] When the Toxics Committee met on August 21, 1991, Peace agreed to amendments, which he said he hadn't even read, merely to keep his bill alive as negotiations continued.[20] The next day the negotiations were temporarily derailed when the host, an aide to California's new Republican Attorney General Dan Lungren, refused admittance to lobbyists for the Sierra Club and two waste companies, prompting

Peace's legislative assistants to walk out, too. Peace's reaction was in character. "This is not the Soviet Union—unless there was a coup that I missed putting Dan Lungren in charge of the state of California." Attendance had been limited to representatives of the state and of the tribes because the Campos had insisted upon conducting the negotiations on a government-to-government basis. The impasse was resolved when the Campos agreed to sit at the table with the interested nongovernmental groups, as well.[21]

AB 240 passed the Senate, but the Assembly refused to concur in the Senate amendments providing for cooperative agreements between tribes and the state. This set the stage for a conference committee hearing to try to draft a compromise bill that both houses could accept. Steve Peace chaired the conference and was the dominating force; other legislators came and went as the hearing, which began at 10:00 A.M., wore on into the early hours of the following day. The manner in which the hearing was conducted was unique in the experience of the participants. The harshest of partisans up to this point, Peace now adopted the role of a mediator, presiding over a marathon negotiating session in which all of the interested parties, in full view of the public and the press, worked through their differences. Instead of the usual practice of having the parties testify to the committee, Peace had them sit around the table, where the legislators usually sat, facing one another and confronting the divisive issues one by one. Each of the parties, including Peace, threatened to walk out at one point or another, but by 4:00 A.M. a compromise had been forged that everyone was prepared to support.

"If you had asked me 48 hours ago if we thought we could get to this point, I would have said no," Peace commented at the time.[22] Two years later Corey Brown of PCL recalls the experience as "one of the best negotiating processes I've ever seen," and Joel Mack, lawyer for Mid-American, says he is still amazed that there was the political will on everyone's part to reach agreement.[23] During that long night, clearly, the former antagonists came to respect one another insofar as each of them contributed to their now-common goal. The Campos' lobbyist John Grattan says that Peace, once he had decided he wanted a veto-proof bill, was "masterful" in facilitating the compromise. Corey Brown says that whenever the parties came close to impasse, Mid-American's Joel Mack would find a way of bridging the differences. Paul Helliker, who represented Cal/EPA and its constituent state agencies, credits Mike Connolly as "a reason why the negotiations ended up being as successful as they were." Mike, Helliker says, is "a very competent individual, and he assembled a good team. He's a low-key . . . congenial person. I think that helped a lot."[24]

Four days after the compromise was reached, AB 240 was overwhelmingly passed by both houses, and Governor Wilson signed it on October 10, 1991.[25]

AGREEING TO DISAGREE BUT COOPERATE

These are the key elements of a state-tribal cooperative agreement under AB 240:

Jurisdiction. The parties preserve their positions on jurisdiction. That is, they agree to disagree over the question of whether the state has authority to regulate a reservation waste project in the absence of the tribe's consent. The war is not over; the parties have simply entered into an armed truce. As Taylor Miller, the lawyer for the Campo EPA, puts it: "Everyone keeps their powder dry."[26] We shall return to this point.

Functional equivalency. In order to enter into a cooperative agreement with a tribe, the state environment secretary must make a good-faith determination, based on the advice of the state water, air, and waste boards, that the tribal regulatory program for hazardous or solid waste is functionally equivalent to the state's—that is, that it provides "at least as much protection for public health and safety and the environment as would the state requirements."

Permit review. In addition to determining whether the tribal regulatory program itself is functionally equivalent to the state's, the state will review draft permits issued by the tribe for the construction or operation of the waste facility to determine whether they:

1. meet the functionally equivalent standards set forth in the agreement;
2. provide not less than the level of protection for public health, safety, and the environment that a state permit would require; and
3. implement all feasible measures to mitigate the adverse environmental consequences of the project.

State enforcement. The state may exercise its enforcement powers over a reservation waste facility if the following conditions are satisfied:

1. a violation of the applicable standards or regulations has occurred or is occurring;
2. the violation has been brought to the attention of the tribe and of the owner and operator of the facility in writing; and
3. the tribe, after having received notice, has failed to take action to correct the violation within a reasonable time.

However, the state may take enforcement action immediately, if immediate action is required to avoid an imminent and substantial threat to public health or the environment, and the tribe has been notified.

Access and data. The tribe is to allow state agency personnel reasonable access to the reservation for the purposes of carrying out their responsibilities under the agreement, and the parties are to share with one another such information as inspection reports and monitoring data.

Technical assistance. Subject to reimbursement, the state will provide the tribe with technical assistance in designing

and implementing its permitting, monitoring, and enforcement programs.

Dispute resolution. The state or the tribe may bring a civil
action to enforce the terms of the cooperative agreement, and
the parties waive their sovereign immunity for the purposes of
such suits. Alternative dispute resolution mechanisms, like
mediation, are to be included in a cooperative agreement, so
that litigation will be a last resort.

The Campo Environmental Protection Agency (CEPA)
submitted a proposed cooperative agreement to the California
Environmental Protection Agency on March 21, 1992, thereby
initiating the formal review, comment, and decision period
provided under AB 240. Recall that a finding of functional
equivalency is a prerequisite to a cooperative agreement. That
is, the secretary of Cal/EPA must be satisfied, based on the
advice of the state water, air, and waste boards, that the tribal
regulatory program will provide "at least as much protection
for public health and safety and the environment as would the
state requirements." Paul Helliker of Cal/EPA coordinated
the comments of the state boards. According to Helliker,
Mike Connolly and his advisers "kind of bent over backwards"
to make the tribal solid waste code conform to the state's. "In
fact, every time the California regulatory staff would say, well,
this is how we think you ought to write it, [the Campos]
would make a modification" to the tribal code.[27]

After a series of formal negotiations between Cal/EPA
and Campo EPA, the proposed agreement was released for
public comment and review, including a public hearing in a
community near the reservation. On December 10, 1992, Secretary James M. Strock, the head of the Cal/EPA, signed a
finding that the proposed cooperative agreement met the requirements of AB 240. Campo EPA's regulatory system, Secretary Strock found, is very closely patterned on California's,
with no material differences between the two. At the signing
ceremony for the cooperative agreement itself, Secretary Strock

commented that the Campo tribe had adopted stringent standards for the design, construction, and operation of the proposed facility, standards that are "at least as protective, and in some cases more so, than those in effect throughout California. To complement these tough standards, we expect CEPA to be diligent in enforcing them," continued Strock. "[CEPA Director Mike] Connolly has assembled a well-trained team at CEPA, and I have confidence that he and his staff are prepared for the task. However, we stand ready to step in, should Cal/EPA action be required to prevent environmental contamination problems." Strock concluded by expressing the hope that the agreement would serve as a model of environmental partnership between states and tribes, largely eliminating jurisdictional disputes as a source of the conflicts that have marred state-tribal relations in the past.[28]

ASSESSMENTS OF THE COOPERATIVE AGREEMENT PROCESS

Two years after they bought into the compromise that resulted in the enactment of AB 240 and made the cooperative agreement between the state and the Campo tribe possible, the interested parties, with the notable exception of BAD, express no buyers' remorse. Corey Brown is the most guarded. Reiterating the view he expressed after he emerged from the marathon negotiating session, Brown says, "If the state agencies are vigilant, it's a good bill; if the state agencies are not vigilant, it's not a good bill."[29]

Karen O'Haire is a lawyer for the state water board, one of the agencies upon whose vigilance Corey Brown and other environmentalists are counting. In order to assess the value of a cooperative agreement under AB 240, she says, you must consider the alternative. Because of the jurisdictional conflict, state agencies have found it difficult, if not impossible, to obtain the information and access necessary to investigate suspected environmental problems on reservations. Under the cooperative agreement, the Campos have agreed to provide the necessary information and access. The greatest benefit, though, is the open dialogue that has developed between the state and the tribe. That will save everybody time and money. The cooperative agreement process, in O'Haire's view, is a "win-win."[30]

Taylor Miller, along with his partner John Grattan, was a lobbyist for the Campo tribe. A lawyer, Miller now represents the Campo Environmental Protection Agency. He emphasizes that AB 240 in its final form is respectful of tribal sovereignty. Cooperative agreements are not mandated by the statute; they are voluntary. Under the cooperative agreement process, a tribe retains the flexibility to craft its regulations to meet its individual circumstances, so long as they are functionally equivalent to the state's. The oversight provisions require appropriate deference. In the absence of an emergency, the state cannot step in until it has given the tribe notice of the suspected problem and a reasonable opportunity to address it. Most importantly, the process provides mutual incentives to focus on real environmental concerns, rather than "jurisdictional posturing." Miller's bottom line: "So far, so good."[31]

Joel Mack, the lawyer for Mid-American, picks up on Miller's last point. From a developer's point of view, one of the principal benefits of a cooperative agreement is that it removes some of the uncertainty surrounding a project. Uncertainty kills projects. A client contemplating an investment of millions of dollars developing a reservation waste project wants to know whether the state will prevail in court if it asserts jurisdiction over the facility. The only honest answer, Mack avows, is that it will depend on what the nine people then on the Supreme Court want the law to be. The high court's cases on tribal sovereignty, Mack asserts, "don't make any sense at all. As a universe. Particular cases do, in particular circumstances. But on the whole there is no unifying theme." And the Campo case, says Mack, "had Supreme

Court written all over it." A cooperative agreement deals with the jurisdictional question by "putting it in the freezer," until a concrete dispute arises under the agreement.[32]

This raises a question deferred until now. What precisely does it mean to say that the parties to a cooperative agreement have "agreed to disagree" over the issue of state jurisdiction? The following hypothetical case may help us think this question through. Suppose that a serious violation of a Campo EPA regulation, one that poses a substantial risk of environmental damage, comes to the attention of Calfornia authorities. Suppose that the state properly notifies CEPA and Mid-American of the violation. Suppose that CEPA fails to take action to address the problem within a reasonable period. Finally, suppose that the state properly exhausts the possibilities of alternative dispute resolution and then goes to a court of competent jurisdiction to enforce the terms of the cooperative agreement as a contract. Would it be inconsistent with the terms of the cooperative agreement for CEPA to argue to the court that the state has no jurisdiction to take an enforcement action to abate the environmental problem?

Taylor Miller, the lawyer for CEPA, believes that CEPA would be free under the cooperative agreement to raise the jurisdictional issue. "The state at that point, in order to do anything about [the alleged violation of a CEPA regulation], would have to win the jurisdictional issue."[33] Perhaps surprisingly, when asked the same hypothetical question, representatives of the state confirmed that the cooperative agreement would not bar CEPA from contesting the state's jurisdiction. Jurisdiction, says Karen O'Haire, a lawyer for the state water board, "is one argument [a tribe] can bring. We would hope they wouldn't and that they would believe in the process and the agreement."[34] Paul Helliker of Cal/EPA believes that a cooperative agreement under AB 240 does not in itself give the state any additional enforcement authority over a reservation waste facility.[35]

If it is not enforceable as a contract, isn't a cooperative agreement illusory? Not so, say Miller, O'Haire, and Helliker. The very fact that the state and a tribe have entered into a cooperative agreement means that the state has been satisfied that the tribe has adopted waste regulations that are at least as protective as the state's. That is not chopped liver. Moreover, the state and the tribe may be able to resolve any disputes regarding enforcement without resorting to court. If state and tribal regulatory officials are equally committed to protecting the environment, and if the experience of working together under the cooperative agreement promotes mutual trust and confidence, such a dispute may never arise. However, if it does, Helliker points out, the facts stated in the hypothetical case would give the state a compelling record on which to litigate the question of jurisdiction.

Joel Mack, the lawyer for Mid-American, makes a related point. If the Supreme Court were to review the question of state jurisdiction over a reservation waste project in the absence of a cooperative agreement, Mack predicts, it would use a balancing test: Are the federal and tribal interests in tribal self-government, self-sufficiency, and economic development outweighed by the state's interest in protecting the off-reservation environment? However, a balancing test assumes that the competing interests have a sort of materiality, a concreteness, a "heft." Weighing abstract interests in a vacuum, Mack points out, leads to unpredictable results.

On the other hand, under a cooperative agreement the parties articulate their interests with particularity and their rights and responsibilities with specificity. Therefore, if the question of jurisdiction arose under a cooperative agreement, the court might inquire, along the lines of our hypothetical case, into the following questions: Was there a violation or threatened violation of a specific regulation set forth in the agreement? Did the state notify the tribal regulatory authority and the facility operator in writing of the problem? Did the tribal agency fail to address the problem within a reasonable time? If the parties are to spend their limited resources in litigation, says Mack, then let them litigate such questions of genuine environmental concern, concrete questions appropriate to judicial review, rather than the abstract and ultimately political question of tribal sovereignty. The cooperative agreement process under AB 240, concludes Mack, is a "terrific process."[36]

The most significant holdout from the chorus of approval is BAD. BAD did support AB 240 in its final form, while making it clear that the organization was not dropping its opposition to the Campo project.[37] However, BAD has since filed suit in state court against the state water and waste boards, contending that the agencies abused their discretion in approving the construction permit issued by Campo EPA to Mid-American. The gist of BAD's complaint is that CEPA, inconsistently with the cooperative agreement, split the permitting process into two parts—authority to construct and authority to operate—and that the defendant state boards approved the construction permit while deferring the critical issues until they review the operating permit.

The state legislative process resulting in the cooperative agreement was one of the two major fronts in the Campo landfill war. The other was a federal administrative process— the study of the likely environmental effects of the project, to which we now turn.

CHAPTER NINE

CONSIDERING THE CONSEQUENCES

BECAUSE RESERVATION LAND IS LEGALLY CONSIDERED TO BE held in trust by the federal government for the benefit of a tribe, the proposed lease of the Campo site to Mid-American required the approval of the Department of Interior's Bureau of Indian Affairs. And because this landfill project was a political landmine, the question of approving the lease was ultimately decided by the Secretary of Interior himself. In the end, each side would use the access and exercise the influence at its disposal to win the secretary's heart and mind. Initially, however, because of the National Environmental Policy Act, the contest had to be waged in the open, in a process that guarantees the public an opportunity to participate—an environmental impact study that would serve as the basis for the secretary's decision.

THE NATIONAL ENVIRONMENTAL POLICY ACT

Under the National Environmental Policy Act (NEPA), any federal agency proposing a major project that may significantly affect the environment must disclose to the public the possible environmental effects of the project. The environmental impact statement (EIS) must also discuss alternatives to the proposed project that could reduce or eliminate any adverse environmental consequences it might have. It must be emphasized that NEPA is procedural, not substantive. That is, although NEPA requires an agency to consider alternatives to its proposed project, the statute does not require the agency to pick the least environmentally damaging alternative. The rationale of NEPA is that the process of examining a proposed action and its alternatives in a public forum will lead to better decisions by the federal agency.

Congress gave EPA a watchdog role under NEPA, directing EPA to review and comment upon the environmental effects of major actions proposed by other federal agencies. Some would say that EPA is a toothless watchdog, because EPA cannot require another agency to choose the least environmentally damaging alternative to its proposed project, nor even require it to prepare an environmental impact statement on the project. EPA can refer questions of NEPA compliance to the President's Council on Environmental Quality (CEQ), which is responsible for resolving interagency disputes concerning the implementation of NEPA. However, if EPA is toothless, so is CEQ, because CEQ also lacks authority to require federal agencies to comply with its rulings. Ultimately, EPA's role under NEPA is hortatory, encouraging other federal agencies to prepare honest environmental impact statements, and EPA's authority is limited to the persuasive force of its comments and its consequent ability to leverage the power of informed public opinion. There are cases, of course, where EPA has regulatory authority independent of its role under NEPA. The limits of EPA's regulatory authority over municipal solid waste landfills were outlined in chapter two, and will be discussed further in chapter ten.

Some federal agencies have come to terms with NEPA because it has become so clear (although litigation may well have served as the clarifying agent) that their actions have significant environmental consequences—for example, lease sales by the Interior Department's Minerals Management Service for oil wells off the California coast, adoption by the National Park Service of a new management plan for Yosemite

National Park, or incineration by the U.S. Army of chemical weapons stored on Johnston Atoll in the Pacific. EPA's role in reviewing the environmental impacts of such actions is accepted, even if its specific comments are sometimes unwelcome.

In other arenas, the importance of NEPA compliance and the legitimacy of EPA's role under NEPA is still contested. An agency or the constituency it serves will contend that environmental considerations should not drive the agency's decisions; permitting that to happen, the argument goes, would be to let the tail wag the dog. For example, the appropriateness of EPA's commenting under NEPA upon the environmental effects of mergers has been questioned. In EPA's Region 9, which I headed, one of the contexts in which that question arose was the proposed merger of electrical utility companies in southern California. The Federal Energy Regulatory Commission and the California Public Utilities Commission were considering a merger application filed by Southern California Edison and San Diego Gas & Electric Company.

The stakes were high: the surviving utility, Southern California Edison, would have been the nation's largest investor-owned electrical utility, with 4.8 million customers; Edison asserted that efficiencies made possible by the merger would result in $1.7 billion in cost savings that would be passed through to utility customers; and before it was over the two utilities would report spending $87 million in their attempt to win regulatory and legislative approval at local, state, and federal levels for the proposed merger.[1]

Commenting upon such a controversial project places EPA in a very vulnerable position. One of the risks is that EPA's comments will be seized upon by project opponents, whose opposition may spring from entirely different considerations. For example, the opposition of the mayor of San Diego and utility consumer groups to the proposed merger of Southern California Edison and San Diego Gas & Electric was not motivated by environmental considerations, but doubtless they welcomed the fact that the utilities would have to fight on yet another front. It is a natural human reaction for the proponents of a project, having been beaten about the heads and shoulders with a stick provided by EPA, to lump the agency in with their other tormenters. And, frankly, EPA doesn't need more enemies. Unlike other federal agencies—the Department of Agriculture, for instance—EPA has no natural constituency. Certainly the regulated community does not lobby Congress to increase EPA's budget or regulatory reach. And the environmental community seems to feel that EPA, under any administration, will respond only to sticks, not to carrots. Be that as it may, Region 9 did comment on the likely environmental consequences of the proposed merger.

One of the efficiencies claimed for the proposal was that electrical energy production could be shifted from San Diego to newer, more efficient plants near Los Angeles. That was precisely what caused EPA concern. Region 9 pointed out that the shift in power production to the Los Angeles area threatened to increase significantly emissions there of nitrogen oxide, a precursor of smog. This in the region with the worst air quality in the nation.[2] A federal administrative law judge shared EPA's concern, recommending that the merger be prohibited on the ground that it would further degrade air quality in southern California, as well as stifle competition and generate few benefits for utility customers. Before the federal energy commission acted on the judge's recommendation, the state utilities commission rejected the merger, leading the utilities to withdraw their application to the federal agency.[3]

SURGERY ON MOTHER EARTH:
NEPA AND INFORMED CONSENT

A landfill may significantly affect the environment. Indeed, as BAD claims, the adverse environmental consequences of an ill-considered landfill project may be devastating and irreversible. Therefore, under NEPA an EIS is required for the approval of a lease of reservation land for a commercial landfill, and given the BIA's fiduciary responsibility to tribes, one would expect it to comply with NEPA as a matter of course. Such expectations have been disappointed before, however, because of the BIA's conflicting missions.

As indicated, EPA makes enemies in carrying out its statutory responsibility to review environmental impact statements, and the agency does not need any more enemies. In practice, the NEPA process is even more stressful for the lead agency, the agency whose contemplated action is being reviewed, than it is for EPA. The federal Bureau of Reclamation, for example, traditionally regarded the NEPA process as an impediment to the accomplishment of its primary mission—building dams—and it was not career-enhancing for the bureau's environmental staff to be perceived by their superiors as being part of the NEPA problem. EPA, by contrast, has the advantage of a unified mission—protecting human health and the environment.

Admittedly, long before James Carville made it a mantra for the Clinton campaign, every cabinet-level official in the Reagan and Bush administrations knew that his or her other priority had to be "the economy, stupid." Indeed, while William Reilly was contemplating an offer to join the Bush Administration, one of his predecessors in office warned him that being EPA administrator in a recession would be no prize. And the pressure to consider jobs as well as the environment is inevitably felt by rank-and-file EPA employees just as by political appointees.

Nevertheless, for the BIA the preparation of an environmental impact statement on an economic development project can be especially traumatic because the agency has trust responsiblities both to protect the reservation environment and to promote tribal economic development. The latter responsibility was underlined during the Reagan Administration with the issuance of an Indian Policy Statement, the goals of which are recited in the environmental impact statement prepared for the Campo project:

This Administration intends to remove the impediments to economic development and to encourage cooperative efforts among tribes, the federal government, and the private sector in developing reservation economies.

Growing economies provide jobs, promote self-sufficiency, and provide revenue for essential services.

The federal government's responsibility should not be used to hinder tribes from taking advantage of economic development opportunities.

It is the policy of this Administration to encourage private involvement, both Indian and non-Indian, in tribal economic development.[4]

The conflict within the BIA between promoting development and protecting the environment came to a head in an unlikely place—the tiny Cortina reservation, just one mile square, of the Wintun Indians, about 120 miles north of San Francisco. National Environmental Corporation had contracts to dispose of building-rehabilitation waste containing asbestos. Such material is considered hazardous waste by the state of California, but is subject to less stringent regulation by the federal government; this made it less expensive to dispose of the material on an Indian reservation insofar as reservations are subject to federal but not state regulations. The tribal president, Mary Norton, supported the project. Norton did not live on the reservation. Tribal members who did— including Norton's daughter, Carmeno Bill—vehemently opposed the project and felt terribly threatened by potential exposure to asbestos.

Subjected to considerable pressure to hurry through the environmental review process, the local office of the BIA contented itself with an *environmental assessment*, which is a much less rigorous study than an environmental impact statement. On the basis of the environmental assessment, the local BIA office issued a "Finding of no significant impact" (FONSI), NEPA terminology for the conclusion that the potential environmental impacts of a project are so negligible that an EIS is not warranted. Cortina members wrote to the district BIA superintendent, complaining that the agency had not complied with NEPA.[5]

Don Knapp is a natural resource specialist with the regional office of the BIA in Sacramento whose duties include the review of FONSIs prepared by the local BIA offices. On this occasion, according to Knapp, the local office had issued the FONSI "boom out with it and sent us an information copy." The regional office overruled the FONSI. "The more we looked," says Knapp, "the worse it got. Can of worms. We wrote a huge, major report on it [to BIA headquarters]. Thirteen pages of things that were wrong and not done right that [the company] said they were going to do."[6]

Eventually, the asbestos really hit the fan. During the summer, Carmeno Bill complained that National Environmental was improperly disposing of the asbestos waste, simply dumping bags of it in a ravine, a charge the lawyer representing the tribe denied.[7] On December 6, 1988, Bill told the *Colusa Sun Herald* that torn bags of asbestos waste were exposed to the elements on the reservation, and that heavy equipment used by National Environmental was contaminated with asbestos, spreading the contamination on and off the reservation. Bill complained that her family and others on the reservation had already begun to suffer from symptoms of asbestos exposure. She added that the tribe's spiritual ground had been contaminated with asbestos, preventing Bill and her family from visiting the site to do honor to a nephew who had died recently. Bill phoned BIA and other federal agencies from the *Sun Herald* office, but received no help. Again the tribal lawyer dismissed Bill's charges, characterizing them as "wild hallucinations."[8]

The next day Carmeno Bill, her sixteen-year-old son, and her fourteen-year-old daughter were arrested on the reservation after they confronted two men who were about to use the heavy equipment that Bill believed to be contaminated with asbestos. The sheriff's office gave the *Colusa Sun Herald* the following account of the alleged incident: Bill told her daughter to get an ax and use it on a car, which "obediently, she did," inflicting three hundred dollars' worth of damage to a 1979 Cadillac that apparently belonged to one of the men. Then Bill told her son to get a shotgun; the shotgun was fired into the air several times, although no one was injured. The arresting officers took Bill to a hospital because she had gone into a trance and could not be awakened.[9] Because of the controversy the tribe and the company agreed to close the landfill.

Martin Topper, EPA's national Indian coordinator, had been one of the federal officials receiving Carmeno Bill's increasingly frantic phone calls. In the wake of the incident, Topper told George Farris, his contact in BIA headquarters, that this sort of thing could not be permitted to happen again. There had to be a more open process that guaranteed public participation—the process involved in an EIS. In the meantime, Farris had been getting the same message from the BIA's regional office in Sacramento. Believing that "political" decisions had been made and anticipating that the region's decision to overrule the FONSI would be appealed to Washington, Don Knapp and the regional director had urged BIA headquarters to adopt a consistent policy requiring the preparation of an EIS in cases like Cortina. Knapp says the region sought the directive "to slow these things down, they were being ramrodded, just like that one was, shoved down our throat."[10]

This was an unusual alignment of the planets, with the BIA regional office lining up with EPA headquarters. It exerted sufficient gravitational pull to elicit the policy that governed the Campo case—that an EIS is required as a matter of course for a commercial landfill project on a reservation.

EPA's Topper likens the process to the informed consent that should be obtained before major surgery. Surgery is an assault on the body for therapeutic purposes. An informed patient can make a rational decision as to whether the prospective benefits of surgery outweigh the adverse consequences that may ensue. Often referred to by tribal environmental activists as raping Mother Earth, a landfill project is, indeed, an assault upon the land. In order to make a responsible decision as to whether the prospective benefits of such a project outweigh the possible adverse environmental consequences, the tribe needs the information that would be developed in an EIS.

THE CAMPO EIS

The government agencies, nonprofit organizations, and private citizens who commented on the Campo EIS raised a wide variety of concerns: the alleged lack of demand for additional landfill capacity in San Diego County; the effect of the project on the value of surrounding properties; the possibility that earthquakes might lead to a catastrophic failure of the containment systems; and the litter, noise, traffic congestion, and air pollution that the project might generate.

The comments ranged from the ethereal to the earthy. The San Diego Astronomy Association, a nonprofit educational organization whose observatory is within two miles of the project site, expressed concern that landfill operations would raise dust, which would scatter light, degrading viewing conditions at "one of the finest locations for observational astronomy on the North American continent."[11] One BAD supporter eschewed technical comments, simply characterizing the two-volume draft EIS as an "abhorrent waste of taxpayer monies by the leeches of society representing a bloated bureaucracy."[12]

The unifying themes of the critical comments were an overriding concern with the possibility of groundwater contamination, a distrust of government, and a defiant resolve to stop the project. A Boulevard resident addressed an open letter to "all the 'BIG WHEELERS' and 'DEALERS' who have been lying to us" concerning the project. "This is the only water and air we've had, have, or ever will have out here," he wrote. *"We've worked* all our lives for what we have, and we are not going to 'roll over' at the 'whim' of some 'self-important, arrogant' people or companies with a great deal of *money to buy* '*boot-lickers.'"*[13]

Donna Tisdale's mastery of the EIS process would be the envy of any environmental lawyer. BAD submitted lengthy comments on every aspect of the EIS and coordinated with other organizations submitting comments. Donna testified at all three of the public hearings held on the EIS by the Bureau of Indian Affairs, and at times almost seemed to function as the hearing officer as she orchestrated the order of witnesses and asked the forbearance of the more unruly of her supporters. Nevertheless, Donna seemed no more inclined than other BAD members to trust the system she had mastered or to accept its outcome if it were adverse to her cause. "I have also heard that Ron Jaeger, the California Director of B.I.A., has called me a troublemaker," she testified at one of the hearings. "And in defense, well, I could be. Just don't cross me. All we're trying to do is cooperate with the system. And if the system doesn't work, then we will be troublemakers."[14]

By far the most serious concern raised by BAD is the possibility of groundwater contamination. Just how high the stakes are for Donna and her neighbors was established in a separate administrative proceeding. Under a provision of the federal Safe Drinking Water Act, BAD submitted a petition asking EPA's Region 9 to determine that the proposed landfill would be located above an aquifer that is the "sole source" of drinking water in the vicinity.

At the public hearing conducted by EPA, the supporters of BAD again expressed a sense of alienation from government, with one witness declaiming: "This is the age of Ross

Perot. This is the grass roots people that are fed up with you politicians telling us how it's going to be. We're tired of you stickin' shit down our throat. We ain't havin' it anymore. You know, people are rising up and we're throwing you out of office. If you don't start wisin' up and doin' what the people want, you're history."[15]

After reviewing hydrogeological studies of the area, Region 9 determined that the Campo/Cottonwood Creek aquifer does meet the statutory criteria for designation as a sole source aquifer: the people in a four-hundred-square-mile area draw almost all of their drinking water from domestic wells tapping into the aquifer. Economically feasible alternative sources of drinking water are not available. Building a pipeline to the isolated, sparsely populated area would be prohibitively expensive; a comparable project in San Diego County a decade earlier had cost approximately $170 million. Moreover, the exploding population of southern California has long since outstripped the water supply; the water supply agencies serving San Diego County would not be willing to annex the area. In the absence of practicable alternative sources of drinking water, contamination of the aquifer would create a significant hazard to public health.[16]

As Donna had understood it would be, the sole source aquifer designation was largely a symbolic victory for BAD. Under the federal Safe Drinking Water Act, the practical effect of a designation is that federal financial assistance is not available to a project that the EPA administrator determines may contaminate a sole source aquifer. However, the Campo landfill project is not federally financed. Therefore, the designation gave EPA no additional leverage.

OF OPEN DUMPS, DRIP COFFEE MAKERS, AND WITCHES' BREW

A facility of the sort proposed by the Campos is known as a *municipal solid waste landfill*. The change in terminology reflects more than an exercise in euphemism. The open dumps in which most United States waste was deposited until recently lacked important pollution controls that are incorporated into many modern landfills.

One of the most common pollution problems associated with an open dump is that rainwater seeping through the garbage may contaminate the groundwater underneath the dump, with a poisonous plume of contaminated leachate possibly spreading well beyond the boundaries of the facility. The formation of leachate can be illustrated by comparing an open dump with a drip coffee maker. The dry coffee is the garbage, the water poured into the top is rainwater, and the dark, brewed coffee dripping out of the bottom is leachate.[17] Leachate is a witch's brew because the waste through which it percolates is laced with toxic substances.

Unlike dumps, which accepted industrial waste as well as municipal garbage, modern municipal landfills do not accept hazardous waste, as such. The major source of potential contamination in the waste that would be accepted by the Campo landfill is household hazardous waste. There is no standard definition of this term. However, *household hazardous waste* is generally understood to include such common items as home maintenance products (e.g., paint, paint thinner, stain, varnish, and glue) and yard maintenance products (e.g., pesticides, insecticides, and herbicides). In most cases these products are not hazardous while in storage, or during use if properly handled, but they release potentially toxic substances after they have been discarded. More than one hundred substances listed as hazardous under the federal Resource Conservation and Recovery Act are present in household products, including metals (e.g., mercury, lead, and silver) and organic chemicals (e.g., trichlorethylene, benzene, tuolene, and parathion).

The United States Congress' Office of Technology Assessment summarized a number of studies of the household hazardous waste component of municipal solid waste. In two

communities—New Orleans and California's Marin County—
the household hazardous waste was sorted out of the trash
from single-family dwellings and weighed. Between 0.35 and
0.40 percent of the total municipal solid waste was considered
hazardous, and each household threw away an average of fifty
to sixty grams (approximately two ounces) of household hazardous waste each week. Other studies in Albuquerque and
the Puget Sound area in Washington reached similar conclu-
sions: In general, household hazardous waste comprises less
than one percent of municipal solid waste.

Data from other communities indicated that the hazardous constituents themselves were present in even lower quan-
tities—less than 0.2 percent.[18] Assume for the sake of argument that 0.2 percent is the correct figure. There would still
be ample cause for concern, for if the Campo landfill were to
accept waste at the projected rate of 3,000 tons per day, it
would receive 12,000 pounds of household hazardous waste
each day.

THE CAMPO DESIGN EXCEEDS
STATE AND FEDERAL REQUIREMENTS

The Campos do not deny that household hazardous waste
leaching from a landfill can pose a serious threat of groundwater contamination. The Campos contend, however, that
their facility would not pose such a threat because the design
specifications of the landfill regulations the tribe has adopted
are more protective than the standards required by either the
federal government or the state of California. To explain the
design features of the proposed Campo facility, we shall return
to the comparison of an open landfill with a drip coffee
maker. Again, the dry coffee is garbage, the water poured into
the top of the coffee maker is rainwater, and the brewed coffee dripping out the bottom is leachate. A modern landfill
might be described as a kind of anti–coffee maker. That is,
there is a "lid" on the top of a modern landfill to prevent the

infiltration of moisture into the garbage, and one or more liners on the bottom to prevent the escape of any leachate that does form. The design of the Campo landfill incorporates both of these features. It would have a cover to prevent rainwater from entering the landfill and forming leachate, and it would have a *double* liner and leachate collection system.

The final cover over the landfill would be eight feet thick. There would be three feet of soil over the waste, including twelve inches of low-permeability soil. That layer of soil would be covered by a 40-mil synthetic liner. (By comparison, the "commercial strength" lawn bags one buys at the grocery store are 1.4 mil thick.) The liner, in turn, would be covered by another five feet of soil.

There would be two *liner systems* underneath the waste. The primary liner system is intended to collect any leachate that forms in the landfill. The primary liner would be a 60-mil high-density polyethylene. The leachate collection system above the primary liner would consist of twelve inches of gravel containing six-inch perforated collection pipes. A two-foot layer of soil would be placed above the gravel to protect the collection system and primary liner from the overlying waste. The secondary liner system is intended to detect and remove any leachate that migrates through the primary liner system. Leachate from both collection systems would drain to sumps; when the sumps were full, the leachate would be tested to determine whether it was hazardous and it would then be disposed of appropriately.[19]

The importance of these design features should not be underestimated. When the Campo project was announced, only one percent of existing landfills had synthetic liners to prevent the escape of leachate, and only eleven percent had systems to collect and remove leachate. In the absence of such safeguards, it is not surprising that 184 municipal landfills had by 1986 made the United States Environmental Protection

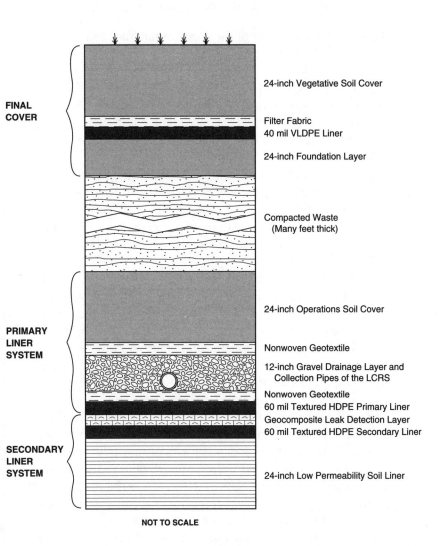

FINAL COVER
- 24-inch Vegetative Soil Cover
- Filter Fabric
- 40 mil VLDPE Liner
- 24-inch Foundation Layer

Compacted Waste
(Many feet thick)

PRIMARY LINER SYSTEM
- 24-inch Operations Soil Cover
- Nonwoven Geotextile
- 12-inch Gravel Drainage Layer and Collection Pipes of the LCRS
- Nonwoven Geotextile
- 60 mil Textured HDPE Primary Liner
- Geocomposite Leak Detection Layer
- 60 mil Textured HDPE Secondary Liner

SECONDARY LINER SYSTEM
- 24-inch Low Permeability Soil Liner

NOT TO SCALE

Typical profile of landfill containment system

Agency's Superfund list of the most contaminated sites in the nation.[20] Nor is it surprising, though it is tragically ironic, that the legacy of contamination at older landfills has made it next to impossible to gain community acceptance for proposals to open new, safer facilities.

Some critics believe that modern landfills that comply with the latest federal requirements still pose an unacceptable risk of groundwater pollution. They point out that landfill covers may deteriorate; that synthetic liners are not perfectly impermeable and may be defectively manufactured or improperly glued at the seams; and that leachate collection systems may become clogged with silt or microorganisms, corroded by chemicals in the leachate, or simply smashed by the tons of overlying waste.[21]

For those of us who are not scientists or engineers, the difficulty of maintaining landfill covers may be more easily understood than the problems associated with landfill liners or leachate collection systems. Because a landfill cap is designed to be relatively impermeable, rain will run off it at a velocity determined by the quantity of the rain and the slope of the cap. Unfortunately, some of the cap soil may be carried away with the runoff, contributing to sheet and rill erosion, and, ultimately, gullying of the cap. Moreover, as the soil dries, cracks will form. Subsequent rains will penetrate the cracks. In winter, moisture in the cracks may freeze and expand, widening the cracks. To minimize rain and wind erosion, vegetation may be planted. However, as the roots of the plants penetrate the cap, they may compromise its physical integrity. Moreover, plants provide cover and food for burrowing animals. One study revealed that mice, shrews, and pocket gophers can move 10,688 pounds of soil to the surface per acre per year. Earthworms alone can have a substantial impact, passing from two to fifteen tons of soil through their digestive tracts per acre per year. The holes left as earthworms move through the soil increase water infiltration.

Writing in the industry publication *Waste Age*, David I. Johnson of Michigan State University observes: "At this point, you may well say, 'If we plant, we're encouraging plant and animal penetration of the clay cap. If we don't plant, we get erosion or freeze-thaw destruction of the cap.'" "Unfortunately," Johnson points out, "that is one of the fundamental dilemmas left us by the normal processes of change in the natural world, be they the progressive conversion of a grassy field to a forest or the utilization of cracks in concrete sidewalks by ants and dandelions. This same successional development process," Johnson concludes, "will detrimentally affect long-term landfill cap integrity."[22]

Potential problems with the landfill cover, liners, and leachate collection systems were raised by some of the organizations and individuals who commented upon the draft environmental impact statement. The final environmental impact statement included responses to comments raising such concerns. For example, penetration of the landfill cap by roots or burrowing animals was acknowledged to be a "serious concern." To address the concern, Campo EPA regulations require that the vegetation growing on the landfill be of a type having roots "no deeper than the top layer of cover soil, and that the soil be deep enough to prevent penetration of the cap by burrowing animals." For this reason, the response explained, Campo EPA had decided to require that the top layer of soil be five feet deep, rather than the two-foot depth originally proposed.[23] As for the liners, the response to comments stated that appropriate quality control/quality assurance measures would be taken during the manufacture and installation of the liners to ensure their integrity. For instance, all the seams in a liner would be field tested and a certain number of the seams would be laboratory tested.[24] Turning to the leachate collection systems, the response to comments indicated that, for example, clogging would be prevented by flushing the systems periodically.[25]

The Campo landfill would be significantly safer, the final environmental impact statement concluded, than a landfill satisfying minimum federal design criteria, which require less durable covers and specify single-liner rather than double-liner containment systems. The probability of a *failure* in one or more cells of the Campo landfill was analyzed. A failure was defined as a breach of all lines of defense. In the case of the Campo landfill, this would mean, simultaneously, failure of the final cover, which would permit rainwater to enter the landfill and migrate through the waste; failure of the leachate collection and removal system; failure of the primary liner; failure of the leak detection system; failure of the secondary liner; and failure of the low-permeability soil underlying the secondary liner. Failure of less than all of these components within a single phase of the landfill was not considered likely to result in release of leachate from the landfill.

The cumulative probability of a failure of a landfill meeting the minimum federal design criteria is about 70 percent over a period of 150 years, according to the final environmental impact statement, whereas the cumulative probability of a failure of a landfill of the Campo design is only 3 percent over the same time period. "In terms of reliability, this means that the proposed Campo design is 97 percent reliable when considered over the time period that includes 30 years of operation, 30 years of post-closure maintenance, and 90 years of no activity. . . . At 100 years after startup, the proposed Campo design is expected to be 99.8 percent reliable, compared to a reliability of 78 percent for a federally compliant design."[26]

BUT IS THE SITE FATALLY FLAWED?

Though a landfill of the Campo design may be significantly less likely to experience a failure than a landfill merely meeting minimum federal design criteria, the Campo landfill would still be required by EPA's municipal solid waste landfill regula-

tions to have a system of wells to monitor whether contaminated leachate is escaping into the groundwater.

If there is a fatal flaw in the proposed Campo landfill, it
inheres in the nature of the rock underlying the project site.
There are two types of rock, differentiated by their degree of
weathering and decomposition. Weathered and highly de-
composed bedrock extends to a maximum depth of 110 feet
beneath the surface of the proposed facility. The weathered
bedrock is soft and crumbles easily. Unweathered bedrock,
which is resistant to the blows of a hammer, lies beneath the
weathered bedrock.

It is the unweathered bedrock that is the cause of concern.
It is igneous rock—that is, it was formed by the cooling and
consolidation of magma. Igneous rocks tend to form *fracture
systems* as they cool or react to other geologic forces. These
fracture systems serve as conduits for groundwater while making it difficult, perhaps impracticable, to monitor its movement and quality.

Under EPA's regulations, the system of monitoring wells
surrounding a landfill must be adequate to detect whether the
groundwater passing underneath the landfill is becoming contaminated. When the regulations were proposed in 1988, EPA
sought comment on the question of whether landfills should
simply be prohibited in certain sorts of hydrogeologic formations because of the inherent difficulty of monitoring groundwater in such formations. The preamble to the proposed rule
stated: "Some geologic settings that could preclude effective
groundwater monitoring are fractured bedrock where complex fractures and joint systems impeded flow direction prediction."[27]

In response to comments that landfills should be fore-
closed from locating in unmonitorable areas, EPA said that it
agreed. However, rather than adopting a rule that would have
precluded siting a landfill above fractured bedrock, EPA sought
to deal with the matter on a case-by-case basis through its

groundwater monitoring requirements. Under the regulations, a landfill cannot be sited above fractured bedrock, unless the developer can demonstrate the feasibility of adequate groundwater monitoring. In other words, the burden of proving that the groundwater monitoring requirements can be satisfied at the proposed site is on the project proponent.[28] In its comments on the final environmental impact statement prepared on this project, EPA Region 9 concluded that Mid-American had not carried that burden of proof.

WHAT ARE DNAPLS, AND WHY SHOULD WE CARE?

To illustrate its concerns about the feasibility of monitoring groundwater in fractured bedrock for possible contamination, EPA hypothesized that leachate containing a *dense non-aqueous phase liquid* or *DNAPL*, like the tetrachloroethylene found in cleaning solvents, made its way through the landfill's two liner and leachate collection systems.

Nonaqueous phase liquids are organic compounds that tend not to mix with water, dissolving very slowly. A dense nonaqueous phase liquid—that is, one having a density greater than does water—tends to sink through groundwater. Common dense nonaqueous phase liquids include chlorinated solvents like tetrachloroethylene—a man-made substance widely used for dry cleaning fabrics and textiles and for metal-degreasing operations.

Spot remover containing tetrachloroethylene is likely to be included in the household waste reaching the proposed Campo landfill. Tetrachloroethylene is thought to be capable of causing cancer in humans.[29] Accordingly, health-based standards for maximum concentrations of DNAPLs in groundwater have been established at five parts per billion. The release of just sixteen ounces of spot remover containing tetrachloroethylene could contaminate twenty-five million gallons of water to levels unsafe for human consumption.

If a failure of the Campo landfill containment systems resulted in a release of a DNAPL like tetrachloroethylene, a slug of the material would migrate downward through the unsaturated zone above the groundwater table and then through the pore spaces of the weathered bedrock within the saturated zone. The slug of DNAPL would dissolve slowly into the groundwater as it penetrated the saturated zone of the weathered bedrock. The groundwater contaminated by the dissolving DNAPL is known as the *dissolved phase*. The dissolved phase of the contaminant would be carried along with the groundwater as it flowed through the weathered bedrock toward the boundary of the landfill.

Where groundwater flows through relatively homogenous, porous rock, such as the weathered bedrock at the Campo site, a plume of a dissolved-phase contaminant disperses across a wide volume of an aquifer. Therefore, the system of wells Mid-American has designed to monitor the groundwater flowing through the weathered bedrock should detect the release of a contaminant that dissolved sufficiently. However, because DNAPLs dissolve very slowly, a concentrated slug of tetrachloroethylene might migrate through the unweathered bedrock undetected.

Upon reaching the base of the weathered zone, the slug could drain into any one of the numerous fractures in the unweathered bedrock, further dissolving into the groundwater contained within the fracture as it continued to migrate downward. In its comments on the final environmental impact statement, EPA Region 9 expressed serious misgivings as to whether a slug of DNAPL migrating down such a fracture would be detected by the system of monitoring wells Mid-American planned to drill into the unweathered bedrock.

A monitoring well along the landfill boundary would have to be drilled to a depth of over four thousand feet, EPA pointed out, to intercept a slug of DNAPL seeping down a continuous fracture that dipped at an angle of sixty degrees. "The footprint of the facility overlies the traces of approximately 50 such fractures, some greater than 0.5 mile in length. Because fractures are intercepted by other fractures at depth, groundwater contaminants would likely follow an unpredictable path from fracture to fracture beneath the site," EPA noted.[30]

In explaining his concerns to me, an EPA staff hydrogeologist used the following illustration: Detecting the release of a DNAPL in the fractured bedrock underlying the Campo landfill site "would require interception of a moving line (the slug) along a plane (the fracture) by a point (the well). If one of the numerous fractures were likened [to a] football field inclined below the surface, the chance of finding the contaminants from the facility boundary with a [monitoring well drilled into the unweathered bedrock] would be similar to successfully spearing a worm crawling along the fifty-yard line with a needle from over a distance of four thousand feet above while wearing a blindfold."

The comments filed by the staff of the California Integrated Waste Management Board regarding the final EIS echoed EPA's concerns regarding the monitorability of groundwater in fractured bedrock. "The proposed composite liner will eventually leak due to construction flaws, seismic events, and operator error. This is a reality and an unavoidable event," the waste board emphasized. The landfill's groundwater monitoring system, therefore, must be capable of "detect[ing] the escape of pollution quickly and prevent[ing] its entering the complex fracture aquifer. [However, w]ithout an exact knowledge of the location and nature of the fracture zones beneath and adjacent to the proposed landfill, such a ground-water monitoring system cannot be properly designed," the waste board continued. Important tests performed by Mid-American concerning the fracture zone were "inconclusive," the waste board found. "Until the location and nature of the fractured bedrock system can be accurately described it is not possible to propose measures that will assure mitigation of potential groundwater contamination. Additional hydrogeologic studies need to be conducted to provide that kind of information," the waste board concluded.[31]

Mike Connolly believes that the waste board staff spoke out of turn in making these comments. He notes that AB 240 gives the State Water Resources Control Board, not the state waste board, responsibility for water quality issues arising under a cooperative agreement between the state and a tribe concerning a reservation landfill project. The waste board itself, as distinguished from its staff, has not addressed the question whether the site is monitorable, and because of the division of duties under AB 240, is not expected to. Nor has the state water board addressed the monitorability issue, although it may do so when it reviews the license to operate the Campo landfill, assuming that the Campo EPA in fact grants such a license to Mid-American.

DID EPA DISCRIMINATE AGAINST THE CAMPOS?

Mike and the lawyers for the tribe believe that EPA Region 9 discriminated against the Campos in the agency's comments on the EIS. Recall that EPA's regulations do not establish an outright bar against the siting of landfills above fractured bedrock. Instead, the regulations provide that each case is to be decided on its own merits, with the project proponent having the *burden of proving* that EPA's groundwater monitoring requirements can be satisfied at a particular site.

Mike does not quarrel with requiring Mid-American to prove that its groundwater monitoring system will satisfy EPA's regulations. He insists that the Campo EPA will not issue Mid-American a permit to operate the landfill unless the company makes the required showing. However, Mike feels that EPA discriminated against the Campo project by rushing to judgment; that is, by requiring the tribe and Mid-American to shoulder the burden of proof prematurely, at the EIS stage.

It would have made more sense, and it would have been

consistent with Region 9's comments in similar cases, Mike contends, for EPA simply to have flagged the monitorability issue in its EIS comments, but then suspended judgment until the Campo EPA acts on Mid-American's application for permission to operate the landfill. At the EIS stage, Mike argues, the information available to regulators is necessarily limited; preliminary designs for the groundwater monitoring system have been prepared and some data is obtainable from test wells. However, by the time Mid-American applies for the operating license, the Campo EPA and the federal and state agencies that review its action will have much more information upon which to base their judgments. The actual monitoring well network will have been completed, and the information developed in the course of designing, redesigning, and implementing the monitoring plan will be at hand.

Mike supports his charge of bias by pointing to comments made by EPA Region 9 three months earlier with regard to the EIS prepared on another landfill project—a proposal by non-Indians to develop a municipal solid waste landfill in an old open-pit iron ore mine located at Eagle Mountain in Riverside County, California. Like the Campo site, the proposed Eagle Mountain landfill is located above fractured bedrock. Region 9's comments on the Eagle Mountain EIS noted that "there is insufficient information to fully assess the feasibility of full compliance" with EPA's groundwater monitoring requirements. Indeed, Region 9 went on to say that "it does not appear that groundwater monitoring can be accomplished by methods described in the EIS." However, rather than treating the EIS as the definitive document on which the case for monitorability had to stand or fall, as the region would arguably do later in its comments on the Campo project, Region 9 expressly stated that the deficiencies of the Eagle Mountain EIS could be remedied in the subsequent permitting process. "The record of decision, landfill permit application and draft landfill permit decision should therefore specify how a groundwater monitoring program will be implemented to meet the requirements" of EPA's regulations.[32]

At the time, I was aware that the Campos were charging Region 9 with bias and that they cited the Eagle Mountain comments in support of their accusation, but I failed to understand the precise character of their grievance. I thought that the crux of the Campos' complaint was that Region 9 had raised concerns regarding the monitorability of groundwater in fractured bedrock in its comments on the Campo EIS, while remaining silent on the point in its comments on the Eagle Mountain EIS. I obtained a copy of the region's Eagle Mountain comments, satisfied myself that we had raised the monitorability issue there, too, and concluded after discussion with my staff that the charge of bias was groundless. One of the major responsibilities of the regional administrator, I believe, is protecting the staff from intimidation. Region 9 had not pulled its punches in EIS comments when wealthy developers invoked their friends in high places, and we were not going to do so in response to what seemed to me to be a baseless charge of racial bias.

I now understand that Mike's real complaint was that EPA's comments on the EIS seemed to betray a lack of confidence in the Campo EPA to do the right thing when it acted on the landfill permit applications. In the Eagle Mountain case, EPA had identified the monitorability issue in its EIS comments but had then deferred to the state waste and water boards, trusting those agencies to apply EPA's groundwater monitoring regulations appropriately when they eventually ruled on the permit. No such deference, it seemed to Mike, had been accorded to the Campo EPA. To the contrary, EPA seemed to him to have taken pains to imply that the site could not properly be found to be monitorable, usurping the role of the Campo EPA, and doing so long before all the evidence on monitorability was in. The untimely and unwarranted conclusion allegedly implied in Region 9's EIS comments will haunt the Campo project, Mike predicts, because Donna Tisdale will rely heavily upon it in the RCRA citizen suit she will surely file if the Campo EPA ultimately decides that Mid-American has carried its burden of proof on monitorability and should be issued a permit to operate.

What I failed to understand at the time was that Mike was not accusing Region 9 of conventional racial discrimination. He did not think that we were biased against Indians in the sense of intentionally denying them equal protection of the laws we were responsible for administering. He was accusing us of *paternalism*, of assuming that we had to protect the Campos from themselves. And, paternalism, the complacent conviction that we know what is best for others, Mike reminds us, inspired some of the worst sins that whites have committed against the Indians—robbing them of their culture, their religion, and even of their children.

I can speak only for myself, but I suspect there may be an element of truth in the accusation of paternalism, at least in the sense that I had not developed much confidence in Mike or the Campo EPA by the time Region 9 commented on the EIS. On the other hand, I did have great confidence in the Navajo EPA, for example. Were there significant differences between the two tribes and their environmental protection programs that justified different degrees of confidence in their ability and commitment to implement federal environmental laws?

The Navajo nation has a population of over two hundred thousand and a land base the size of West Virginia. The Campo tribe has some three hundred members, and a much smaller reservation—about fifteen thousand acres. The Navajos have had an environmental protection agency since 1972; the Campo EPA was created in 1990. The program offices of the Navajo EPA largely mirror those of EPA Region 9, covering a broad range of environmental concerns—for example, air quality, water quality, pesticides, solid waste and hazardous waste permitting programs, and hazardous waste cleanups. Although it has a broad mandate and has now taken significant steps to assume other responsibilities, the Campo EPA did not then have much of a track record and its primary mission was to regulate the proposed landfill.

The director of the Navajo EPA had an outstanding career with the federal EPA before she joined the tribal government. Mike was an aerospace engineer until he became the chairman of the Campo EPA in 1990. The Navajo EPA director's role within the tribal government has always been clear. She is a regulator, not a proponent of the tribe's business interests. I have since learned that Mike was doing his very best to draw the same bright line and to stay on the side reserved for regulators, but his role seemed ambiguous to me at the time. When reporters asked the tribe to comment on the latest accusation made by Assemblyman Steve Peace, Supervisor Dianne Jacob, or Donna Tisdale, the Campo answering the charges was likely to be Mike, not Ralph Goff; Ralph had largely abandoned his role as the tribe's public spokesman for the project, having despaired of getting a fair hearing in the press.

I am not drawing these distinctions in order to belittle the smaller tribes, or to suggest that they are inherently incapable of assuming responsibility for implementing some or all of the federal environmental protection programs. I am suggesting that it is fair to inquire whether a particular tribal program has the critical mass, resources, trained personnel, and track record to merit confidence. To fail to distinguish among tribal programs on such grounds would be, it seems to me, an indefensible lack of discrimination. The Campos have demonstrated that it is possible for a small tribe with sufficient resources and resolve to develop a landfill regulatory system that a very tough critic, the state of California, has come to recognize as at least as protective as its own. Moreover, as we shall see in chapter ten, EPA later tentatively approved the Campo Environmental Protection Agency's landfill regulatory program as meeting or exceeding federal environmental standards. The system worked; it gave the Campo EPA an opportunity to be judged on its own merits.

THE SECRETARY OF INTERIOR'S DECISION

The decision whether to approve the lease of the Campo site to Mid-American was elevated to the Secretary of Interior himself. The leaders of both BAD and the Campo tribe met with Secretary of Interior Manuel Lujan. BAD's meeting was arranged by Congressman Duncan Hunter. Awarded the Bronze Star for participating in twenty-five helicopter assaults in Viet Nam, Hunter was first elected to the House in 1980 in the Reagan landslide. A leader of the Conservative Opportunity Society, founded by Georgia Republican Newt Gingrich, Hunter was elected chairman of the House Republican Research Committee—the fifth-highest GOP position—in 1989. Hunter has an unusual background for a conservative Republican. For three years before being elected to Congress, he lived and worked in the Hispanic section of San Diego. Running his own storefront law office, Hunter often gave free legal advice to poor people. When President Reagan called for abolition of the Legal Services Corporation, Hunter was one of the dissenters.[33]

Donna Tisdale says that Secretary Lujan repeatedly assured her and Congressman Hunter that the Campo project would not be approved. According to Donna, after she met with the secretary in Washington, Lujan pulled Congressman Hunter aside and said, "Tell your people not to worry, the project isn't going to happen." Donna was also encouraged by a secondhand report of a meeting that Lujan had with proponents of the project. One of Congressman Hunter's staff members told Donna that a BIA official who had been present at that meeting had told the staffer that Lujan had said that he would not approve the project, that it was not environmentally sound. On the other hand, Mike Connolly says that when the Campos met with Secretary Lujan, they did not get the impression that he was opposed to the project. However, when the secretary came to California to speak at a fundraiser for Congressman Hunter, Donna met with him one-on-one for ten or fifteen minutes. Lujan told her: "Relax. This is wrong, and it's not going to happen."[34]

As it turned out, Secretary Lujan did not act on the Campo project before leaving office, because the period for public comment on the final environmental impact statement did not close until just two weeks before the inauguration of President Clinton. Congressman Hunter, Donna says, tried to get the secretary to write a memo to the incoming administration, putting it on guard concerning the project, but Lujan refused.[35] Two days after the Clinton Administration took office, Congressman Hunter wrote Interior Secretary Bruce Babbitt, advising him of "serious flaws" in the Campo project, principally the threat of groundwater contamination. Hunter later said that he had received assurances from Interior Department officials that Babbitt himself would make the final decision whether to approve the landfill lease. "I will continue to press this issue with the new Administration," Hunter vowed. "This is a life or death situation for the individuals living near the reservation, and I'm confident Secretary Babbitt will be willing to listen to our arguments."[36]

Donna met Secretary Babbitt on March 17, 1993. The meeting was to have been on March 26, but Congressman Hunter's office told her that Babbitt was expected to act on the project on the nineteenth, so the meeting had been moved up to the seventeenth. The last-minute change of plans meant that Donna had to exchange her $500 roundtrip ticket to Washington for one costing $1,200.

At the meeting, Donna was accompanied by Congressman Hunter and Hunter's chief of staff; Secretary Babbitt had no staff with him. The meeting lasted half an hour. Babbitt seemed to be unaware of the arguments against the project—

for example, the dependency of the Campo region on groundwater, and EPA's comments concerning the monitorability of groundwater in fractured bedrock. Indeed, Babbitt seemed to Donna to be "genuinely shocked" by the information she brought to his attention. At the conclusion of the meeting, Donna had the sense that she had received a fair hearing, and that Babbitt was "sincere." Expected to act by March 19, Secretary Babbitt did not announce his decision until April 27, leading Donna to believe that he did look into the issues she raised with him.[37]

According to Mike Connolly, when the Campos met with the secretary, Babbitt asked Chairman Ralph Goff several questions: How long had he been in office? (Nine years.) When was he last reelected? (April 1991.) What was his margin of victory? (Ninety-eight percent.) Was the tribe still behind the project? (Yes, the most recent referenda were unanimous.)[38]

On April 27, 1993, Secretary Bruce Babbitt approved the lease of the landfill site to Mid-American. "The Campos' substantial efforts over many years, encouraged by the prior Administration, and my conclusion that the project has almost universal support among tribal members were important factors in my decision," the secretary said.[39] Secretary Babbitt's statement struck Donna Tisdale as disingenuous insofar as it referred to the prior administration's encouragement of the project, because Secretary Lujan had asssured her of his opposition to it. To Donna, Babbitt "sounded like he was making excuses for saying 'yes.'"[40]

Secretary Babbitt took the opportunity presented by the Campo case to announce significant new policy guidelines that are to govern the Department of Interior's exercise of its trust responsibilities concerning proposals to develop commercial waste projects on Indian reservations during his tenure. Indeed, the Interior Department's press release announcing the secretary's decision in the Campo case emphasized that "it would be a mistake for the waste disposal industry to look upon the decision as encouraging the targeting of Indian lands for dumps for non-Indian waste."[41] For the moment we will concentrate on Secretary Babbitt's decision in this case, before returning in chapter twelve to the broader policy guidelines he announced.

Secretary Babbitt's formal act was approving a document called the *record of decision* (ROD) prepared by the Bureau of Indian Affairs. In the record of decision, the BIA concluded that, despite the fractured bedrock, the groundwater passing beneath the landfill could be adequately monitored for contamination. The BIA was satisfied that, given the available information concerning the direction in which the groundwater flows within both the unweathered and weathered bedrock, "monitoring well networks can be targeted to encounter fractures such that representative groundwater samples can be collected." Additional engineering studies would be required, the BIA noted, to define the orientation of the fractures more fully and to determine where the monitoring wells should be located. The fractured character of the unweathered bedrock, the BIA recognized, requires "many more monitoring wells than typically found at other solid waste landfill sites."

The detailed design of such a system of monitoring wells is, the BIA contended, "beyond the scope of the NEPA process," and would be reviewed by the Campo EPA prior to the installation of the wells and prior to excavation of the first phase of the landfill. However, the BIA continued, the record of decision "does identify the general requirements of such an engineered system." Moreover, the BIA said that it would review the monitoring plan when it was prepared, "pursuant to its trust responsibility to ensure protection of human health."[42]

Secretary Babbitt's decision was denounced by a chorus of federal, state, and local elected officials representing the Campo area. "This process is far from over," said Congressman Hunter. "With the health risk that this dump poses to the reservation and the surrounding communities, we simply can't give up this fight."[43] Jan Goldsmith, who has represented the Campo vicinity in the California Assembly since the area was redistricted, characterized Babbitt's decision as "outrageous." Anything I can do at the state level, I will do," Goldsmith pledged. The most outspoken official was San Diego County Supervisor Dianne Jacob, who suggested that campaign contributions might explain why Secretary Babbitt's decision was announced just before the California waste board was due to act on the project. "That was no coincidence. It was obvious to me that they had the political skids greased," Supervisor Jacob charged. "This is not over," Jacob added. "The Board of Supervisors will meet on this issue in closed session to discuss legal action," Jacob said, including the possibility of suing Secretary Babbitt.[44]

THE COUNTY TAKES SECRETARY BABBITT TO COURT

Following Secretary Babbitt's approval of the lease to Mid-American, the County of San Diego filed a motion for a preliminary injunction in the federal district court in San Diego to enjoin the Department of Interior and the Campo tribe from issuing any additional leases or permits, or engaging in any other activities in furtherance of the construction of the landfill. The county claimed that the environmental impact statement prepared by BIA did not satisfy the requirements of the National Environmental Policy Act, principally because it failed to analyze adequately the possibility of groundwater contamination.

A preliminary injunction is intended to maintain the status quo until the court has the opportunity to consider the merits of a case more fully. Federal courts in California employ a two-pronged test in determining whether to grant such extraordinary relief. To make the case for a preliminary injunction, the moving party must demonstrate either: (1) a combination of *probable success* when the merits of the matter are considered in a subsequent hearing, and the possibility of *ir-reparable injury* if the preliminary injunction is not granted in the interim; or (2) that serious questions are raised and the *balance of hardships* tips in the moving party's favor.[45] These formulations are not considered to be separate tests, but rather the opposite ends of a single continuum.[46] In essence, the standard for granting a preliminary injunction is a sliding scale: as the probability of success on the merits decreases, the required degree of irreparable harm increases.[47]

The Department of Interior and the Campo tribe scored a lopsided victory over the county and its silent partner, BAD. The court denied the preliminary injunction on the following grounds: "First, it does not appear likely that the County will succeed on the merits, as the BIA's action seems to have adequately considered the EIS, which appears reasonably thorough. Second, the County has failed to show a possibility of irreparable injury. Third, the balance of hardships tips in the Tribe's favor. Finally, the public interest seems best served by permitting the Campo Band to proceed with the project."[48]

In determining the likelihood of the county's prevailing on the merits, the court was guided by the standard of judicial review applicable to cases involving the National Environmental Policy Act (NEPA). NEPA is, as discussed earlier, essentially a procedural statute.[49] That is, NEPA itself does not mandate particular results, but simply prescribes the process that a federal agency proposing a major project must follow. Accordingly, if the environmental impact statement adequately identifies and evaluates the adverse environmental consequences of the proposed action, the agency—which is not constrained by NEPA from deciding that other values outweigh the environmental costs—may decide to proceed with the project.[50] In other words, if an agency has taken a hard look at the likely environmental consequences of its proposed action, its decision must not be disturbed by the courts.[51]

The court ruled that the BIA did appear to have taken the

requisite "hard look" at the likely environmental consequences of approving the landfill lease. "It has issued a lengthy and detailed Environmental Impact Statement, which complies with NEPA's requirements of a fairly detailed analysis of environmental effects and alternatives." Specifically, the County's greatest concern—the possibility of groundwater contamination—"appears to have been a particular concern of the BIA as well, and the measures designed to prevent groundwater contamination are discussed in full in the EIS." The court noted that a landfill of the Campo double-liner design appeared to be significantly less likely to fail than one meeting minimum federal standards. With regard to the question of monitorability of groundwater in fractured bedrock, the court concluded that "the EIS and ROD indicate that [BIA] has seriously examined the question of site monitorability."[52]

Turning to the other factors to be considered in determining whether to grant a preliminary injunction, the court held that the county had not shown a real possibility of irreparable damage. The EIS was adequate in itself and more detailed groundwater monitoring studies would be required by the Campo EPA before Mid-American would be granted a permit to operate the landfill. Moreover, the court noted, the BIA's record of decision was conditioned upon the completion, review, and approval of the groundwater monitoring plan. "If the required further studies indicate that the project poses serious environmental risks, the BIA and the Campo Band may still halt the Project, as the Court assumes they would do if the landfill threatened the tribe's water supply."[53]

By contrast, the court held, the potential of harm to the Campos was "concrete and immediate" if an injunction were to be granted. "Delay in the construction of the Project will deprive the Campo Band of much-needed revenue and employment. As the Tribe also points out, delay of the project may jeopardize negotiations with potential customers of the landfill. Further, the costs of the project could increase substantially."

Such factors, the court noted, are commonly considered when deciding whether to grant an injunction halting construction of a project.[54]

Finally, the court held, a preliminary injunction did not appear to be in the public interest. "Rather, halting construction would harm the public interest in Indian sovereignty and economic security. In addition, there is public benefit to increasing landfill capacity, as well as providing a competitive alternative to the County's waste management system."[55]

The denial of the county's motion for a preliminary injunction came as no surprise to anyone familiar with either the showing required to support such a motion or the standard of review applicable to cases involving the National Environmental Policy Act. Indeed, even before the court ruled, Mike Connolly said that he thought the county was "just going through the motions, so that [Supervisor] Dianne Jacob can come back to Donna and say, 'Well, I tried everything I could.' . . . It's kind of a shame," Mike continued. "I don't think Donna is politically sophisticated enough to really see when they're kind of stringing her along, these politicians, just doing enough to mollify her. We saw that with Duncan Hunter and Steve Peace, too, at various times." For example, Mike said, "I heard Steve Peace say at various times that he was going to stop the landfill, and then after the cooperative agreement was negotiated, then all of a sudden his position was, 'Why, I never said I was going to stop the landfill. I just said I would make sure that it was regulated as stringently as California's.'"[56]

The defendants—the Campos and the Department of Interior—followed up on their victory by asking the court to render *summary judgment* in their favor, a procedure for deciding a case on the written pleadings without conducting a trial. After she attended the hearing on the motions for summary judgment, Donna permitted herself to hope again. "I think the judge is seeing things from our side now," she said. "I was shocked." The outlook had changed, Donna was convinced, because the judge seemed finally to have focused on the fact that the aquifer at risk is the sole source of the region's drinking water. "So it's looking good for us," she concluded.

A judge's remarks at oral argument, Donna was cautioned, are a notoriously unreliable indicator of the eventual ruling; the judge may be playing the devil's advocate simply to test the strength of various positions. However, Donna was convinced that the judge had tipped her hand. The judge had made "some pretty strong statements, and by the looks on the [opposing attorneys'] faces . . . whew! Even the reporter for the *Union* told me as he left [the courtroom], 'Well, it looks like the winds have shifted here.' It wasn't just me," Donna insisted.[57]

Donna was, she would say later, optimistic for a whole week. Her hopes were then dashed; the defendants' motions for summary judgment were granted. Summary judgment is appropriate when the record reveals no disputed issues of *material fact* and the moving party is entitled to judgment as a matter of law. There certainly are disputed issues of fact in this case, most notably whether the landfill poses an unacceptable risk to the area's water supply. However, the disputed issues of fact, the judge held, were not material to the narrow question a court may consider in reviewing an environmental impact statement—whether the agency took the requisite "hard look" at the likely environmental consequences of its proposed action. The fact that the aquifer underlying the proposed landfill is the sole source of the area's drinking water was, the court observed, the premise underlying most of the analysis in the EIS. Moreover, it is well established that in determining whether an agency has complied with NEPA, the court is not to resolve a conflict between scientific experts.[58]

A federal district court's scope of review of agency action is limited; essentially, it may only set aside agency action that is "arbitrary, capricious, an abuse of discretion, or otherwise not in accordance with law."[59] The court found that NEPA's requirements were satisfied here. "Specifically, the EIS provides sufficient detail to inform the decisionmakers of the environmental impact of the Project. The BIA's approval of the Project was neither 'arbitrary or capricious,' nor undertaken 'without observance of procedure required by law.'"[60]

Donna has the character trait coaches admire most—she does not seem have any "quit" in her. Her reaction to the order granting summary judgment was simply to rally her troops one more time—to lobby the county Board of Supervisors to appeal the judge's order. Steve Peace and two other state senators provided letters of support, Congressman Duncan Hunter manned the phones, and Dianne Jacob led the fight from within the Board of Supervisors.[61] On March 14, 1994, the county filed its notice of appeal.

Though others may admire her for it, Donna's refusal to admit defeat dismays Mike. "There's been this pattern: She'll make these accusations. They turn out to be unfounded. But it doesn't seem to change any attitudes." For example, the Campos were alleged to be dupes of the landfill developer, who was said to be seeking a haven from stringent state standards. However, when the dust settled, the state itself concluded that the standards adopted by the Campos for the design, construction, and operation of their landfill are at least as protective as California's. "I think that what we're dealing with here is a case of people believing what they want to believe. It doesn't really matter what you say," Mike laments. "You're just beating your head against the wall trying to get it across to them. But it's my job to try to get it across to them; I've got to do it anyway. I guess I've just got to put shock absorbers on my skull and keep plugging away."[62]

Donna's attitude was perhaps best captured by a statement she made following Secretary Babbitt's decision. She was undaunted, she insisted, as were other members of BAD. "Out of countless neighbors I've talked to, not one has expressed a defeatist attitude." She pointed out that other hurdles—regulatory and financial—remained for the project. "They have a helluva long row to hoe, and we will be dogging each and every step they take."[63]

CHAPTER TEN

THE TIDE OF BATTLE

ON OCTOBER 12, 1993, EVEN BEFORE THE JUDGE DENIED SAN Diego County's motion for a preliminary injunction in the federal lawsuit challenging the environmental impact statement, Mike Connolly was increasingly optimistic that the project would be realized and increasingly pessimistic that the tribe and its neighbors would be reconciled. The impediment to reconciliation, Mike believed, would be Donna Tisdale.

"The way it is now we have absolutely nothing going on between the communities," Mike lamented. "Donna's pitch among the local businessmen is, if you do anything with the Campos, you're supporting the landfill. As long as she is where she is now, it will go that way. It will be confrontational. It's a pity." Actually, Mike contended, Donna "doesn't have a whole lot of support from the regular people. It's mainly kind of the elite people, the ruling clique" of the business community. By contrast, "we have a pretty good relationship with the Joe Blows in Boulevard. A lot of them have friends on the reservation. They're the ones where the Indian [kids] go and spend the night with their kids, they eat dinner together, they go to ball games, they go on fishing trips. . . . There's a lot more of them than there are of BAD."

Looking ahead to the shift in the region's economic center of gravity that would result from the landfill operation, Mike argued that off-reservation business leaders were cutting their own throats. Rather than benefitting from the new wealth of their old customers, they would find that their unremitting antagonism had goaded the Campos into investing much of their landfill income into competing tribal-owned businesses. "Who do you think is going to be running and controlling every one of those businesses on the reservation? It's going to be the Campo tribe," Mike declared. "And are they going to rely on any of these businesses in Boulevard or Campo? No, they're going to compete with them." The off-reservation business owners "are going to end up losing a tremendous amount because they don't have any kind of rapport or relationship established with the reservation."

For example, the tribe will open a supermarket on the reservation, Mike predicted. To get supermarket prices now, residents of the region have to drive thirty miles to Alpine, which is still rather pricey, or forty-five miles to El Cajon. The mom-and-pop grocery stores in Boulevard and Campo have to charge high prices and their profit margins are still "pretty slim"; a supermarket on the reservation will drive them to the wall, Mike anticipated. The tribe will have a number of competitive advantages. It will have the proceeds of the landfill for capital investment; it will not have to pay land costs or property taxes; and it will have a built-in customer base. "The tribe is about ten percent of the [region's] population, and just pulling our ten percent off the market and going to tribal businesses is going to be a pretty good blow to a lot of these businesses out here. Whatever we draw from off the reservation is going to be even more of an impact." And a tribal supermarket would draw off-reservation customers, Mike is convinced. "We'll be going after the consumers in Boulevard and Campo. The vast majority of them will go where they can get the best prices. They are not going to boycott tribal businesses just because they're against the dump. They're going to go where it's cheaper for them."[1]

Mike's optimism concerning the project seemed to be warranted. The California EPA, as we have seen, had found the tribe's landfill regulations to be at least as protective as the state's. In April of 1994, the Campo EPA issued Mid-American the permit to construct the landfill.[2] (As noted in chapter nine, another permit would be required to *operate* the landfill. The Campo EPA had not acted upon Mid-American's application for that permit.) On May 2, 1994, EPA announced that it had tentatively approved, subject to public comment, the Campo Environmental Protection Agency's landfill regulatory program as meeting or exceeding federal environmental standards.[3]

To qualify for program approval, a tribe must demonstrate, among other things, that its standards are technically comparable to EPA's municipal solid waste landfill criteria, that its monitoring and enforcement authorities are adequate to deal with violations of its regulations, and that it is capable of administering the regulatory program.[4] Jeff Zelikson, the director of Region 9's waste division, stated that the agency was satisfied that the Campos' program met the same regulatory criteria that EPA requires of state programs. "Indian tribes are sovereign nations," Zelikson noted. "We respect this sovereignty. Their environmental protection programs must meet the same stringent standards as our states—no more and no less."[5]

EPA acknowledged that the Resource Conservation and Recovery Act (RCRA) is silent on the question of whether tribes should have the authority to grant permits for municipal solid waste landfills on their reservations. "RCRA does not explicitly define a role for Tribes . . . and reflects an undeniable ambiguity in Congressional intent." Nevertheless, EPA decided that tribes were entitled to the same opportunity as states to apply for approval of their landfill permitting programs. The underlying ground for the decision was that tribal landfills would otherwise be unregulated, because EPA does not have direct permitting or enforcement authority over landfills, wherever located, and states lack such authority in Indian territory.

Allowing tribes to apply for federal approval of their regulatory programs for landfills is consistent with EPA's Indian Policy, which recognizes tribes as the primary sovereigns responsible for regulating reservation environments and commits the agency to working with tribes on a government-to-government basis to effectuate that recognition. A major goal of the policy, EPA noted, is the elimination of all statutory and regulatory barriers to tribal assumption of federal environmental programs. The tentative approval of the Campo landfill permitting program, EPA stated, manifested its "continuing commitment to the implementation of this long-standing policy."[6]

In the factsheet announcing its tentative decision and soliciting public comment, EPA emphasized that approval of the Campos' solid waste landfill permitting and enforcement program would *not* constitute "approval or disapproval of the municipal solid waste landfill proposed by Mid-American Waste Systems, Inc." That decision would be up to the Campo Environmental Protection Agency (CEPA), EPA stressed.[7]

While approving the Campos' landfill permitting program, EPA apparently continued to have severe misgivings concerning the proposed landfill itself. EPA had said as much a year earlier in a letter to Mike Connolly that responded to Mike's request for comments on CEPA's tentative decision to issue Mid-American a permit to construct the landfill. CEPA was under no legal obligation to seek such comments, nor was EPA obliged to provide them. Mike was seeking technical assistance from EPA, a second opinion, and both of the agencies were bending over backwards to be collegial. However, when the EPA comments repeated the agency's misgivings about the project, Mike may well have regretted that he had bent over quite so far.

EPA prefaced its comments by stating that they were being provided at the request of CEPA for technical assistance purposes only, that they in no way indicated approval or disapproval of the proposed facility, and that EPA recognized that CEPA had bifurcated its permitting process, with the result that the concerns that EPA was expressing regarding the proposed permit to *construct* the landfill might be addressed when CEPA considered Mid-American's subsequent application for a permit to *operate* the facility. That said, EPA reiterated its concerns about the monitorability of the site. "Given the heterogeneity and complexity of the site, we believe it is unlikely that the ground-water can be characterized, monitored and remediated in accordance with" the requirements of RCRA.[8]

The significance of EPA's comments is not that the agency was thereby signaling its intention to withdraw its approval of the Campo program if CEPA issued Mid-American permits to construct and operate the landfill. EPA may withdraw approval of a state or tribal landfill permitting program under appropriate circumstances. However, EPA has never done so, and it is highly unlikely that the agency would do so here. Politically, withdrawal of approval would be virtually impossible. Mike has become one of the most respected tribal environmental officials in the nation; he is the co-chair of the environmental subcommittee of the National Congress of American Indians and serves as a representative from Region 9 to EPA's Tribal Operations Committee. In approving the Campos' landfill permitting program, EPA would have approved the tribe's laws and regulations, their monitoring and enforcement authorities, and their capacity to administer them. If EPA were to withdraw its approval of the program because it disagreed with CEPA over the issuance of these permits to Mid-American, EPA would be vulnerable to a charge of paternalism. The agency would be accused of trusting tribes to protect their reservation environments, so long as they exercised their discretion—made the same decisions in important cases—as EPA would. The lie would have been given, critics would charge, to the Indian Policy in which EPA has taken such pride. Moreover, withdrawing approval of the Campos' landfill permitting program would create a regulatory vacuum that neither EPA nor California could fill.

Therefore, the practical significance of the fact that EPA again placed on the record its misgivings about the monitorability of the Campo site is not that EPA will itself act to stop the project, but that the agency provided more ammunition for the "citizen suit" that Donna Tisdale and BAD are sure to file if CEPA issues Mid-American a permit to operate. As EPA has noted repeatedly in its public statements regarding the Campo case, failure to comply with the federal municipal solid waste landfill criteria leaves owners and operators of landfills vulnerable to lawsuits brought by individual citizens in federal court.[9]

THE BORDER WAR

Stymied so far by U.S. agencies and courts, the opponents of the Campo landfill have enlisted the good offices of the Mexican government.

The proposed Campo landfill is less than a mile from the United States–Mexico border. Hydrogeologically, the Campo–Cottonwood Creek aquifer extends into Mexico. Legally, the sole source aquifer designated by EPA stops at the border because the agency concluded that Congress did not intend, and that Mexico might object to, extraterritorial application of U.S. law—the Safe Drinking Water Act. The Campos' neighbors in Baja California oppose the landfill for the same reason that BAD does; they are concerned that it may contaminate the aquifer upon which the residents of the area, north and south of the border, are equally dependent.

On November 11, 1993, the Baja California legislature called upon Mexican President Carlos Salinas de Gotari to oppose the landfill. President Salinas responded by asking Mexico's representative to the United States–Mexico International Boundary and Water Commission (IBWC) to investigate the landfill project. Following a meeting of U.S. and Mexican officials—including members of the IBWC—hosted by Congressman Duncan Hunter, Mexico's commissioner for the IBWC notified his U.S. counterpart of Mexico's opposition to the landfill. The Mexican commissioner based his objection on two grounds. First, that "storage of hazardous wastes" along the border zone would violate the 1983 La Paz Agreement. Second, that the fractured character of the bedrock underlying the site would preclude adequate monitoring for groundwater contamination.[10]

The United States commissioner, Narendra N. Gunaji, replied that he had kept the Mexican commissioner fully informed concerning the project. Specifically, Commissioner Gunaji responded that "the proposed project is not intended to handle hazardous wastes and would only accept municipal solid wastes. One should expect municipal solid wastes facilities to be available in border communities in both the United States and Mexico." With regard to the difficulty of monitoring for groundwater contamination in fractured bedrock, Gunaji noted that he himself had previously expressed "somewhat similar" concerns and that the concerns had been addressed by the responsible U.S. and tribal regulatory authorities. He concluded by stating that copies of the correspondence between the commissioners were being provided to EPA.[11]

A month later a spokesman for the U.S. commissioner's office stated that no further action was contemplated. Asked about communications with the U.S. State Department concerning the matter, he responded that it had "not been elevated beyond a routine case."[12] However, on June 5, 1994, more than two hundred Mexican citizens blockaded the border crossing at Tecate, near the Campo reservation, for two hours; they were protesting what their spokesman characterized as the "short shrift" given to the Mexican IBWC commissioner. The protesters were joined by Gustavo Davila Rodriguez, the chairman of the Baja California legislature's ecology committee, who carried a protest sign along with his constituents.[13]

Cutting the Rail Line

Engaging the Campos on another front in the border war, Donna and her Mexican allies urged the Mexican government to ban solid waste shipments on the transborder rail line providing the only direct rail access between the landfill and San Diego. The rail line crosses the border from the United States to Mexico and back again, running south of the border for about forty-five miles between Tijuana and Tecate (see figure 3). "If [the Campos] don't use a railroad, their landfill becomes economically unfeasible," Donna asserted. "If they lose the rail line, it basically shuts them down."

The general counsel of the railroad argues that the proposed ban would violate the North American Free Trade Agreement (NAFTA), but Chairman Rodriguez of the Baja California legislature's ecology committee disagrees. "Before NAFTA, the Mexican government was afraid to raise a finger to oppose anything against the United States," said an aide to the chairman. "Now . . . I think we have a little more power." Among Donna's allies in Mexico is Martha Rocha, leader of Amas de Casa de Playas de Tijuana (Housewives of the Beach of Tijuana). Rocha says that her environmental justice group, which halted the construction of a chemical waste incinerator in Tijuana in 1991, is willing to block the tracks physically if the Mexican government does not ban waste shipments to the Campo landfill.[14]

An editorial in the *San Diego Union-Tribune* criticized BAD for "whip[ping] up groundless fears" about the risks of hauling municipal waste by rail. "[T]heir futile effort to stop this promising project on such a flimsy pretext . . . risks creating a pointless international misunderstanding."[15] In a letter to the editor, Donna explained that "Baja's opposition is not so much about rail safety as it is about water. Asking the Mex-

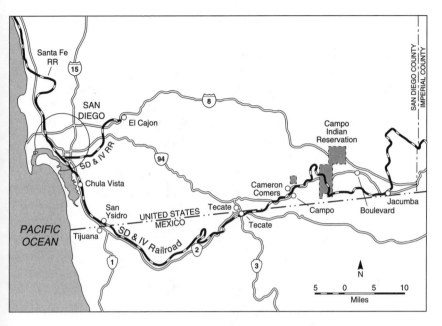

Route of San Diego & Imperial Valley Railroad

ican government to deny the permit to haul waste to Campo is the only real leverage Baja has to stop what it sees as a threat to the transboundary aquifer that we share." Rather than a "pointless international misunderstanding," Donna argued, "[w]hat there is is an educated, united effort by BAD, the county of San Diego and our allies in Mexico to defend and protect the most valuable commodity on earth—a fresh, reliable water supply."[16]

The opponents of the landfill have apparently won this skirmish. The Mexican rail authority has advised the railroad that it does not want the line used to haul waste to the Campo landfill. However, whether the denial of rail access is a mortal blow to the project, as Donna claimed it would be, remains to be seen. Mike Connolly acknowledges that originally the Campos had considered delivery of waste by rail to be not only environmentally but also economically preferable to truck delivery. However, Mike says that the railroad had priced itself out of consideration before the Mexican rail authority had made its position known, and that Mid-American's bids to cities were already predicated exclusively on trucking by then. Mike tells the following story with the air of a man who believes that he has disappointed his opponent's expectation that he has been placed in check. Donna Tisdale remarked to Jay Powell, the project manager for Mid-American, that she had noticed that Mid-American's bid to the city of Chula Vista was based on delivery of waste to the Campo landfill by truck, not rail. Powell confirmed that was so, saying that the company had found rail haul to be too expensive. Donna seemed crestfallen. Powell wondered why, until he learned of the position taken by the Mexican rail authority.[17]

MEXICO CARRIES THE BORDER WAR INTO CALIFORNIA

Perhaps the most significant effect of Mexico's opposition to the Campo landfill is that it has exacerbated Mid-American's already considerable difficulties in securing customers for the facility. The case of Chula Vista illustrates the point. Chula Vista—a city of 150,000 south of San Diego—is one of several cities in San Diego County that started searching for alternatives to the county landfill system when the tipping fees charged by the county began skyrocketing. The proposed Campo landfill was one of the alternatives considered by Chula Vista.

On September 11, 1993, Donna Tisdale wrote to Chula Vista City Council Member Jerry Rindone. Stating that it was a "known fact" that Mid-American had approached Chula Vista and that it was also a "known fact" that the city was considering the Campo landfill as an alternative to the county system, Donna urged Rindone and the other council members not to consider the Campo facility. Having fought the Campos in many arenas, Donna had developed the knack of putting her punches together in swift combinations. On September 13, Congressman Duncan Hunter wrote to Chula Vista Mayor Tim Nader of his opposition to the Campo project, and a week after that Assemblyman Steve Peace also wrote to Mayor Nader, with copies to each of the council members.[18]

In October 1993, the Chula Vista City Council voted to retain a consultant to draft a request for bids from private disposal firms, as an alternative to continued use of the county's landfill system.[19] Never missing a trick, Donna wrote to the consultant to convey BAD's opposition to the Campo project; she enclosed a copy of a letter that BAD's attorney, Alan Waltner, had written to the county Interim Solid Waste Commission "regarding the liabilities cities will face if they choose to use the Campo landfill."[20]

However, on April 5, 1994, the consultant presented the city council with proposals from three waste companies, each one predicated on use of the Campo landfill. Addressing the council, Donna urged the rejection of the Campo site on a variety of grounds, perhaps the most significant being the opposition of Mexico. Donna stated that Mexican authorities had assured her that they would not permit the rail line through Mexico to be used to haul waste to the Campo landfill. She added that Baja California officials concerned about cross-border groundwater contamination were looking into legal action to stop the landfill. Unwilling to limit their alternatives to a landfill that might never be in business, the council voted unanimously to instruct each of the original five bidders to go back to the drawing boards and present cost estimates based on landfill sites other than Campo.[21]

On April 21, 1994, Chairman Gustavo Davila Rodriguez wrote to Chula Vista Mayor Tim Nader of the Baja California legislature's ecology committee's "strong opposition to [the Campo] project, due to the threat to our groundwater resources."[22] Subsequently, the city council voted to take certain preliminary steps to prepare the way for leaving the county landfill system, should that be the city's ultimate decision, but to defer the question of what private landfill would be used in that eventuality. Stephanie Snyder, the staff member in the Chula Vista city manager's office responsible for this project, reports that the council members decided to delay as long as possible the choice of a landfill site, "because right now they are not very comfortable about some of the disposal options, particularly about the Campo option." The council maintains that it is interested in the most cost-effective solution to the city's waste problems and the Campo site, being the closest to the city, would be the least expensive alternative, Snyder acknowledges. However, the environmental concerns expressed by the opponents of the Campo landfill, especially the Baja California legislature, made the council "very uncomfortable." Therefore, the council seemed to be leaning toward a site in La Paz County, Arizona, even though the added cost of transporting the city's waste to that distant site would make it more expensive.[23]

A WAR OF ATTRITION

Donna asserts that Mid-American will have to abandon the Campo project because it cannot afford to keep investing millions in a landfill that will not open in the foreseeable future and has not been able to sign up customers. "Because of their lease agreement with Campo, Mid-American is (now) paying Campo $4,500 a day—for nothing. It's breaking Mid-American. Their stocks are so far down, it would really hurt them to admit they're writing this project off (as a loss). Mid-American can't afford to hold out much longer."[24]

Donna's prediction may be more than wishful thinking. In May 1994, Mid-American was forced to sell $175 million in notes at 12¼ percent interest, to retire short-term debt carrying a 6 percent interest rate.[25] In its 1993 annual report, Mid-American gave the following rationale for the refinancing:

"The Company anticipates that it will not be able to meet expected 1995 debt service obligations from cash flow from operating activities and cash on hand." In the absence of refinancing, Mid-American said, the company might have to "reduce discretionary capital expenditures, including the $15,000,000 to construct a new landfill in California."[26]

The *Wall Street Journal* explained why Mid-American was forced to refinance at junk-bond rates. Founded in 1986, and taken public in 1990, Mid-American raised hundreds of millions of dollars from investors who counted on the "capacity crisis" then prevailing in the waste industry to guarantee large profits. Unfortunately for Mid-American and its investors, the market system worked only too well. Despite the NIMBY phenomenon, the supply of disposal space increased to satisfy the demand. Moreover, because of the recession and increased recycling, demand was significantly below projections.

In hindsight, Christopher L. White, the chairman and chief executive officer of Mid-American, appears to have been too successful at raising capital and acquiring disposal capacity. "He's been one of the most successful guys at raising capital," says Stephen L. Schweich, a waste industry analyst at Robertson Stephens & Co. who was with Alex Brown & Sons when that firm underwrote Mid-American's stock offerings. "His biggest sin is he got handed all this money and bought landfills at the top of the market."

Indeed, Mid-American has already had to write down or write off significant assets it acquired when the waste industry was booming. "Two recycling-processing plants in Ohio, opened in 1991 and 1993 at a cost of $4.5 million each, were written off completely; a Philadelphia trash-transfer station bought in 1990 was written down by $6 million and put up for sale; and a sludge processing business acquired in 1991 was written down by $26 million and sold," the *Journal* reported. Mid-American's White admits that the company greatly overspent. "We could've not invested $100 million," he says.

The average tipping fee paid Mid-American last year—$16.41 a ton—was far below the price the company anticipated when it acquired many of its landfills. Moreover, Mid-American had agreed to pay "host fees" of between one and four dollars a ton to local governments in order to secure permits. "We gave a lot away," laments White. "We've got a major-league squeeze going on."

Finally, Mid-American has major investments in two projects that have been long delayed: $21.6 million in the Campo project and $11.2 million in a Jacksonville, Florida project. "We've got a lot of dollars that aren't working for us," White concedes.

As Mid-American's debts have risen faster than its revenues, its stock price has plummetted. The stock reached its high in 1990, closing on one occasion at $26.625. By the time the *Wall Street Journal* article appeared in 1994, Mid-American's shares were trading at $4.875.

White insists that Mid-American's debt is manageable because the company remains profitable. "We can earn our way out of it," he maintains.[27]

David Trossman, a waste industry analyst with Alex Brown & Sons, the firm that underwrote Mid-American's stock offerings, agrees. Trossman concedes that Mid-American's refinancing package was "very dilutive" and hurt the company's earnings as well as its stock performance.[28] However, "there is still ample cash flow in the organization to pay that interest," Trossman asserts. "The solid waste business tends to be a steady, cash-generating business. So . . . will Mid-American be around in eighteen months? Yeah, they'll be around in eighteen months. If they choose not to grow, they'll be around for a long, long time," he predicts. "What they don't have is the capital capacity to go out and make acquisitions and grow rapidly. But they do have the financial capacity to (a) build out [the Campo] landfill, or (b) wait, if they have to, or that is the right thing to do," he concludes.[29]

However, Vishnu Swarup, a waste industry analyst with Prudential Securities, is not so bullish on Mid-American. Asked if Mid-American can afford to keep pouring money into the Campo landfill without either a projected opening date or waste contracts, Swarup reponds, "I think it's going to be very tough for them." Mid-American, in Swarup's opinion, has "too much debt as it is . . . [and] their earnings outlook continues to get worse. Campo was expected to open a year and a half ago, two years ago," Swarup notes. "I don't know how long they can wait." There are other landfills being developed in southern California that will compete with Campo for the waste from the cities of San Diego County, as will distant sites served by rail, Swarup notes; "the value of the Campo site goes down by the day."[30]

In June 1994, the combatants seemed exhausted but unwilling or unable to loosen their holds on one another. After five years of fighting the Campo landfill, Donna's life is still consumed by it. In May, she had attended the Mid-American stockholders' meeting in Columbus, Ohio, and then toured the company's landfill sites for five days, staying with leaders of local grassroots groups having Mid-American as a common enemy. In the next several weeks, a partial list of Donna's activities would include helping her Mexican allies organize the protest at the border crossing in Tecate, organizing and presiding over the annual pit barbecue fundraiser for BAD, and marshaling her forces and testifying at the public hearing EPA would conduct on its tentative decision to approve the Campo landfill permitting program. While Donna remained committed to waging a war of attrition, what worried her now was that the project would "quietly fade away, and never really be eliminated, just sort of hang over our heads," quiescent until the demand for landfill space once again outstrips the supply.[31]

The day after the *Wall Street Journal* article on Mid-American appeared, Mike seemed subdued. If not completely preoccupied by the clouds on the horizon, he did at least seem to be searching for a silver lining. He spoke not of the fruits of victory but of the consolations of defeat. Heat is required to temper steel, Mike observed. The unity that the Campos now enjoy, Mike is convinced, was forged in the fire of the opposition to their project and may be its most significant legacy.[32]

PART FOUR

THE LESSONS OF THE WAR

CHAPTER ELEVEN

WAR AND REBELLION: CAMPO AND LOS COYOTES COMPARED

POVERTY DOES NOT DISTINGUISH THE CAMPOS FROM THE TRIBES that have rejected landfills; neither does the lack of economic development alternatives, nor the indifference or even hostility of the off-reservation community. So what does? The answers, for there is no one answer, will emerge when we compare the Campo case with that of the Los Coyotes tribe.

The Los Coyotes appear to be well chosen as a comparison group. Their reservation is also in rural San Diego County, and is about the same size as the Campos'. Approximately the same number of tribal members live on or adjacent to the two reservations. The Los Coyotes may be even poorer than the Campos were before they began receiving development fees from their landfill project. Of the 105 Los Coyotes reservation residents potentially in the labor force, only six have jobs, and none of them make more than seven thousand dollars a year.[1] Like the Campos, the Los Coyotes considered leasing a site on their reservation for a large commercial solid waste landfill.

LOS COYOTES: THE DEAL THAT WOULDN'T DIE

The facts of the Los Coyotes case are bitterly disputed. The developer was the Chambers company, a Pennsylvania-based waste management firm. Under the lease with Chambers, which the tribal chairman consistently defended but denied having signed, the tribe would have received the following consideration: $5,000 per month while environmental studies were being conducted to determine the suitability of the site; $20,000 when the Secretary of Interior approved the lease; $100,000 when landfill operations began; and then, depending upon the volume of waste received, royalties that Chambers claimed would have amounted to $1.2 to $2.4 million a year.[2]

What is not in dispute is that the Los Coyotes reservation is desperately poor. According to tribal members who opposed the project, their mountainous twenty-five-thousand-acre reservation is rugged and beautiful, providing a home for a wide variety of plants and animals, some of them classified as endangered, but its economic development has been limited to "a primitive campground and a Christmas tree business."[3] In defending the deal he claims he did not make, Los Coyotes chairman Banning Taylor explained that the tribe's economic situation made the opportunity difficult to resist. "Why not? Don't everybody want money?" he asked. "They offered these guys [the tribe] $5,000 a month just to do environmental studies. Who wouldn't accept it? Tell me who wouldn't? In these old woods up here where you can't get 50 cents a year out of there. We thought we were doing the reservation good by getting some money."[4]

In February 1991 opposition to the project crystalized. The Los Coyotes tribe does not have a written constitution or bylaws. Under the customs and traditions of the tribe important decisions are to be made by the tribal members acting as the general council; routine business is conducted by tribal officers.[5] The tribal members who opposed the project felt that Chairman Taylor should have sought the approval of the general council before signing the landfill lease. On February 10, the general council voted to direct Taylor to cease all activities related to the landfill project until tribal members received copies of the lease, and to prohibit the Chambers company from entering the reservation until a decision was taken concerning the project. Taylor, who was then eighty-five years old and had been the tribal chairman for fifty years, later defended his failure to heed the general council's directions by saying that it had neglected to express them in a formal motion.[6]

On February 15, the Coalition for Indian Rights, a grass-roots organization with members on nearly all the reservations in San Diego County, staged a demonstration in front of the federal building in San Diego, protesting what it saw as a conspiracy by waste companies to target Indian reservations. Standing in front of a "Protect Mother Earth" banner, Marina Ortega, a resident of the Santa Ysabel reservation, implored the Indian people considering such projects to "take into consideration the effect on future generations." The waste companies are "trying to poison us for money," added Steve Banegas, a resident of the Barona reservation.[7]

On February 19, members of the Los Coyotes tribe joined their non-Indian neighbors for Chambers' first presentation to the off-reservation community. The town hall meeting was the largest assembly ever held in tiny Borrego Springs. The Los Coyotes members in attendance expressed concern over ancient burial grounds at one of the proposed landfill sites, and medicinal plants found only in the high mountain region. "Some of us are not for this; that's why we are here. We want to stop it," Kevin Siva said. His uncle, Alvino Siva, said that the lease should have been approved by the general council of the tribe before it was signed, but that tribal members were "never notified."

The primary concern expressed by the off-reservation community was the possibility of groundwater contamination. The two sites on the reservation that Chambers had under consideration both directly feed the Borrego area's underground aquifer, the county groundwater geologist told the crowd. John Sasso, the president of the Borrego water district, criticized the preliminary environmental study Chambers had prepared. "We live or die on our ground water. How could this

feasibility study miss or dismiss the significance of our depen-
dence on ground water?" Sasso asked. Richard Chase, a consultant to Chambers, insisted that the company had a valid
agreement with the tribe, approved by a majority of the tribal members. Chase assured the audience that if anybody at
Chambers believed that the proposed landfill would have the
"slightest impact" on the area's groundwater, "we would not
do the project. I would be the first to say we should not do the
project."

Asked why Chambers was trying to site the landfill on a
reservation, Chase conceded that avoiding state and local
regulations was a factor. "To site these facilities through a normal course . . . has been notably unsuccessful." However,
Chase continued, the corporate policy of Chambers was to
"meet or exceed all state and federal standards." A lawyer
named Susan Trager later analyzed the lease—dated October
18, 1990, and apparently bearing Banning Taylor's signature—
for Katherine Saubel and other Los Coyotes tribal members
who opposed the project. Noting that the lease referred only
to federal regulations, Trager concluded that the tribe would
not be able to hold Chambers to its public statements that it
would also meet the stricter California standards. In a letter to
Chairman Taylor, which Taylor then distributed to tribal
members, Edwin K. Wiles, Chambers' manager for corporate
development, wrote that Trager's memorandum was "so bla-
tantly misguided and incorrect that it is beyond comprehen-
sion that she had any proper intentions in authoring it." On
its face, the Wiles letter appeared to be a point-by-point rebuttal of the Trager analysis. For example, Wiles made much
of the fact that trucks delivering trash to the landfill would
enter the reservation at the rate of once every five minutes
during the working day, not every two minutes as Trager had
asserted. However, the Wiles letter was conspicuously silent
on the question of whether the lease obligated Chambers to
comply with California's regulations.[8]

On March 15, BIA Superintendent Virgil Townsend gave Chambers permission to enter the reservation to conduct environmental studies. Confrontations ensued with tribal members who opposed the project. Two brothers, Gilbert and Milton Campbell, ordered survey and seismic crews off the reservation. "I told them the general council didn't want them there," Milton Campbell said later. "I told them, 'You're not going to do any more work,' and we escorted them out." Chambers' response was to hire security guards to accompany the crews. "We're going to have drilling rigs and other equipment that we don't want vandalized," explained Richard Chase, the Chambers consultant. "We don't want our equipment being vandalized and we don't want our people being hassled." Milton Campbell characterized the arrival of the security guards as an ominous sign. "It's like bringing a police state into our country."9

By March 27 the environmental studies had been suspended, pending resolution of the dispute. Tribal Chairman Banning Taylor did little to advance that cause. On the one hand, Taylor confirmed Chambers' right to conduct the preliminary studies; he had signed an agreement to that effect, Taylor said, and tribal members had approved it. On the other hand, Taylor claimed that he had not signed the lease to which tribal members were objecting. Chase insisted that there were two agreements in force—one for testing and another for a lease, should the testing prove the project feasible.10

On April 14, the members of the Los Coyotes tribe voted, by a margin of twenty-seven to two, to invalidate the lease upon which Chambers was relying. The resolution embodying the action concluded by directing Taylor to inform Chambers and BIA of the tribe's decision. It began by reciting the rationale of that decision: "WHEREAS it is the Custom and Tradition of the Los Coyotes Band of Mission Indians to live in harmony with their land; and WHEREAS the Los Coyotes Band depends on its reservation for its spiritual and economic sustenance." The next day Taylor refused to comment on the tribe's action, "I can't tell you anything. That's the rules of the reservation," he said. Chambers insisted that the lease was valid, despite the fact that Taylor denied having signed it, and the tribe had declared it "voided and invalidated." Chambers had not been told by either the tribe or BIA to stop work on the project, according to Richard Chase. "As far as we know, the project is still a go. We still believe that a majority of the members support the project," he said.[11]

On May 19, having refused until then to honor it, Taylor and three officers of the tribe signed a document certifying the action taken by the tribal membership on April 14, the vote to invalidate the lease. In addition, Taylor signed a document denying that the notarized signature on the lease was his. The lease had been canceled, reported Andrew Chaparosa, one of the tribal officials who signed the certification: "It was too one-sided." "This will save our land," rejoiced Katherine Saubel. "That dump was going to destroy the land of our ancestors."

The next day Taylor confused matters even further. He again denied having signed the lease. "My name was forged on that lease," he claimed, although he could not say by whom. On the other hand, he defended the lease, and said the tribe forced him, on pain of having to resign, to certify the vote declaring the lease void.

Constance Maxey, a tribal member who attended the May 19 meeting, recalled the response of tribal members to Taylor's repeated denials that he had signed the lease. "I said, 'Banning, the lease was notarized.' And one of the other members said, 'Do you mean that somebody forged your signature? Do you think it was the company?' He said, 'I didn't sign it.' She said, 'Banning, I will type up an affidavit. We'll support you 100% if somebody's forging your signature.' And he signed it." If Taylor was telling the truth, then someone not only forged his signature but also impersonated him before the notary.

The certification of the notary, who works for California Indian Legal Services in nearby Escondido, recited that a person "proved to me on the basis of satisfactory evidence" to be Banning Taylor, chairman of the Los Coyotes tribe, had appeared before her in person on October 18, 1990, and acknowledged to her that he had signed the lease "as his free and voluntary act." Asked about Taylor's claim that his signature was forged, the notary said that she notarizes so many documents each day that she could not specifically remember the event in question, six months earlier. However, she said, if her stamp appears on the document, she executed it correctly. "I go strictly by the rules," she insisted. "If I need an I.D., I would ask for one."

Ed Wiles of Chambers seemed incredulous upon hearing of Taylor's claim of forgery. He did not himself witness Taylor's signature, Wiles said, but other company officials did. Wiles rejected the decision of the tribal general council to renounce the lease. "You can't go buy an automobile and drive it for months and then sit down and say I hereby invalidate this purchase agreement for this car. It doesn't exist." Wiles, it appeared, was undaunted. "Hopefully this is simply a matter of ongoing review," he said. "We remain optimistic that we can proceed."[12]

On June 30, Taylor asked the tribe to reverse its decision of April 14, but the motion for reconsideration was voted down. Chambers again refused to take "no" for an answer. In a letter to the Bureau of Indian Affairs, Ed Wiles characterized the significance of the June 30 tribal vote as "uncertain." He asked that the bureau "temporarily suspend" the work of its consultants on the project "until the issue is clarified." "At such time," Wiles said, "we would plan to resume work." For public consumption, Chambers remained upbeat. "As far as we're concerned, we still have an executed [lease]," insisted a Chambers spokesman. "We're still going to pursue the project. The project is not over."[13]

On February 23, 1992, the landfill project appeared to rise from the dead. Having upped the ante to ten thousand dollars a month, Chambers won the tribe's permission to resume preliminary environmental studies. To secure its majority, Chambers flew in "prodump" tribal members from other states, a project opponent charged.[14]

Two years later, the Los Coyotes project had dropped out of the news. Asked the status of the project, BIA Superintendent Virgil Townsend said that it seemed to be moribund again. The tribe had taken the unusual step of asking BIA to sign off on its February 23, 1992, resolution authorizing the resumption of environmental studies, Townsend said, and when BIA undertook to consult Chairman Taylor concerning the matter, "nothing came of it." The project was in a sort of bureaucratic limbo. It had not been officially canceled, but neither was there any further action being taken. Townsend referred further questions to Chairman Taylor.[15]

Queried as to the fate of the project, Banning Taylor said that the tribe "made a decision to turn it down." Asked why the tribe had rejected it, Taylor replied that he didn't know. "They didn't explain nothing; they just voted it down." Taylor, who is now eighty-eight and has been reelected twice since the controversy began, continues to believe in the project, but thinks it really is dead this time.[16]

Perhaps it is. If so, the Los Coyotes may have dodged a bullet. On October 21, 1992, the *Wall Street Journal* reported that Chambers was "scrambling for cash and trying to sell off its assets. . . . It faces a slew of shareholder suits and pending investigations by the Securities and Exchange Commission and the American Stock Exchange." The "charade" collapsed, the *Journal* stated, when an outside audit disclosed that in every year since Chambers went public in 1985, "the company reported strong profits but actually lost money. Now, a chastened Chambers, once hailed on Wall Street as a waste management star, has restated its net income going all the way back to its inception, reducing its reported results by $362 million on an after-tax basis."[17]

Unlike the Campo case, the critical opposition to the Los Coyotes project came from within the tribe itself. Why did the tribes, whose material circumstances seem so similar, react so differently? There appear to be four significant grounds of distinction: (1) whether tribal members were satisfied that the *process* of reaching important decisions was consistent with their tribal constitution or their customs and traditions; (2) whether the tribal chairman acted *competently* in representing the tribe's business interests; (3) whether concerns of the members regarding the environmental impacts of the project were allayed by a *credible tribal regulatory program*; and (4) whether opposition to the project by non-Indians was perceived by tribal members as an attack upon *tribal sovereignty*.

PROCESS

Some members of the Los Coyotes tribe, the Campbell brothers and Katherine Saubel, for example, would probably have opposed the project under any circumstances, because they are convinced that having a commercial landfill on their reservation is inconsistent with their tribal culture and land use traditions. But their ranks were clearly swollen by the fact that Chairman Taylor was perceived to be violating the tribal custom and tradition of submitting all important questions to the general council. Taylor had, apparently, signed the landfill lease without seeking general council approval. Worse yet, he repeatedly defied clear directions from the general council to suspend or reverse his actions.

By contrast, the Campo chairman, Ralph Goff, seems to have honored scrupulously the tribal constitutional provision that vests all of the legislative and proprietary powers of the tribe in its general council. The general council of the Campo tribe functions as a committee of the whole; all adult members of the tribe may vote on any matter that comes before the general council at its monthly meetings. During the formative stages of this project, the general council voted on dozens of matters relating to the landfill proposal. The general council supported the project on every occasion; the lease of the landfill site, for example, was approved by all but one of the twenty-three tribal members who voted.[18]

Taylor Miller provides a glimpse of Ralph Goff's leadership style. Miller, who was once the the president of the John Muir Society, is a non-Indian lawyer who represents the Campo EPA. (To avoid a conflict of interest, the Campos made the commendable decision to have different law firms represent the tribe in its capacities as promoter and as regulator of the proposed landfill.) Miller had the opportunity to attend a meeting of the tribal general council at which the landfill project was discussed. A lobbyist in the state capitol as well as an environmental lawyer, Miller is accustomed to political leaders who try to dominate discussions. He found the general council meeting "painful, in the sense that [Goff] did not make proposals. He would sit there and wait for five minutes, and no one would say anything before he would make a proposal." During the silences that Miller found so awkward, Goff was apparently waiting for a consensus to develop, for someone to say, "Well, I think we should do such and such."[19]

Ralph Goff's nondomineering leadership style is in keeping with Campo tradition. As discussed in chapter four, the anthropologist Florence Shipek has studied and served as an advocate for the Kumeyaay Indians, of which the Campos are a band, since the 1950s. Shipek learned from tribal elders that a traditional Kumeyaay band leader, called the *kwaaypaay*, did not give orders but was followed because of his greater knowledge or managerial abilities. For example, most band members would follow the kwaaypaay in his seasonal journeys, believing him best quaified to find food throughout the year, but those who thought they knew better would go their own way.[20] Ralph Goff conducts himself, Shipek says, like a traditional kwaaypaay.

One difference between the two cases, then, involves process. The process by which decisions were reached concerning the two projects tended to unify the Campos but divide the Los Coyotes. Ralph Goff submitted important decisions to his general council; Banning Taylor did not. Beyond process, however, there is the question of competence. Ralph Goff seems to be a much better businessman than Banning Taylor.

COMPETENCE

Because of their poverty, Indian tribes are at a profound disadvantage in dealing with would-be developers of reservation resources. A tribe with an annual budget of $15,000 simply cannot retain the independent consultants that would be required to protect its interests in a complex undertaking like a landfill project. But a tribe with an income of $700,000 can. Ralph Goff recognized the handicap the Campos suffered, and he found a way to overcome it. The Campos required their corporate suitors to pay large development fees that enabled the tribe to retain its own experts—a financial adviser, a nationally recognized law firm specializing in the representation of Indian tribes, and a highly regarded environmental engineering and consulting firm.[21]

While he was overbearing with tribal members, Banning Taylor appears to have been passive in his relationship with the Chambers company. Recall his defense of the lease: "They offered these guys $5,000 a month just to do environmental studies. Who wouldn't accept it?" The Campos, by contrast, took the initiative and framed the terms of their negotiations with waste companies.

The Campos formed a tribal development corporation—Muht-Hei, Inc., its board consisting entirely of tribal members—to handle the business interests of the tribe in the project. With the assistance of its consultants, Muht-Hei prepared a prospectus for the landfill project, detailing the proposed terms of the lease. In addition to the terms of compensation, the Muht-Hei proposal included requirements regarding compliance with tribal environmental laws, Indian preference in employment and training, indemnification, and insurance. Muht-Hei then opened negotiations with seven solid waste management firms. The pivotal terms turned out to be the amount of compensation and compliance with tribal environmental regulations. One company offered only fifty cents per ton for garbage taken to the landfill, and another insisted that the tribe's landfill regulations be no stricter than California's. After a search lasting eighteen months, Muht-Hei selected Mid-American Waste Systems, Inc., which had offered three dollars a ton and had agreed to abide by the tribe's environmental regulations.[22]

The lease that Banning Taylor defends but denies having signed runs thirty-four pages, plus exhibits. It covers such critical subjects as fees, the design, construction, operation and closure of the landfill, and remedies for breach. Nevertheless, asked whether he had a lawyer review the lease, Taylor replies: "No. The band don't want no lawyers." Neither did he consult any technical experts. How had he come to the conclusion, for example, that $5,000 a month was a fair price for the privilege of conducting the preliminary site studies? "The band agreed to that." But what did he himself think? "I never had nothing to do with it. It's up to the band. They do all the business part."[23]

Ed Wiles of Chambers rejects charges that the company sought to take advantage of Banning Taylor's incompetence. Confronted with Taylor's statement that he had obtained neither legal nor technical advice concerning the lease, Ed Wiles objects: "Incorrect. Incorrect. All of those things were processed through the BIA, and there were attorneys and other disciplines within the BIA who looked at and provided input and comment."[24]

However, if there is one point upon which Banning Taylor and Virgil Townsend, the district superintendent of BIA, are agreed, it is that BIA is of absolutely no help to a tribe during its negotiations with a landfill company. Taylor's characterization of the agency—"BIA won't do nothing"—may seem harsh. But Superintendent Townsend confirms that doing nothing that would involve the agency in negotiations is official BIA policy.

Townsend acknowledges that the Campos were wise to demand large development fees up front, in order to hire independent experts to advise them in subsequent negotiations. Asked whether BIA did not have a fiduciary responsibility to the Los Coyotes to advise them to seek a similar deal, Townsend replies that it would be inappropriate for BIA to advise a tribe while it was considering a project. Even if it were appropriate, Townsend says, BIA doesn't have the staff to attend council meetings and provide advice. "We [the Riverside district office that covers San Diego County] have one environmental specialist. Period. And that's somebody brand new, and we're lucky to get that."

Superintendent Townsend points out that BIA does play a role, eventually, in reviewing the environmental impact statement and determining whether to approve a proposed landfill lease. However, he acknowledges, the preparation of an environmental impact statement takes years, and by that time, "it's often too late. The tribe has already bought into the decision. Unfortunately, that's just the nature of the business. These companies have much more staff to influence tribal members." Moreover, "I don't think it would be appropriate," says Townsend, "to emphasize one point or another before they've reached a decision."

Asked whether BIA could not at least have whispered to Banning Taylor, "Hey, did you know that the Campos got a lot of money up front so that they could hire their own experts?" Townsend replies: "I don't know. I don't know if that's ethical [to reveal] a business practice that another tribe has negotiated." BIA, Townsend is concerned, might seem to be endorsing one company or deal over another. In fact, although Banning Taylor knew that the Campos were also considering a landfill project and he did discuss it briefly with Ralph Goff, Taylor did not know that the Campos had managed to get the developer to underwrite the costs of independent experts.[25]

Put to one side the question whether, in the ordinary case, BIA should get involved in a reservation waste project while the proposal is still under discussion within the tribe. There were allegations of serious misconduct, perhaps criminal wrongdoing, in the Los Coyotes case. Did Banning Taylor sign the lease, and then repeatedly lie about it to tribal members? Did a Chambers official forge his signature? There are other, innocent explanations, of course, but they are hardly more reassuring. Banning Taylor was quite elderly. Perhaps he did not know what he was signing, or did not remember. Did BIA not have a fiduciary responsibility to the members of the Los Coyotes tribe to get to the bottom of the matter? "No," says Superintendent Townsend, "it's an internal matter." Besides, he says, "the project never got that far." An environmental impact statement would have been required before BIA would have had to review the lease, Townsend notes, and that would take years. The project died, apparently, well before it reached that point. Therefore, BIA never had to inquire into the question of whether Banning Taylor signed the lease, Townsend concludes, "and thank God!"[26]

Ralph Goff took the initiative in dealing with waste firms, demanding large development fees that enabled the Campos to hire independent experts to advise them in subsequent negotiations. Banning Taylor did not even take the elementary precaution of having a lawyer review the lease prepared by Chambers. Taylor defends his conduct by saying the tribe did not want lawyers involved. However, the opponents of the project thought fit to consult a lawyer and they received a very critical analysis of the lease. Taylor's response was to circulate a rebuttal prepared by a Chambers official. After the debacle involving Taylor's claim that his signature on the lease was forged, even tribal members favoring the landfill project must have questioned whether he was competently representing their interests.

CREDIBLE TRIBAL REGULATORY PROGRAM

Another distinction between the Los Coyotes and Campo cases involves the ability and determination of the tribes to assume responsibility for regulating their landfill projects. The federal EPA has historically delegated the authority for regulating solid waste landfills to the states. But the states, arguably, do not have jurisdiction over landfills on reservations. The Los Coyotes tribal government was not prepared to exercise that responsibility, nor did it indicate any interest in doing so. Therefore, the project opponents feared, Chambers would be allowed to operate in a regulatory vacuum.

The Campos, on the other hand, intended from the outset to exercise regulatory authority over the proposed landfill themselves. Pursuant to that plan, the tribe formed the Campo Environmental Protection Agency, enacted the Campo Environmental Policy Act and the Campo Solid Waste Management Code, and issued solid waste management regulations. At the cost of half a million dollars, the consultants retained by the Campos drafted the laws and regulations; the development fees required by the Campos subsidized the regulatory development process. Statutes and regulations are, of course, valueless unless they are enforced. By all accounts, Mike Connolly inspires confidence in tribal members that he is committed to protecting the reservation environment, and that he is competent to discharge his responsibilities as the chairman of the Campo EPA.

To inform tribal members regarding the environmental issues associated with the landfill project, Mike organized a series of six seminars. Concerns raised at one meeting would be the subject of a presentation the next week by the environmental consulting firm retained by the tribe. Mike does seem to have been scrupulous in providing information to tribal members concerning the environmental risks of a landfill project. For example, among the publications that are available to tribal members in a rack in Mike's outer office is *Rachel's Hazardous Waste News*. *Rachel's Hazardous Waste News*, which describes itself as "[p]roviding news and resources to the Movement for Environmental Justice," is extremely critical of the reliability of landfill technology, the motives of the waste industry, and the integrity of government regulators, so much so that BAD appended several articles from the newsletter to its comments on the Campo environmental impact statement.

Just before the vote was to be taken on the lease of the landfill site, Mike addressed the tribal general council and emphasized that, despite the strict landfill regulations the tribe intended to enact and enforce, environmental risks could not be entirely eliminated, and that the only foolproof way to protect the reservation environment would be to turn down the project. The general council proceeded to approve the project by a vote of twenty-two to one.[27]

Environmental justice leaders give Mike high marks for presenting the environmental issues fairly and they consider his credibility with tribal members to be a critical factor in uniting the tribe behind the project. Although he is "horrified" by the landfill project, Bradley Angel of Greenpeace confirms that the Campo tribe "did open itself up to informed and respectful critiques" of the proposal. Angel says that Mike contacted him and asked him to provide information to the tribe on an ongoing basis. Despite his profound misgivings about their project, Angel feels that the relationship between Greenpeace and the Campos is an "open one" and "more than cordial."[28]

As was mentioned in chapter two, Peter Montague, a scientist who is a technical adviser to the Indigenous Environmental Network (IEN), went to the Campo reservation and later reported to Tom Goldtooth, the chair of the IEN, that he believed that the tribal members had been provided information regarding the environmental risks a landfill poses.[29]

Marina Ortega of the Coalition for Indian Rights says that "there's always a question in everyone's mind: Are they [the Campos] really informed? No one knows that but them." However, Ortega's impression is that the Campos had, "right from the beginning," much more information than other tribes considering waste projects. "That would seem to be the difference there. There was a lot more time spent working with the people themselves, you know, just explaining things, and giving them time to consider."[30]

Marina Ortega believes that Mike's credibility has been critical to the tribe's unity. "I would say that the success of the whole project was because of him." Indeed, Ortega fears that the integrity of the project may be too dependent on Mike personally. She reports with concern a remark he made to her: "This project is only as good as those who uphold these regulations that I write. As long as I'm here, I'm not going to let anything go by that's not in the regs . . . but I can't say that will always be the case because if I ever leave this position to go work someplace else, and someone else takes over, it would be up to them."[31]

So far, in our attempt to understand why opposition to the project did not develop within the Campo tribe, we have focused on internal matters, all of a positive character. Ralph Goff consistently deferred to the general council, stimulating in it, to use current jargon, a sense of "ownership" concerning the project. The competence with which the tribe conducted its business blunted the charges of the off-reservation community that it was being exploited by the waste industry. Finally, the tribe took the responsibility for regulating the project itself and found in Mike Connolly a tribal environmental official with high credibility, allaying concerns that the project was inconsistent with tribal values concerning the sacredness of the land.

TRIBAL SOVEREIGNTY

There was, however, an external factor that may have been just as important in unifying the Campos—the approach taken by the off-reservation community. For example, the Campos found the attitude of mainstream environmental organizations paternalistic, at best. The Sierra Club and the Planning and Conservation League were among the principal supporters of legislation to extend state jurisdiction over reservation waste projects. As we have seen in chapters seven and eight, the Campos and many other Indians consider such legislation to constitute an assault upon Indian sovereignty, an attempt to deny them the right to manage the land that is their only tangible economic resource, motivated by a lack of confidence in their competence and integrity. Moreover, Mike says, he tried without avail to open a dialogue with the San Diego chapter of the Sierra Club. After making several attempts, he did succeed in getting a representative of the chapter to make a commitment to come to the reservation, but "she canceled out at the last minute." Thereafter, "I just gave up."[32]

Though she did not come to the reservation and discuss the project with the Campos themselves, the local Sierra Club representative did testify against the project, saying that she had "visited the perimeter" of the proposed site, by which she presumably meant that she had viewed it from the Tisdales' Morningstar Ranch. She also transmitted on behalf of the San Diego chapter highly critical written comments, the shotgun character of which can be illustrated by a few lines dealing with the proposal to transport the waste to the reservation by rail. According to the draft environmental impact statement, the railroad track, which crosses the border from the United States to Mexico and back again, was washed out beyond the reservation, but was in "fair to good condition" between the reservation and San Diego. "What is the nature of the repairs necessary to bring this proposed means of transportation into a condition that exceeds 'fair'?" asked the Sierra Club. "Who will bear the cost of the needed rail facilities upgrade? What is the condition of the railroad west of Tecate? How long will the upgrade take? Will the upgrade be done on both sides of the border to the same standards?"[33] Fair questions, arguably. However, *eighty-three pages* of such questions on this and other subjects may well have suggested to the Campos that the Sierra Club was not really interested in the answers, but was engaged in simple obstructionism.

Interestingly, the approach to the Campo project taken by the Sierra Club's San Diego chapter and Sacramento lobbying office was criticized in the Sierra Club's national magazine. In "Their Mother's Keepers," an article chronicling the efforts of tribal members to fight waste projects on their reservations, Margaret Knox offered this advice to non-Indian environmentalists concerned about such projects: "When a tribe courts dirty industry, the temptation for outside environmentalists is to try and stop it by whatever legal means possible. But that has sometimes meant running afoul of Indian sovereignty and jeopardizing long-term chances for a healthy alliance," Knox cautioned. "The Campo Band of Indians near San Diego, for instance, have hazardous waste disposal standards that are stricter than those of the state of California. Yet when the Campos planned a landfill to accept wastes from San Diego, environmentalists joined the state in attacking their sovereignty," she noted. "'Environmentalists need some education on that,' says George Coling, the Sierra Club's Great Lakes specialist, who works closely with Indian activists. 'You have to respect tribal sovereignty and then pressure the hell out of the tribal council to do the right thing.'"[34]

BAD made the same mistake, according to Mike—attacking the tribe's right to make the decision, rather than trying to influence the decision. Had the project been under consideration by the county, BAD would doubtless have appealed directly to the county officials responsible for making the decision. Here the tribe was the responsible authority but BAD ignored it, focusing its efforts, instead, on lobbying state and federal elected officials to author legislation that would remove decision-making authority from the tribe.

The Campos had been involved in a gallingly similar case several years prior to the inception of the landfill project, Mike recalls. A company approached the tribe with a proposal to build a processing facility on the reservation to extract PCBs (polychlorinated biphenyls) from old electrical transformers in which the material was used as an insulator. Because PCBs are a suspected carcinogen, the Campos' neighbors were understandably concerned. In that case, too, local and state elected officials ignored the tribal government, according to Mike, engaging, instead, in a "tremendous amount of grandstanding" about how they were going to stop the project. In the end, the tribe itself decided against the project. However, "to this day, people in the off-reservation community still think that they were the ones who stopped the project, and they can't even begin . . . to acknowledge that the tribe even had a role in that decision."[35]

Where tribal waste projects have been stopped, says Mike, they have been stopped by the tribal members themselves. Insofar as non-Indian environmental activists have played a role, it has been in support of concerned tribal members. By refusing to believe that Campo tribal members were genuinely open to argument, Mike is convinced, BAD forfeited its best opportunity to influence events. Contrary to BAD's impression, says Mike, there were members of the tribe who "questioned a lot of issues regarding the landfill. There was still a group . . . that weren't sure they even wanted to pursue it."[36]

Marina Ortega of the Coalition for Indian Rights agrees with Mike that BAD blundered by making tribal sovereignty the issue. Ortega, who has relatives on the Los Coyotes reservation, traces her involvement in the environmental justice movement to, among other things, a proposal by the Mesa Grande tribal chairman to site the MRS facility for nuclear waste three miles from her home on the nearby Santa Ysabel reservation. Ortega is not prepared to say that BAD was motivated by racism in asking the state to thwart the Campo project. She notes that when the Campo controversy arose, the notion of tribal sovereignty, in the context of regulating commercial waste projects on reservations, "was a new thing. So it kind of caught everyone unprepared, I think."

"I know Donna Tisdale," Ortega continues; "we try to work together on issues, just mostly sharing information. Some of the mistakes they made, you know, were just out of ignorance, not knowing that the tribes really did have this right." Referring to "a lot of racist statements" made by BAD members, Ortega says, "I sat down and tried to determine, is this out of lack of knowledge, or is this out of hate? And most of the time it is out of lack of knowledge." When non-Indians learn of a reservation project that may affect their lives, "it upsets them, because they know many [Indian] people lack education. . . . And they get very paternalistic, and that's something that they're going to have to leave behind [because] all they'll be doing is pushing these kinds of projects."[37]

Moreover, Ortega acknowledges, some of her Indian allies joined BAD in asking the California legislature to assert regulatory authority over reservation waste projects. Katherine Saubel, one of the leading tribal opponents of the Los Coyotes project, was by all accounts the most effective witness who testified in support the Peace legislation. Los Coyotes members supported the bill because they believed that reservation waste projects fell between the cracks, Ortega says. Regulating a project like this seemed entirely beyond the capacity of a small, poor tribe like Los Coyotes. Proponents of the project claimed that EPA would oversee it "every step of the way." However, when an EPA representative spoke to the tribe, he explained that the agency had neither the personnel nor the budget to get out to the reservation more than once or twice a year. "There wasn't any other laws. Everybody got panicked out when they looked to see what kind of regulatory laws were there. They were very weak; they were not developed. The BIA was not up to coping with all of this," Ortega continues. "So people got desperate and figured, well if federal can't do it, we'll go with the state. And everyone says California has the best environmental protection laws in the whole nation. So people probably figured that would be better than nothing, which was basically what we were looking at."[38]

Ortega's colleague in the Coalition for Indian Rights, Steve Banegas, was no more inclined than Donna Tisdale to permit waste projects to hide behind tribal sovereignty. Accusing the Bureau of Indian Affairs of breaching its fiduciary duties to tribal members, Banegas said: "They are using our sovereignty literally to kill us. The BIA won't listen to the people, and the Tribal Councils don't care about the people either. They only talk to each other."[39]

Although Steve Banegas testified in support of the Peace bill, Ortega says the Coalition for Indian Rights did not itself take a position on the legislation. However, the coalition did support legislation introduced by Congressman Duncan Hunter that would have declared a moratorium on commercial waste projects on the reservations in San Diego County. Although Ortega believed the bill "would not go anywhere," the coalition supported it for two reasons. First, "there were hardly any rules or regs in place" regarding reservation waste projects; it "was really a gray area." Second, opponents of reservation waste projects "needed to show [waste companies] we had clout to get that sort of thing introduced if we needed it." For four days Ortega and Katherine Saubel "went door to door" in the Congress lobbying for the Hunter bill. "Everyone we talked to said, 'Well, Campo wants this project,' and based everything on Campo. We said, 'Campo is a one-in-a-million kind of project. It's rare. They went out looking for the waste company. They spent all this money developing [their regulatory program]. Most tribes don't go through that; it's done for them by the company.'"[40]

Marina Ortega's experience with tribal governments would not inspire much confidence in Donna Tisdale that they can be trusted to do the right thing. "They're capable of making your life very difficult if you live on the reservation," Ortega observes. "If you don't support the current political party, you can be denied housing, you can be denied electricity, you can be denied sanitary facilities, water." Indeed, on some reservations, Ortega asserts, "opposing the chairman could cost you your life." Asked if she has been threatened with violence herself, the young grandmother responds laconically, "Oh, yeah." After the Los Coyotes proposal was voted down, Ortega says she "had a rifle pointed at my head" by a tribal member who supported the project. "I looked at him, and he looked at me, and he just walked away." While trying to organize opposition to the siting of a medical waste incinerator on the Santa Rosa reservation in neighboring Riverside County, Ortega received a threatening phone call at midnight "almost every night for weeks."

Throwing the rascals out often proves impossible, Ortega claims. Asked how Banning Taylor could be reelected chairman of the Los Coyotes tribe, despite the controversy over whether he signed the landfill lease, Ortega responds: "That's what happens when you give loans. . . . [W]hen you have a tribal government that is so corrupt, how could you possibly hope to hold a fair election?" Ortega claims that the Mesa Grande tribe voted three times to throw its chairman out of office over his involvement in the MRS program, but the BIA refused to recognize the validity of the tribe's actions. "So I don't think that just because a chairman gets back into office that it indicates that he's a good leader or that he has tribal support. It just indicates that he is in control of the ball at that moment."[41] Ortega's colleague Steve Banegas concurs. "These guys are like little kings, once they get into office they try to take all the power, and do anything to avoid losing it. They have the power to determine who gets what . . . , and when they don't like you they can cut you off."[42]

Bradley Angel of Greenpeace also agrees with Mike that BAD's approach was misconceived. Angel would seem to have been a natural ally for BAD; he has never seen a landfill proposal that he liked, on or off a reservation. And, working with tribal members, he has been instrumental in stopping many of the more notorious reservation waste projects. However, from the first call he received from a representative of BAD, asking him "to help us fight the Indians," Angel had a premonition that BAD was going to "blow it." "You've got it all wrong," Angel warned his caller. "If you pursue that approach, you'll wind up with a garbage dump."

Just as Angel has never seen a landfill he liked, he seems never to have met a government official he trusted. And, despite his respect for ordinary Indians, he seems no more sanguine about tribal officials; he recounts case after case in which tribal members forced their government to recant its support for a waste project. Nevertheless, Angel counsels non-Indian environmentalists not to attack a tribe's right to site a commercial waste facility on its reservation.

This deference is surprising. While some environmental organizations typically work within the system, Greenpeace seems to prefer disrupting it. While others lobby or litigate, Greenpeace organizes community groups and orchestrates demonstrations. Guerilla theater, preferably with television coverage, appears to be its preferred medium. However, "on Indian reservations we recommend the exact opposite," Angel says. "Where you attack sovereignty, that becomes the issue." In his experience, tribal members ultimately reject waste projects, "in pretty much every case," so long as they are given "breathing room" and, if they want it, information. BAD's attempts to go over the head of the Campo tribal government to the California legislature and the Congress "backfired," and united the tribe behind the project.[43]

Donna Tisdale rejects Angel's criticism. "Greenpeace is totally upset with us; they call us racist. They look at Indian governments as different from any other government, and we don't," Donna declares. "We're saying, look, this tribal government made a decision. We disagree with it, and we have a right to fight. They're saying, 'No, you don't. The Indians are supposed to be able to make their own decisions without any outside interference.' . . . But their decision will impact us," Donna objects, "and so we have a right to fight it. And they [Greenpeace] disagree." Donna feels that Greenpeace is guilty of a "double standard." Greenpeace will help anybody fight a waste project, unless it happens to be on a reservation. Then they will help only if asked by a tribal member. "That's discriminatory," Donna feels. Moreover, she believes that Greenpeace's policy may backfire itself, promoting the siting of waste projects on Indian reservations, because the organization pulls its punches with regard to projects on reservations, while raising such hell over projects anywhere else.[44]

The irony, perhaps the tragedy, is that Angel is just as convinced as Donna that the proposed Campo landfill would be an environmental disaster. "The white community there . . . , I think, have every right to have incredible concerns, because they will get poisoned, just like the Campos themselves."[45]

CHAPTER TWELVE

SUMMING UP

THE ISSUES PRESENTED BY THE CAMPO CASE WILL LIKELY PERSIST. Because of the potential regulatory vacuum on reservations and the difficulty of siting landfills elsewhere, waste companies will continue to be attracted to Indian country. And landfill proposals will continue to be attractive to some tribes. Many are desperately poor. Their reservation land is their only material community asset. It is often an asset of marginal economic value; generally, whites ceded back to Indians only lands considered to be valueless. Therefore, the other economic development alternatives available to tribes may not offer anything like the promised payoff of a landfill project.

Ironically, the expense of complying with EPA's rigorous new landfill regulations provides an additional incentive for a tribe to accept a commercial landfill proposal—to cover the costs of closing their existing open dumps and to secure free use of the commercial facility for the municipal waste generated on the reservation. According to Tom Goldtooth, the chairman of the Indigenous Environmental Network and the environmental director of the Red Lake nation in Minnesota, it cost $450,000 to close Red Lake's open dumps, not counting the sixteen monitoring wells that the tribe installed. And that was less than many tribes would have spent, because Red Lake had its own heavy construction equipment. A neighboring tribe spent more than three times as much. Waste companies, Goldtooth predicts, will capitalize on these compliance costs. "We'll handle it. We'll close all your landfills.

We'll cap them. We'll put in monitoring wells. We'll do the [operation and maintenance]. And we'll even site you a new facility. However, this is going to cost money." To raise the money, some tribes may be forced to open their reservations to commercial waste projects.[1]

In these circumstances, the danger of exploitation is apparent, as Secretary of Interior Bruce Babbitt recognizes. In approving the lease of the landfill site on the Campo reservation to Mid-American, Secretary Babbitt announced policy guidelines intended to "prevent the wholesale targeting of tribal lands across America for waste disposal."

After careful consideration I have decided to approve the lease between the Campo Band of Indians and a solid waste disposal company that will allow the proposal to build a large solid waste facility on tribal land to proceed.

Building large facilities on Indian reservations to handle largely non-Indian–generated waste, however, elicits a disturbing image of "wasting" Indian lands. Also, a project of this magnitude can permanently change the character of a reservation, particularly a comparatively small one.

And there is always the possibility, no matter how tightly regulated, of long-term environmental risks. The Bureau of Indian Affairs is not an environmental regulatory agency, and existing law and practice do not always provide clear answers to questions concerning the extent to which tribal, federal and state environmental regulatory laws apply. Indeed, the exploitation of potential regulatory loopholes or vacuums may be behind some proposals to site such projects in Indian country.

At the same time, these projects can provide significant economic benefits to tribal governments and reservation residents, many of whom may be impoverished.

Exercising the federal trust responsibility in this context is challenging. While respecting tribal self-determination, I must also seek to prevent exploitation of tribal resources for the benefit of non-Indians, and must take longer-term costs and risks fully into account, balancing them against shorter-term benefits.

Weighing these considerations, I have decided that my approach to such proposals as Secretary and trustee will be as follows:

In general, I do not believe the Department should be in the business of encouraging proposals to build large waste facilities on Indian reservations primarily to handle non-Indian waste. I will be especially concerned when a waste project is large in relation to the size of the reservation, and when cultural, scenic and other special qualities of a particular reservation would be dramatically altered.

I will approve such projects only when I am convinced that
—tribal members have been fully apprised of the terms, conditions, and risks, and have approved them, through their tribal governments or, preferably (at least where large facilities are located on small reservations), through a referendum election specifically addressing the issue;
—a first-class regulatory system (tribal, federal, state, or some combination thereof) has been approved by the Tribe, is in place, and will exercise clear supervisory power over the facility, including long-term monitoring and the ability to bring effective enforcement; and
—the financial terms of these arrangements, including potential long-term liability of the Tribe and the United States from environmental contamination, are protective of tribal and federal interests.

I am instructing the BIA to apply these principles in carrying out its responsibilities to provide advice and other assistance to the Tribes.[2]

While not addressing each of these factors in explaining his decision to approve the Campos' lease, Secretary Babbitt did say, "The Campo's substantial efforts over many years, encouraged by the prior Administration, and my conclusion that the project has almost universal support among tribal members were important factors in my decison."[3]

Secretary Babbitt's policy is commendable. And unlike most statements attributed to high government officials, the language used summons the voice of a specific human being, encouraging one to believe that the secretary personally struggled with the issues and thought through the policy. However, as I suspect he would be the first to admit, the policy is not a complete answer to the questions presented by the Campo case.

First, it does not address the fact that the impoverished tribes most likely to be attracted by landfill proposals are the ones least likely to have the resources themselves to evaluate the financial, legal, and technical aspects of the proposals, or to establish and operate the "first-class regulatory system" Secretary Babbitt rightly considers to be indispensable. The federal government does not underwrite the development of tribal regulatory programs for commercial landfills now, and because of the enormous expense that would be involved, is extremely unlikely to do so in the future. Federal funding of tribal environmental programs has been grossly inadequate.[4] Any increases are likely to be marginal. Under the circumstances, to divert funds from basic tribal environmental programs in order to subsidize commercial ventures intended primarily to serve off-reservation communities would not be a wise allocation of scarce resources.

Therefore, if tribes are going to entertain and adopt landfill proposals, the Campo approach of requiring a would-be developer to subsidize the tribe's expenses in assessing the proposal and in developing and implementing its regulatory program is likely to become the model. As was discussed in chapter two, this approach is not a perfect solution, because it entails an inherent conflict of interest.

Admittedly, the Campo EPA is not unique in relying on "user fees." As raising broader-based taxes has become politically impossible, government at all levels has resorted increasingly to fees imposed on regulated communities to supplement general revenues. The problem is that Mid-American is a community of one. If Mid-American were to pull out and another developer did not take its place, the Campo landfill regulatory program would lose its funding along with its reason for being, its employees would lose their jobs, and the tribe might be reduced again to grinding poverty. The conflict of interest is, therefore, inherent and significant. In fairness, however, it is also significantly mitigated by the fact that the Campos have voluntarily subjected their regulatory actions to outside review by entering into the cooperative agreement with the state.

Second, Secretary Babbitt's policy is not a complete answer because the Interior Secretary's approval authority over a proposed landfill lease is a blunt instrument. As Secretary Babbitt points out, the Bureau of Indian Affairs is not an environmental agency. It does not have the expertise or the resources to oversee tribal involvement in a commercial waste project. Superintendent Townsend made this point plaintively in defending BIA's action or inaction in the Los Coyotes case. The BIA office responsible for the district that includes San Diego County and its eighteen reservations has, Townsend complained, "one environmental specialist. Period. And that's somebody new, and we're lucky to get that."5 Moreover, when BIA reviews an environmental impact statement in order to advise the secretary whether to approve a lease of a landfill site, the agency cannot reasonably be expected to anticipate and resolve the many technical questions that may arise later, like the adequacy of a subsequently designed groundwater monitoring system. Finally, long after the secretary has approved a lease, the performance of a tribe's regulatory enforcement program may come into question.

EPA is not going to step into the breach. The agency does not have the authority to regulate commercial landfills directly on reservations or anywhere else. Moreover, EPA's Indian policy favors the assumption of responsibility by tribes for reservation environments. Once a tribal landfill regulatory program is approved by EPA, it will be very difficult, politically, to revoke the approval on the ground that EPA disagrees with a particular decision made by tribal regulators, even assuming that revocation would be legally justified.

While it is an unsettled question, states probably do not have independent authority to regulate reservation landfill projects. Therefore, state-tribal cooperative agreements seem to be the most promising alternative. State environmental agencies have expertise to share with their tribal counter-parts; unlike the federal government, states are in the business of directly regulating commercial landfills. And states will be motivated to enter into such agreements; the citizens of the area surrounding a proposed reservation landfill are likely to insist that the state negotiate as active a role for itself as the tribe will accept.

After having worked under it for more than a year and a half, the state of California considers its cooperative agree-ment with the Campos to be "an outstanding success." On December 10, 1992, Secretary James M. Strock of Cal/EPA found that the Campo EPA's landfill regulatory requirements were "at least as protective, and in some cases more so, than those in effect throughout California." Strock expressed the hope that the cooperative agreement would serve as a model of environmental partnership between states and tribes, largely eliminating jurisdictional disputes as a source of the conflicts that have marred state-tribal relations in the past.[6] On July 1, 1994, in a meeting convened by EPA and prompted by Mexico's concerns regarding cross-border groundwater pol-lution, Paul Blais, a special assistant to Secretary Strock, as-sured the Mexican delegation:

So far everything has gone very well under [the] cooperative agreement. There's been excellent cooperation by the Campo EPA. There's been excellent communication in regards to any issues that we've raised, and so far from the state's perspective at least the Campo cooperative agreement has been just an outstanding success for us. We feel that we're getting the type of opportunity to review and comment and participate on their development that we think is fully protective of the state's interests.

So in that regard if we have any other tribes that were to start out with other major projects, we would be very anxious to try and get into this kind of cooperative agreement with other . . . tribes.[7]

Of course, as was discussed in chapter eight, even with the best of good faith on both sides, a dispute may develop that the state and the tribe will be unable to resolve themselves. The state would then go to court, if it considered the environmental threat to be sufficiently serious. And the Campos would be free to object to the court that the state has no jurisdiction over the landfill, independent of the cooperative agreement.

Although the outcome of such litigation is unpredictable, the court would not be reduced to weighing abstract interests in a vacuum. The issue of tribal sovereignty would be raised in the context of the cooperative agreement and the parties' performance under it. The court's perception of the competing state and tribal interests would inevitably be colored by the answers to questions like the following: Was there a violation of a Campo Environmental Protection Agency regulation, a violation that posed a substantial risk of significant environmental damage? Did CEPA fail to address the problem within a reasonable period of time after being properly notified of the state's concerns? If the parties are to spend their limited resources in litigation, then as the attorney for Mid-American remarked, let them litigate such questions of genuine environmental significance, concrete questions appropriate to judicial review, rather than just the abstract and ultimately political question of tribal sovereignty. Indeed, the prospect of trying the sovereignty issue in the light of their performances under the cooperative agreement may well reinforce the parties' inclinations to work through their problems without resorting to litigation.

Donna takes no comfort from the cooperation between the state and the tribe. Because she is convinced that the proposed landfill would inevitably leak and contaminate the aquifer, she considers the only acceptable role for the state to be aggressive and unrelenting opposition to the project. For her part, Donna will continue to dog every step taken by the tribe and the state. If CEPA issues Mid-American an operating permit, either with the state's approval or over its objection, BAD will file a citizens' suit under RCRA, alleging violation of the landfill regulations promulgated by EPA. Donna will also continue to wage a war of attrition. The objective is forcing Mid-American to cut its losses by abandoning the project. In this campaign, Donna has powerful and aggressive allies among the elected officials on both sides of the border. One of their principal tactics is trying to convince municipal officials in the region that any savings their cities might realize from using the Campo landfill would be more than offset by the political price they would have to pay.

The Campos have lived in dire poverty for more than a century. They believe that the landfill project offers the first real hope they have had since the coming of the whites that their children's lives can be better than their own. Donna and her allies are just as convinced that the project represents the death of hope for everyone in the region, that no one's children will be able to live there if the groundwater is poisoned.

Whom should we be rooting for? Would the proposed landfill be safe or not? The short, though frustrating, answer is that we don't really know yet, because the information necessary for an objective judgment is not yet available.

As was noted in chapter nine, under EPA's regulations, a landfill cannot be sited above fractured bedrock, unless the developer can demonstrate the feasibility of adequate groundwater monitoring. That is, the burden of proving that the groundwater monitoring requirements can be satisfied at the Campo site is on Mid-American.[8] In its comments on the final environmental impact statement, EPA Region 9 concluded that Mid-American had not carried the burden of proof at that time.

Mike objects that EPA required the tribe and Mid-American to shoulder the burden of proof prematurely, at the EIS stage. It would have made more sense, and it would have been consistent with Region 9's comments in similar cases, Mike contends, for EPA simply to have flagged the issue in its EIS comments, but then suspended judgment until the Campo

EPA acts on Mid-American's application for permission to operate the landfill. At the EIS stage, Mike argues, the information available to regulators is necessarily limited; preliminary designs for the groundwater monitoring system have been prepared and some data is available from test wells. However, by the time Mid-American applies for the operating license, the Campo EPA and the federal and state agencies that review its action will have much more information upon which to base their judgments. The actual monitoring well network will have been completed, and the information developed in the course of designing, redesigning, and implementing the monitoring plan will be at hand.

Whether EPA should have suspended judgment on the monitorability issue in its EIS comments is a moot point now. What is clear is that a good deal of new information has been developed in the interim, that CEPA has yet to make a decision on Mid-American's application for a permit to operate, and that the state will have an opportunity to review the matter, pursuant to the cooperative agreement. Ultimately, the monitorability issue is likely to be a close question about which reasonable professionals can and will disagree. If the state concurs in the issuance of an operating permit to Mid-American, the decision should carry considerable credibility with anyone who has any confidence in "the system." At the very least, the question of whether CEPA's action was tainted by a conflict of interest should be considered moot. If CEPA issues the operating permit over the objection of the state, the conflict in expert testimony will have to be resolved by a court in litigation brought by the state or BAD.

The lessons that environmental justice advocates take from this case may depend largely upon the convictions they bring to it. Many are unalterably opposed to commercial landfill projects on reservations. Some, like Bradley Angel, consider landfills to be inherently unsafe. Others, like Katherine Saubel, consider commercial landfills to be incompatible with

Indian values. If the objective is simply to "stop" a reservation waste project, then the lesson of this case is that the approach that is most likely to be successful is to work directly with the tribal officials and members, lest an "us versus them" mentality develop.

Others in the environmental justice movement, however, may question whether simply trying to stop reservation waste projects is an adequate strategy. Some tribes may well decide to follow the Campos' lead in selecting a commercial landfill as the most viable economic development opportunity available to them. The question then becomes whether such a tribe will also follow the Campos' lead in establishing even stricter regulatory standards than would be required under state and federal law. The answer to this question may depend upon the tribe's relationship with environmentalists from within and without the tribal community. If environmentalists insist that any tribal official willing to consider a waste project must be either ignorant or corrupt, then dialogue is impossible. A proud people will not parley on such terms.

Ultimately, whether a commercial waste project is an acceptable means of economic development is a question each tribe must resolve in light of its cultural and religious values and the best available environmental, financial, and legal advice.

EPILOGUE

ONE OF THE PITFALLS IN WRITING A BOOK ABOUT ISSUES RAISED by current events is that the events continue to unfold after the manuscript leaves the author's hands.

In chapter two, the saga of the MRS project concludes with the announcement in April 1994 that the Mescalero Apache tribe had entered into a tentative agreement with a consortium of utility companies to develop a private interim storage facility for spent fuel rods from nuclear power plants. On January 31, 1995, tribal members rejected the agreement, despite proponents' claims that the project would have yielded $250 million and 300 to 500 jobs over its 40-year lifetime. Two thirds of the tribe's 1,200 eligible voters participated in the referendum—the largest turnout of any election in recent years—with 362 voting for the project and 490 opposing it.[1]

Congress, at the instance of Senator Jeff Bingaman of New Mexico, had effectively vetoed the participation of the Mescaleros in the government's MRS program by barring the expenditure of Energy Department funds for a grant to the tribe. Nuclear Waste Negotiator Richard Stallings had then concentrated his efforts on the Skull Valley Goshutes. However, the very day that the Goshutes chairman agreed to enter into formal negotiations, Stallings learned that his office was going to be shut down, as it was on January 21, 1995.[2]

The president of the utility consortium said that the Mescalero vote "closes out the opportunity" to build a private centralized dry storage facility for the spent fuel now stored in pools at nuclear power plants.[3] The pressure on utilities to secure off-site storage has eased, however. In 1990, the Nuclear Regulatory Commission ruled that dry storage facilities could be built at existing nuclear generators without conducting site-specific environmental impact studies, provided that the utilities used storage casks of a sort approved by the commission. The commission's rationale was that each site at which the casks would be used had already been the subject of an environmental impact statement in connection with the licensing of the plant. On January 11, 1995, the United States Court of Appeals for the Sixth Circuit held that the commission's failure to prepare a site-specific environmental analysis concerning the use and operation of commission-approved dry storage casks at a Michigan nuclear power plant did not violate the National Environmental Policy Act.[4]

The evidence presented in chapter six suggests that the opposition of San Diego County officials to the Campo landfill project has been motivated at least in part by their desire to maintain monopolistic protection for a county system that is unable to compete successfully with private landfills. The county system has not yet pulled out of its "death spiral." In October 1994, the joint powers authority (JPA) now managing the county's landfills began charging nonmember cities $74 per ton, rather than the $55 charged member cities.[5] Again the rate hike backfired, reducing rather than raising revenues. Escondido became the fourth city to leave the county system, entering into a $55-per-ton contract to send half of its waste to a landfill in La Paz County, Arizona.[6] Again the JPA backed down, promising to repeal the discriminatory rates.[7] It remains unclear how the county system, saddled with the debt service on the $139 million San Marcos recycling plant, can ever compete with private landfills on price. A scheme has been floated to subsidize the county system, in order to make lower rates possible, by enacting a special land-use fee that would raise $25 million a year. Proponents of the fee say that money taken out of one pocket would be put back into another.[8] However, the county system's record of runaway rate increases inspires fear that more money would be taken out than would be put back. Moreover, taxpayers seem to be in no mood to have their pockets picked in any event.[9]

The Campos remain unable to sign up the cities abandoning the county system because the tribe's landfill is not open for business or due to open in the foreseeable future. The latest roadblock is a change in EPA policy regarding issuance of air quality permits.

The federal Clean Air Act requires that major sources of certain pollutants employ control technologies to reduce their emissions as much as possible. On May 16, 1994, EPA announced that it proposed to issue an air permit to Mid-American for the construction and operation of the Campo landfill. The draft permit that EPA submitted for public comment was predicated on the assumption that the air pollutants of concern were volatile organic compounds (VOCs) like benzene and tuolene. VOCs, which landfills generate along with methane as waste decomposes, react with sunlight to form ground-level ozone or smog. The San Diego air basin, which includes the rural Campo area, does not meet federal air quality standards for ozone. Under the draft permit, gas collection systems and flares would reduce the landfill's VOC emissions by 90 percent, with the remaining thirty-eight tons a year to be more than offset by emission reductions elsewhere in the air basin. Such offsets can be purchased from businesses that have managed to reduce their VOC emissions more than is required under their own permits.[10]

On December 6, 1994, EPA informed Mid-American that a recent decision by the agency's appeals board in an unrelated case meant that "fugitive" dust raised by, for example, truck traffic or unloading operations has to be taken into account in deciding whether a landfill will be considered a significant source of very fine particulate matter that can cause respiratory damage. The significance of the decision is that Mid-American now has to demonstrate that it will use the best technology available to control such emissions. Making that showing will take time, as will holding another public hearing on a revised draft permit. Therefore, EPA's final decision on Mid-American's application for the air permit, which the agency might have made as early as January 1995, will now be delayed at least six more months.[11]

Moreover, EPA has still not given its final approval to the Campo EPA landfill regulatory program, although Regional Administrator Felicia Marcus informed Congressman Duncan Hunter that the agency expected to make its final decision in the fall of 1994.[12] In the meantime, the conflict between the Campos and their neighbors has grown, if possible, even more bitter. In written comments opposing EPA approval of the Campo program, Donna Tisdale stated that testimony in a New York criminal trial "reflects that Ralph Goff, Chairman of the Campo Band, accepted payments from project proponents." Donna added that allegations of another commenter raised "even more concerns regarding payments to Chairman Goff." She asked that EPA or another federal agency investigate the "legality of these payments."[13]

Two executives of Campo Projects, Inc., a company that had hoped to build the recycling component of the landfill project, were prosecuted in New York state for conspiracy to defraud, bribery, and conflict of interest with regard to another project. Campo Projects had financed the initial stages of the Campo landfill project with the understanding that (1) the company would be reimbursed by the landfill developer ultimately selected by the tribe, and (2) its proposal to build the recycling facility would be "looked on favorably" by the tribe.[14]

According to the excerpts from the transcript submitted by Donna to EPA, Ralph T. Barber, president of Campo Projects, testified at his trial that Ralph Goff "was on the payroll." (Barber was acquitted.) Asked about Donna's allegations, Mike Connolly responded that "Ralph was never on (Campo Project's) payroll. . . . They had to pay costs associated with developing the project and . . . they were billing Ralph's time." The tribe, Mike adds, "knew about that." Moreover, "once we got word of those indictments in New York, we just put the brakes on [the Campo Projects recycling proposal]. We stopped it dead in its tracks."[15]

The comments that Donna characterized as raising "even more concerns regarding payments to Chairman Goff" were filed by Joseph M. Lopez. According to Lopez, a Campo tribal member known as Leroy told him that "Ralph Goff their tribal chairman had accepted a sum of approximately $240,000 . . . from the trash company for putting the deal together." Mike exploded in rage when asked whether the tribe would have any comment on this allegation. "A drunk in a bar says that Ralph got $240,000, and another person in the bar signs an affidavit that that other drunk told him that. And they're going . . . to use that as their comments, that's their source of information on the financial dealings. . . . That is sickening!"[16]

In the prologue, I expressed the hope that Mike and Donna will find that I have presented their own views honestly and sympathetically, even if neither will admit the justice of my portrayal of the other's position. As to Mike, that hope seems to have been disappointed because he has come to question the moral legitimacy of endeavoring to present Donna's point of view.

> BAD committed a crime against us. To be apologetic and say that they didn't know or they were just looking out for their families and their children . . . is wrong. . . . [I]t's like apologizing for some other fascist group. Where does it end? Do they . . . line us up and shoot us and throw us in a pit? . . . Regardless of how much Donna Tisdale believes that what . . . she's doing is right, the fact is it's not right. It's wrong.
> To me what you're doing is wrong. It's wrong to take a middle road on that kind of thing. . . . What's there to debate? What's there to discuss? What's there to make your mind up about?[17]

I leave these questions for my readers. As a participant in and commenter on public affairs, I am afflicted by a sort of color blindness. Where others see black and white, I often discern only shades of gray. Where others confidently distinguish between good and evil, I may perceive only competing goods or a choice of evils.

Finding the moral landscape more ambiguous and therefore more treacherous than some others do, I am naturally wary of extremes. However, my personal inclination to take the "middle road" is reinforced by a sense of obligation—to give my readers a clear view in all directions, permitting them to choose sides for themselves.

DAN McGOVERN

Walnut Creek, California
February 28, 1995

NOTES

PROLOGUE

1. U.S. Environmental Protection Agency, *Environmental Equity: Reducing Risk for All Communities, Volume 2: Supporting Document*, 1992, 9–10.

2. U.S. General Accounting Office, *Siting of Hazardous Waste Landfills and Their Correlation with Racial and Economic Status of Surrounding Communities*, 1983.

3. United Church of Christ, *Toxic Wastes and Race in the United States: A National Report on the Racial and Socio-Economic Characteristics of Communities with Hazardous Waste Sites*, 1987.

4. John H. Cushman, Jr., "U.S. Weighs Blacks' Complaints about Pollution," *New York Times*, November 9, 1993.

5. Mary Hager, "Dances with Garbage," *Newsweek*, April 29, 1991.

CHAPTER 1. DRAWING THE BATTLE LINES

1. Donna Tisdale, Interview by author, September 14, 1993.

2. Craig MacDonald, "Boulevard: A Right Turn to Contentment," *San Diego Union*, February 12, 1978.

3. Donna Tisdale, Interviews by author, May 7 and September 14, 1993; Ed Tisdale, Interviews by author, May 7, 1993, and January 6, 1994.

4. Donna Tisdale, Interview by author, May 7, 1993; Arol Wulf, Interview by author, January 6, 1994.

5. Michael Connolly, Interview by author, May 4–5, 1993.

6. Donna Tisdale, Interview by author, January 6, 1994; Arol Wulf, Interview by author, January 6, 1994.

7. Amy Wallace, "Unlikely Allies Fight Indian Landfill," *Los Angeles Times*, October 28, 1989.

8. Bradley Angel, Interview by author, August 17, 1993.

9. Donna Tisdale, Videotape of meeting at Boulevard fire station, October 26, 1989.

10. Wallace, "Unlikely Allies Fight Indian Landfill."

11. Tisdale, Videotape, October 26, 1989.

12. Michael Connolly, Interview by author, January 7, 1994.

13. Wallace, "Unlikely Allies Fight Indian Landfill."

14. Robert Reinhold, "Indians and Neighbors Are at Odds over Proposed Reservation Dump," *New York Times*, January 8, 1990.

15. Tisdale, Videotape, October 26, 1989.

16. Steve Peace, Member of California Assembly, to Donna Tisdale, January 12, 1990.

17. Reinhold, "Indians and Neighbors."

18. Michael Connolly, Interview by author, January 7, 1994.

19. Donna Tisdale, Videotape of meeting of chamber of commerce in Campo, January 16, 1990.

20. Arol Wulf, Interview by author, January 6, 1994.

21. Donna Tisdale, Interviews by author, May 7 and September 14, 1993.

22. *World Monitor*, June 5, 1991.

23. Florence C. Shipek, *Pushed into the Rocks: Changes in Southern California Land Tenure*, 1988, 30–31.

24. U.S. Department of Interior, Office of Indian Affairs, *Annual Report of the Commissioner of Indian Affairs to the Secretary of the Interior for the Year 1875*, 10.

25. U.S. Department of Interior, Bureau of Indian Affairs, Sacramento Area Office, *Campo Solid Waste Management Project: Comments and Responses*, Final Environmental Impact Statement, FES 92-29, vol. 2, Testimony of Florence Shipek, F206.

26. U.S. Department of Interior, *Annual Reports of the Department of Interior for the Fiscal Year Ending June 30, 1905*, 190.

27. Charles F. Lummis, "Three Grains of Corn," *Out West*, January 1905.

28. Melvin C. Mayne, "San Diego Indians May Get Aid," *San Diego Union*, October 2, 1932.

29. Joe Brown, "Area Indian Plight Called 'Intolerable,'" *San Diego Union*, June 9, 1959.

30. Michael Scott-Blair, "Cultural Differences Can Breed Tension, Sometimes Hatred," *San Diego Union*, August 6, 1989.

31. Michael Connolly, Interview by author, June 13, 1993.

32. Michael Scott-Blair, "Giving Indian Kids a Boost up the Education Ladder," *San Diego Union*, August 6, 1989.

33. Florence C. Shipek, Interview by author, June 12, 1993.

34. Michael Connolly, Interview by author, May 4–5, 1993.

35. U.S. Department of Interior, Bureau of Indian Affairs, Sacramento Area Office, *Campo Solid Waste Management Project*, Final Environmental Impact Statement, FES 92-29, vol. 1, S-11, 2-36 to 2-37; vol 2, Testimony of James Lee West, F300; Declaration of James Lee West in Support of Opposition to Plaintiff's Motion for Preliminary Injunction, *County of San Diego v. Babbitt*, No. 93-0986-IEG (LSP) (S.D. Cal.), 2–3.

CHAPTER 2. RESERVATIONS: THE WASTE INDUSTRY'S LAST FRONTIER

1. John Anner, "Protecting Mother Earth," *Minority Trendsletter*, Fall 1991, 4, 5.

2. Paul Schneider, "Other People's Trash," *Audubon*, July–August 1991, 109, 112.

3. Schneider, "Other People's Trash," 113.

4. Pamela A. D'Angelo, "Waste Management Industry Turns to Indian Reservations as States Close Landfills," *Environment Reporter: Current Developments*, December 28, 1990, 1607–1608, 1610.

5. Mark Shaffer, "Paiutes' Waste-Site Plan Alarms Neighbors," *Arizona Republic*, January 28, 1990.

6. Schneider, "Other People's Trash," 114.

7. Thomas A. Daschle, "Dances with Garbage," *Christian Science Monitor*, February 14, 1991.

8. Margaret Knox, "Their Mother's Keeper," *Sierra*, March–April 1993, 51, 81.

9. Susan Traylor, "Choctaw Dumping Decision Worries Other Tribes," *Gannett News Service*, April 1, 1991, 1, 2.

10. Traylor, "Choctaw Dumping," 1, 2.

11. *California v. Cabazon Band of Mission Indians*, 480 U.S. 202, 219–20 (1987), distinguishing *Washington v. Confederated Tribes of Colville Indian Reservation*, 447 U.S. 134 (1980).

12. Bradley Angel, "The Toxic Threat to Indian Lands," Unpublished Greenpeace report, June 1991, 12–13; *Blue Legs v. United States Environmental Protection Agency*, 668 F. Supp. 1329 (D.S.D. 1987).

13. U.S. Senate, Select Committee on Indian Affairs, *Workshop on Solid Waste Disposal on Indian Lands*, 102 Cong., 1st Sess., Committee Print, July 29, 1991, 8, 55.

14. U.S. Senate, Select Committee on Indian Affairs, *Workshop on Solid Waste Disposal on Indian Lands*, 46–48; Michael Connolly, Interviewed by author, September 6, 1994.

15. U.S. Senate, Select Committee on Indian Affairs, *Workshop on Solid Waste on Indian Lands*, 75.

16. Ringe Media Inc., "Campo: Sharing the Future," Videotape, 1991.

17. Bradley Angel, Letter to Assemblyman Steve Peace, June 12, 1991.

18. Bradley Angel, Interview by author, August 17, 1993.

19. U.S. General Accounting Office, *Nuclear Waste: Operation of Monitored Retrievable Storage Facility Is Unlikely by 1998*, 1991.

20. Matthew L. Wald, "Nuclear Industry Seeks Interim Site to Receive Waste," *New York Times*, August 27, 1993.

21. U.S. General Accounting Office, *Nuclear Waste: Operation of Monitored Retrievable Storage Facility Is Unlikely by 1998*; Bureau of National Affairs, "Suit by States Against Energy Department Challenges Failure to

Construct Repository," *Environment Reporter: Current Developments*, June 24, 1994, 404.

22. Wald, "Nuclear Industry Seeks Interim Site to Receive Waste"; Matthew L. Wald, "Nuclear Plant Searches for a Place for Its Waste," *New York Times*, March 28, 1994.

23. U.S. Office of the Nuclear Waste Negotiator, "What Is the Office of the Negotiator," 1993; U.S. Office of the Nuclear Waste Negotiator, "An Invitation for Dialogue and Participation," 1991; Southwest Research and Information Center, "Monitored Retrievable Storage—Questions and Answers," n.d.

24. U.S. Office of the Nuclear Waste Negotiator, "An Invitation for Dialogue and Participation," 1991.

25. U.S. Office of the Nuclear Waste Negotiator, "What Is the Office of the Negotiator," 1993.

26. Juan A. Avila Hernandez, "How the Feds Push Nuclear Waste onto Indian Land," *SF Weekly*, September 23, 1992.

27. Robert M. Mussler, Interview by author, November 23, 1993.

28. Wald, "Nuclear Industry Seeks Interim Site to Receive Waste."

29. Robert M. Mussler, Interview by author, November 23, 1993.

30. Jason Salzman, "The Clinton Administration Should Cancel the MRS Program," n.d.

31. Skull Valley Band of Goshutes, "Taa-Pai: Phase IIa Report," n.d.

32. Matthew L. Wald, "Nuclear Storage Divides Apaches and Neighbors," *New York Times*, November 11, 1993.

33. Wald, "Nuclear Storage Divides Apaches and Neighbors."

34. Tom Goldtooth, Interview by author, September 17, 1993.

35. Wald, "Nuclear Storage Divides Apaches and Neighbors."

36. Katherine Shelley, "Indians Protest N-Waste Idea," *Gallup Independent*, August 12, 1993.

37. Beverly McCutchon, "Nuke Storage Protest Now in Mescalero," *Alamagordo Daily News*, August 26, 1992.

38. Wald, "Nuclear Storage Divides Apaches and Neighbors."

39. Avila Hernandez, "How the Feds Push Nuclear Waste onto Indian Land."

40. Avila Hernandez, "How the Feds Push Nuclear Waste onto Indian Land."

41. Robert M. Mussler, Interview by author, November 23, 1993.

42. Avila Hernandez, "How the Feds Push Nuclear Waste onto Indian Land."

43. Shelley, "Indians Protest N-Waste Idea."

44. Avila Hernandez, "How the Feds Push Nuclear Waste onto Indian Land."

45. Robert M. Mussler, Interview by author, November 23, 1993.

46. U.S. Department of the Interior, Bureau of Indian Affairs, "Indian Service Population and Labor Force Estimates," January 1989.

47. Wald, "Nuclear Storage Divides Apaches and Neighbors."

48. Ellen Miller, "Indian Lands on Dump List," *Denver Post*, May 15, 1992.

49. Skull Valley Band of Goshutes, "Nuclear Natives: The Proposed Storage of High Level Nuclear Waste on Native American Reservations," n.d.

50. Wald, "Nuclear Storage Divides Apaches and Neighbors."

51. Robert M. Mussler, Interview by author, November 23, 1993.

52. Bureau of National Affairs, "Federal Nuclear Waste Negotiator Touts Possible Beneficial Uses of Spent Fuel," *Environment Reporter: Current Developments*, June 17, 1994, 314–15.

53. Angel, "The Toxic Threat to Indian Lands," 12–14; Schneider, "Other People's Trash," 108; Anner, "Protecting Mother Earth," 4, 7.

54. Angel, "The Toxic Threat to Indian Lands," 7; Diane E. Austin, "Knowledge and Values in the Decision Making Around Hazardous Waste Incineration Facilities: Final Report," School of Natural Resources and Environment, University of Michigan, January 1993, 78, 130; Tom Goldtooth, Interview by author, September 20, 1993.

55. Anner, "Protecting Mother Earth," 23.

56. Indigenous Environmental Network, "No Nuclear Waste on Indian Lands: Resolution of the Third Annual Indigenous Environmental Network Gathering, Celilo Village, Oregon, June 6, 1992," *Race, Poverty & the Environment* 3, no. 3 (Fall 1992): 9.

57. Tom Goldtooth, Interview by author, September 17, 1993.

58. Tom Goldtooth, Interview by author, September 17, 1993.

59. Tom Goldtooth, Interview by author, September 20, 1993.

CHAPTER 3. WHITES AND CALIFORNIA INDIANS

1. James J. Rawls, *Indians of California: The Changing Image*, 1984, 64.

2. George Harwood Phillips, *Indians and Intruders in Central California, 1769–1849*, 1993, quoting Salvador Vallejo, "History of California," 1874, C-D 22, 46, Bancroft Library, Berkeley, Calif.

3. Rawls, *Indians of California*, 76.

4. Rawls, *Indians of California*, 76–77, 194; Albert L. Hurtado, *Indian Survival on the California Frontier*, 1988, 73–74; Walton Bean, *California: An Interpretive History*, 1968, 82–83.

5. John Marsh, "Letter of John Marsh to Hon. Lewis Cass," *California Historical Society Quarterly* 22 (1943): 315–22.

6. Rawls, *Indians of California*, 78.

7. Phillips, *Indians and Intruders*, 122, quoting John A. Sutter to ———, New Helvetia, May 18, 1845, published in the *San Francisco California Farmer*, March 13, 1857.

8. Phillips, *Indians and Intruders*, 123, quoting Heinrich Lienhard, A

Pioneer at Sutter's Fort, 1846–1850: The Adventures of Heinrich Lienhard, trans. and ed. by Marguerite Eyer Wilbur, 68.

9. Robert F. Heizer, ed., *The Destruction of California Indians: A Collection of Documents from the Period 1847 to 1865 in Which Are Described Some of the Things That Happened to Some of the Indians of California,* 1974, 220–24.

10. Ferdinand Fernandez, "Except a California Indian: A Study in Legal Discrimination," *Southern California Quarterly* 50 (1968): 164.

11. Hubert Howe Bancroft, *History of California,* 1890, vol. 7, 478, n. 10.

12. Heizer, *Destruction,* 220–21.

13. Heizer, *Destruction,* 220–24.

14. Heizer, *Destruction,* 297.

15. Quoted in Rawls, *Indians of California,* 90.

16. Quoted in Rawls, *Indians of California,* 90.

17. Heizer, *Destruction,* 224–26.

18. Heizer, *Destruction,* 232–33.

19. Heizer, *Destruction,* 230–32.

20. Sherburne F. Cook, *The Conflict Between the California Indian and White Civilization: The American Invasion,* 1943, 57.

21. Rawls, *Indians of California,* 97.

22. Rawls, *Indians of California,* 97.

23. Quoted in Rawls, *Indians of California,* 99.

24. Isaac Cox, *The Annals of Trinity County,* 1940, 112.

25. Hurtado, *Indian Survival,* 100.

26. Sherburne F. Cook, "Historical Demography," in *Handbook of North American Indians,* vol. 8, *California,* ed. by Robert F. Heizer, 1978, 93; Rawls, *Indians of California,* 171.

27. Bean, *California,* 169.

28. Cook, "Historical Demography," 93.

29. Rawls, *Indians of California,* 190, quoting Thomas Butler King, "Report on California," in *Message from the Pesident [sic] of the United States, Transmitting the Report of T. Butler King* (Washington, D.C.: 1850) 8–9.

30. Cook, "Historical Demography," 93; Bean, *California,* 4, 6.

31. Cook, *Conflict,* 26–35; Edward D. Castillo, "The Impact of Euro-American Exploration and Settlement," in *Handbook of North American Indians,* vol. 8, *California,* 108; Richard L. Carrico, *Strangers in a Stolen Land: American Indians in San Diego 1850–1880,* 1987, 44.

32. Rawls, *Indians of California,* 176–77; Hurtado, *Indian Survival,* 122, 134.

33. Cook, *Conflict,* 36.

34. California Legislature, "Governor's Message," *Journal of the Senate,* 2d sess., January 6, 1851, 14.

35. California Legislature, 1851, 15.

36. Rawls, *Indians of California,* 139–41.

37. Hurtado, *Indian Survival,* 132.

38. Rawls, *Indians of California*, 141, quoting "Address of the Indian Agents," *Alta California*, January 14, 1851.

39. Harry Kelsey, "The California Indian Treaty Myth," *Southern California Quarterly* 55 (1973): 230–31.

40. Robert F. Heizer and Allan F. Almquist, *The Other Californians: Prejudice and Discrimination under Spain, Mexico, and the United States to 1920*, 1971, 76.

41. Bean, *California*, 167; Hurtado, *Indian Survival*, 137–39; Rawls, *Indians of California*, 141.

42. Rawls, *Indians of California*, 142–44.

43. California Legislature, "Report of the Special Committee to Inquire into the Treaties Made by the United States Indian Commissioners in California," *Journal of the Senate*, 1852, 3d sess., 597, 600.

44. California Legislature, "Report of the Special Committee to Inquire into the Treaties Made by the United States Indian Commissioners in California," *Journal of the Assembly*, 1852, 3d sess., 203.

45. Carrico, *Strangers*, 48.

46. Rawls, *Indians of California*, 179, quoting the *Humboldt Times*, November 20 and 27, 1858, as well as William Kibbe, *Report of the Expedition Against the Indians in the Northern Part of This State* (Sacramento: 1860) 6, 8, 10.

47. Rawls, *Indians of California*, 180, quoting the *Yreka Herald*, August 7, 1853.

48. J. Ross Browne, *The Indians of California*, 1944, 62.

49. Rawls, *Indians of California*, 185.

50. Castillo, "Impact," 108.

51. Rawls, *Indians of California*, 185–86.

CHAPTER 4. WHITES AND THE CAMPOS

1. Florence C. Shipek, "History of Southern California Mission Indians," in *Handbook of North American Indians*, vol. 8, *California*, edited by Robert F. Heizer, 1978, 610.

2. Katherine Luomala, "Tipai and Ipai," in *Handbook of North American Indians*, vol. 8, *California*, 592.

3. Shipek, "History of Southern California Mission Indians," 610.

4. Florence C. Shipek, *Pushed into the Rocks; Changes in Southern California Indian Land Tenure*, 1988, 12, 18; Shipek, undated letter to author.

5. Luomala, "Tipai and Ipai," 594–95; Florence C. Shipek, "Kumeyaay Socio-Political Structure," *Journal of California and Great Basin Anthropology* 4 (1982): 300.

6. Quoted in Florence C. Shipek, "California Indian Reactions to the Franciscans," *The Americas* 41 (1985): 481.

7. Luomala, "Tipai and Ipai," 595; Shipek, "History of Southern Cali-

fornia Mission Indians," 610; Florence C. Shipek, Interview by author, June 12, 1993.

8. Shipek, "Kumeyaay Socio-Political Structure," 297.

9. Shipek, "Kumeyaay Socio-Political Structure," 297–98.

10. Shipek, "Kumeyaay Socio-Political Structure," 298.

11. Shipek, "Kumeyaay Socio-Political Structure," 297–98.

12. Shipek, "Kumeyaay Socio-Political Structure," 300–01.

13. Shipek, "Kumeyaay Socio-Political Structure," 299, 301.

14. Richard L. Carrico, *Strangers in a Stolen Land: American Indians in San Diego 1850–1880*, 1987, 75, quoting U.S. Department of Interior, Office of Indian Affairs, *Report of Charles A. Wetmore, Special United States Commissioner of Mission Indians of Southern California*, 1875.

15. Carrico, *Strangers*, 3.

16. Shipek, *Pushed into the Rocks*, 30–31.

17. Carrico, *Strangers*, 59, 65; James J. Rawls, *Indians in California: The Changing Image*, 1984, 148–58; Albert L. Hurtado, *Indian Survival on the California Frontier*, 1988, 144–48.

18. Carrico, *Strangers*, 66–69.

19. William T. Hagan, "Justifying Dispossession of the Indian: The Land Utilization Argument," in *American Indian Environments: Ecological Issues in Native American History*, ed. by Christopher Vecsey and Robert W. Venables, 1980, 73, quoting J. Q. Smith in his 1876 annual report, 386.

20. Hagan, "Justifying Dispossession," quoting Carl Schurz in his annual report, Serial 1910, HED, 46th Cong., 2d Sess., 4.

21. Quoted in Carrico, *Strangers*, 75–76.

22. Luomala, "Tipai and Ipai," 595; Carrico, *Strangers*, 88.

23. Carrico, *Strangers*, 76, quoting U.S. Department of the Interior, Office of Indian Affairs, *Annual Report of the Commissioner of Indian Affairs to the Secretary of the Interior for the Year 1875*, 10, 223.

24. Meredith Vezina, "One Hundred Years in Campo Country," Master's thesis, San Diego State University, 12–15; Historical Society, *Historical Guide to the Back Country: A Self-Guided Tour Through the Rugged Mountains of San Diego's East County*, published by Mountain Empire Historical Society, 1988, 9, 33.

25. Vezina, "One Hundred Years," 14, 32; *Historical Guide*, Mountain Empire Historical Society, 34.

26. Vezina, "One Hundred Years," 31, quoting Jacobo Blanco, "A Map Makers Story: A Survey Made for the Congress of Mexican States in 1873," Document 35, trans. by Ila Alvarez, *Brand Book Number 5: San Diego Corral of Westerners*, San Diego: Corral of Westerners, 1978, 125.

27. *San Diego Union*, "On the Eastern Line," February 1, 1880.

28. *San Diego Union*, "Our Trip to the Soda Springs," June 17, 1880.

29. Vezina, "One Hundred Years," 46.

30. M. S. Root, "Atrocious Cruelty," *San Diego Union*, October 7, 1880.

31. Vezina, "One Hundred Years," 47–52.

32. U.S. Department of Interior, Bureau of Indian Affairs, Sacramento Area Office, *Campo Solid Waste Management Project: Comments and Responses*, Final Environmental Impact Statement, FES 92–29, volume 2, Testimony of Florence Shipek, F206.

33. Vezina, "One Hundred Years," 118, quoting U.S. Commission of Indian Affairs, *Annual Report, 31 August 1893, Report of the Mission Tule River Agency*, Government Publication 120.1, San Diego State University.

34. Vezina, "One Hundred Years," 118–19, quoting U.S. Commission of Indian Affairs, *Annual Report, 1 August 1896, Report of the Mission Tule River Agency*, Government Publication 120.1, San Diego State University.

35. U.S. Department of Interior, *Annual Reports of the Department of Interior for the Fiscal Year Ending June 30*, 1905, 104.

36. Charles F. Lummis, "Three Grains of Corn," *Out West* 22 (1905): 3–4.

37. U.S. Department of the Interior, *Annual Reports . . . 1905*, 105.

38. U.S. Department of the Interior, *Annual Reports . . . 1905*, 105.

39. U.S. Department of the Interior, *Annual Reports . . . 1905*, 190.

40. Vezina, "One Hundred Years," 117, n. 38.

41. Florence C. Shipek, Interview by author, June 12, 1993.

42. Florence C. Shipek, *The Autobiography of Delfina Cuero*, 1991, 32–33.

43. Shipek, *Delfina Cuero*, 32–33.

44. Shipek, *Delfina Cuero*, 26, 60–62.

45. Shipek, *Delfina Cuero*, 69–79.

46. Melvin C. Mayne, "San Diego Indians May Get Aid," *San Diego Union*, October 2, 1932.

47. Florence C. Shipek, Interview by author, June 12, 1993.

48. Joe Brown, "Area Indian Plight Called 'Intolerable,'" *San Diego Union*, June 9, 1959.

49. Michael Scott-Blair, "Cultural Differences Can Breed Tension, Sometimes Hatred," *San Diego Union*, August 6, 1989.

50. *San Diego Union*, "Indians Kill White; Fear Campo Riot," July 17, 1927.

51. *San Diego Union*, "Campo Indians Rebel; Two Die," July 18, 1927.

52. *San Diego Union*, "Deputies Exceeded Authority in Campo Indian Fight, Jury at Coroner's Inquest Finds," July 21, 1927.

53. Dan Gregory, "Indian Festival Starts Thursday," *San Diego Union*, July 13, 1959.

54. Ferdinand Fernandez, "Except a California Indian: A Study in Legal Discrimination," *Southern California Quarterly* 50 (1968): 167–68.

55. Terr E. Jacques, "Serving San Diego County's Southern Indians? Campo Agency Schools," *Journal of San Diego History* 29 (1983): 160–61.

56. Edward D. Castillo, "The Impact of Euro-American Exploration and Settlement," in *Handbook of North American Indians*, vol. 8, *California*, 124.

57. Florence C. Shipek, Interview by author, June 12, 1993.

58. Michael Scott-Blair, "Giving Indian Kids a Boost Up the Education Ladder," *San Diego Union*, August 6, 1989.

CHAPTER 5. INDIANS AND THE ENVIRONMENT

1. Alston Chase, *Playing God in Yellowstone: The Destruction of America's First National Park*, 1987, 109.

2. Florence C. Shipek, *Pushed into the Rocks: Changes in Southern California Indian Land Tenure*, 1988, 131.

3. Henry T. Lewis, "Matsuka: The Ecology of Indian Fires in Northern Alberta," *Western Canadian Journal of Anthropology* (1977): 7, 18.

4. Quoted in James J. Rawls, *Indians of California: The Changing Image*, 1984, 26.

5. Quoted in Lowell John Bean and Harry W. Lawton, "Some Explanations for Rise of Cultural Complexity in Native California with Comments on Proto-Agriculture and Agriculture," in *Before the Wilderness: Environmental Management by Native Californians*, ed. by Thomas C. Blackburn and Kat Anderson, 1993, 28.

6. Albert K. Weinberg, *Manifest Destiny*, 1935, 79.

7. Rawls, *Indians of California*, 190.

8. Walton Bean, *California: An Interpretative History*, 1968, 5.

9. Rawls, *Indians of California*, 190.

10. Bean and Lawton, "Rise of Cultural Complexity," 28.

11. Hubert Howe Bancroft, *The Native Races*, vol. 1, 1890, 324.

12. William T. Hagan, "Justifying Dispossession of the Indian: The Land Utilization Argument," in *American Indian Environments: Ecological Issues in Native American History*, ed. by Christopher Vecsey and Robert W. Venables, 1980, 65, quoting *The Texas Monthly*, January 1979, 83.

13. John Locke, *Two Treatises of Government*, 1947, 133–41.

14. Quoted in Weinberg, *Manifest Destiny*, 84.

15. Chase, *Playing God*, 110.

16. Stephen J. Pyne, *Fire in America*, 1982, 71.

17. Jan Timbrook, John R. Anderson, and David D. Earle, "Vegetation Burning by the Chumash," in *Before the Wilderness: Environmental Management by Native Americans*, ed. by Thomas C. Blackburn and Kat Anderson, 1993, 121–25.

18. Timbrook et al., "Vegetation Burning," 126–27.

19. Bean and Lawton, "Rise of Cultural Complexity," 39.

20. Chase, *Playing God*, 93.

21. Chase, *Playing God*, 93.

22. Bean and Lawton, "Rise of Cultural Complexity," 48.

23. Rawls, *Indians of California*, 198.

24. Florence C. Shipek, "An Example of Intensive Plant Husbandry: The Kumeyaay of Southern California," in *Foraging and Farming: The Evo-*

lution of Plant Exploitation, ed. by David R. Harris and Gordon C. Hillman, 1989, 162.

25. Florence C. Shipek, "Kumeyaay Plant Husbandry: Fire, Water, and Erosion Control Systems," in *Before the Wilderness: Environmental Management by Native Americans*, ed. by Thomas C. Blackburn and Kat Anderson, 1993, 383.

26. John W. Caughey, *California: History of a Remarkable State*, 1982, 6–7.

27. Shipek, "Kumeyaay Plant Husbandry," 382.

28. Bean and Lawton, "Rise of Cultural Complexity," 27.

29. Shipek, "Kumeyaay Plant Husbandry," 380.

30. Shipek, "Kumeyaay Plant Husbandry," 380–84.

31. Shipek, "Kumeyaay Plant Husbandry," 384–85.

32. Lowell John Bean and Charles R. Smith, "Cupeño," in *Handbook of North American Indians*, vol. 8, *California*, ed. by Robert F. Heizer, 1978, 588; Shipek, *Pushed into the Rocks*, 13.

33. Shipek, *Pushed into the Rocks*, 15.

34. Shipek, Interview by author, June 12, 1993.

35. Shipek, *Pushed into the Rocks*, 12.

36. Shipek, "Kumeyaay Plant Husbandry," 381.

37. Florence C. Shipek, "The Shaman: Priest, Doctor, Scientist," in *California Indian Shamanism*, ed. by Lowell John Bean, 1992, 90–91.

38. Shipek, "Kumeyaay Plant Husbandry," 386.

39. Shipek, "Kumeyaay Plant Husbandry," 381.

40. Shipek, "An Example of Intensive Plant Husbandry," 166.

41. Shipek, "The Shaman," 91.

42. Timbrook et al., "Vegetation Burning," 130–31.

43. Robert F. Heizer, ed., *The Destruction of California Indians: A Collection of Documents from the Period 1847 to 1865 in Which Are Described Some of the Things That Happened to Some of the Indians of California*, 1974, 222.

44. Shipek, "An Example of Intensive Plant Husbandry," 162.

45. Shipek, "Kumeyaay Plant Husbandry," 387.

46. Shipek, "Kumeyaay Plant Husbandry," 387.

CHAPTER 6. MAKING THEIR STAND ON A LANDFILL

1. U.S. Department of the Interior, Bureau of Indian Affairs, Sacramento Area Office, *Campo Solid Waste Management Project*, Final Environmental Impact Statement, FES 92–29, vol. 1, S-11, 2–36 to 2–37; vol. 2, Testimony of James Lee West, F300; Declaration of James Lee West in Support of Opposition to Plaintiff's Motion for Preliminary Injunction, *County of San Diego v. Babbitt*, No. 93-0986-IEG (LSP) (S.D. Cal.), 2–3.

2. *Campo Solid Waste Management Project*, Final EIS, vol. 1, S-3.

3. Chet Barfield, "Private Landfill Firm Trying to Lure Cities," *San Diego Union-Tribune*, August 7, 1993.

4. Barfield, "Private Landfill Firm Trying to Lure Cities."

5. *Campo Solid Waste Management Project*, Final EIS, vol. 1, S-3, 3-88, 4-77; Michael Connolly, Interview by the author, June 13, 1993.

6. Jana Walker and Kevin Gover, "Commercial Solid and Hazardous Waste Disposal Projects on Indian Lands," in American Bar Association, Section of Natural Resources, Energy, and Environmental Law, Fourth Annual Conference on Natural Resources Management and Environmental Enforcement on Indian Lands, Course Materials, Albuquerque, New Mexico, February 20–21, 1992, 4-87.

7. Michael Connolly, Interview by author, June 13, 1993.

8. *Campo Solid Waste Management Project*, Final EIS, vol. 1, 2-36 to 2-37.

9. *Campo Solid Waste Management Project*, Final EIS, vol. 1, 2-37.

10. *Campo Solid Waste Management Project*, Final EIS, vol. 2, Testimony of James Lee West, F300.

11. *Campo Solid Waste Management Project*, Final EIS, vol. 2, Testimony of Epi Lopez, F285.

12. Jonathan Littman, "And the Dealer Stays," *California Lawyer* 13 (1993): 46.

13. Barry Meier, "Casinos Putting Tribes at Odds," *New York Times*, January 13, 1994.

14. Littman, "And the Dealer Stays," 46.

15. Littman, "And the Dealer Stays," 46.

16. *Campo Solid Waste Management Project*, Final EIS, vol. 1, 2-36.

17. Michael Connolly, Interview by author, June 13, 1993.

18. Backcountry Against Dumps, Comments on the Campo Landfill Final EIS, December 30, 1992, 14.

19. Backcountry Against Dumps, Addendum to Comments on the Campo Landfill Final EIS, December 30, 1992, 6.

20. *Campo Solid Waste Management Project*, Final EIS, vol. 2, A13.

21. Billie Jo Shepherd, "Hunter Suggests Tribe Try Golf Resort," *Alpine (Calif.) Sun*, June 17, 1992.

22. Michael Connolly, Interview by author, May 4–5, 1993.

23. *California Environmental Insider*, "Solid Waste: Waste Board Issues Report on Remaining State Landfill Capacity," February 29, 1992, 11.

24. Walker and Gover, " Commercial . . . Waste Disposal Projects on Indian Lands," 4-79.

25. *Campo Solid Waste Management Project*, Final EIS, vol. 2, Testimony of Florence C. Shipek, F207.

26. *Campo Solid Waste Management Project*, Final EIS, vol. 1, 1-13 to 1-4.

27. County of San Diego, "Comments on the Campo Landfill Final EIS," December 24, 1992, 3–4.

28. U.S. Environmental Protection Agency, *Decision-Makers Guide to Solid Waste Management*, 1989, 1–2; *California Environmental Insider*, "Solid Waste: Waste Board Issues Report on Remaining State Landfill Capacity."

29. C. L. Pettit, "Tip Fees Up More Than 30% in Annual NSWMA Survey," *Waste Age*, March 1989, 101.

30. Declaration of R. Jay Roberts in Support of Opposition to Plaintiff's Motion for Preliminary Injunction, *County of San Diego v. Babbitt*, 93-0986-IEG (LSP) (S.D. Cal.), 3.

31. Jonathan Gaw, "Dump Profit Gets Slashed," *Los Angeles Times*, July 22, 1993.

32. Ernst & Young, "Management Audit of the Solid Waste Division and Financial Review of the Solid Waste Enterprise Fund," Final Report to the County of San Diego, Executive Summary, December 18, 1992, xviii.

33. Ernst & Young, "Management Audit," i.

34. Ernst & Young, "Management Audit," iv.

35. San Diego County Grand Jury, "Grand Jury Report No. 3, San Diego County's Tra$h Cri$is," May 21, 1993, 1, 2, 32, 33.

36. Barfield, "Private Landfill Firm Trying to Lure Cities."

37. Bob Rowland, "El Cajon All But Out of County Trash Net," *San Diego Union-Tribune*, May 19, 1994; Emmet Pierce, "County Tries Price Incentive on Trash," *San Diego Union-Tribune*, May 20, 1994.

38. John Berhman, "Oceanside Pullout Won't Kill Plans to Send Trash to Utah," *San Diego Union-Tribune*, August 5, 1994; Emmet Pierce, "Cities Leaving Trash System Warned," *San Diego Union-Tribune*, August 19, 1994; *California Environmental Insider*, "San Diego Cities Begin to Bolt County Waste Program," July 31, 1994, 13.

39. *Fort Gratiot Sanitary Landfill, Inc. v. Michigan Department of Natural Resources*, 112 S.Ct. 2019 (1992).

40. Rowland, "El Cajon All But Out of County Trash Net"; Pierce, "Cities Leaving Trash System Warned"; *California Environmental Insider*, "San Diego Cities Begin to Bolt County Waste Program."

41. Emmet Pierce, "350% Hike Studied for Landfill Fee," *San Diego Union-Tribune*, July 15, 1994; Emmet Pierce, "Proposed Fee Increase Stinks, Trash Agency Told," *San Diego Union-Tribune*, August 2, 1994; John Behrman, "Authority OKs New Trash-Fee Schedule," *San Diego Union-Tribune*, August 12, 1994.

CHAPTER 7. PEACE DECLARES WAR ON THE CAMPOS

1. Stephen Green, ed., *California Political Almanac, 1991–1992*, 303.

2. Richard Zeiger and A. G. Block, "The Decline and Fall of Speaker Willie Brown, Jr.?" *California Journal*, April 1988, 154.

3. Zeiger and Block, "Decline and Fall," 154.

4. Green, "Almanac," 303.

5. Richard Zeiger, "Rating the Legislators," *California Journal*, March 1990, 133; Richard Zeiger, "The Capitol's Best," *California Journal*, April 1992, 173; Richard Zeiger, "California Journal's Third Biennial Survey Spotlights the Legislature's Best," *California Journal*, March 1994, 9.

6. Zeiger and Block, "Decline and Fall," 154.

7. Steve Peace, Letter to Donna Tisdale, January 12, 1990.

8. *California v. Cabazon Band of Mission Indians*, 480 U.S. 202 (1987).

9. Rudy Corona, Interview by author, October 20, 1993.

10. David Takashima, Interview by author, October 20, 1993.

11. *San Diego Union*, "Bill Aims at Tribe's Dump Plans," March 6, 1990.

12. *United States v. Wheeler*, 435 U.S. 313, 323 (1978).

13. *Washington v. Confederated Tribes of Colville Indian Reservation*, 447 U.S. 134, 156 (1980).

14. Charles Warren, *The Supreme Court in United States History*, vol. 2, 1923, 189.

15. Felix S. Cohen, *Handbook of Federal Indian Law*, 1982, 81.

16. Cohen, *Handbook*, 82.

17. *Cherokee Nation v. Georgia*, 30 U.S. (5 Pet.) 1 (1831).

18. *Worcester v. Georgia*, 31 U.S. (6 Pet.) 515, 561 (1832).

19. *Rice v. Rehner*, 463 U.S. 713, 718 (1983), quoting *Organized Village of Kake v. Egan*, 369 U.S. 60, 74 (1962).

20. *Rice v. Rehner*, 463 U.S. 713, 722–23.

21. *Rice v. Rehner*, 463 U.S. 713, 724.

22. *Rice v. Rehner*, 463 U.S. 713, 726.

23. Carole E. Goldberg, "Public Law 280: The Limits of State Jurisdiction over Reservation Indians," *U.C.L.A. Law Review* 22 (1975): 535, 541.

24. *Bryan v. Itasca County*, 426 U.S. 373 (1976).

25. *California v. Cabazon*, 480 U.S. 202, 207–12.

26. *California v. Cabazon*, 480 U.S. 202, 214–15.

27. *California v. Cabazon*, 480 U.S. 202, 216.

28. *California v. Cabazon*, 480 U.S. 202, 216.

29. *California v. Cabazon*, 480 U.S. 202, 218–19.

30. *Washington v. Colville*, 447 U.S. 134, 155.

31. *California v. Cabazon*, 480 U.S. 202, 219.

32. *New Mexico v. Mescalero Apache Tribe*, 462 U.S. 324, 341 (1983).

33. *California v. Cabazon*, 480 U.S. 202, 220.

34. *California v. Cabazon*, 480 U.S. 202, 220.

35. *California v. Cabazon*, 480 U.S. 202, 220–22.

36. *State of Washington, Dept. of Ecology v. United States Environmental Protection Agency*, 752 F.2d 1465, 1472 (9th Cir. 1985), citation omitted.

37. U.S. Environmental Protection Agency, "EPA Policy for the Administration of Environmental Programs on Indian Reservations," William D. Ruckelshaus, November 8, 1984.

38. *Blue Legs v. U.S. EPA*, 668 F.Supp. 1329 (D.S.D. 1987), aff'd, *Blue Legs v. U.S. Bureau of Indian Affairs*, 867 F.2d 1094 (8th Cir. 1989).

39. *California v. Cabazon*, 480 U.S. 202, 216.

40. *California v. Cabazon*, 480 U.S. 202, 219.

41. *California v. Cabazon*, 480 U.S. 202, 216, quoting *New Mexico v. Mescalero Apache Tribe*, 462 U.S. 324, 333–34 (1983).

42. Ralph Frammolino, "Lawmakers and Indians Wage War over Dump," *Los Angeles Times*, July 5, 1990.

43. Ralph Frammolino, "Indian Environmental Bill Clears Hurdle," *Los Angeles Times*, July 6, 1990.

44. Corey Brown, Letter to California State Senator Robert Presley, Chairman of the California Senate Appropriations Committee, August 16, 1990.

45. Darryl Wilson, "Five Hundred Years from Now," *News from Native California*, February–April 1991.

46. Corey Brown, Interview by author, October 19, 1993.

47. Frammolino, "Indian Environmental Bill Clears Hurdle."

48. Ron Roach, "Garbage-Dump Limit for Indian Lands Advances in Senate," *San Diego Tribune*, July 6, 1990.

49. Frammolino, "Indian Environmental Bill Clears Hurdle."

50. Ralph Frammolino, "Campo Indians Accuse Peace of Cheap Shots at Landfill Hearing," *Los Angeles Times*, August 14, 1990.

51. Donna Tisdale, Interview by author, October 9, 1993.

52. Corey Brown, Letter to California Senator Robert Presley, emphasis in the original.

53. Kevin Gover, Letter to California State Senator Alfred Alquist, August 15, 1990.

54. Gover, Letter to California State Senator Alfred Alquist.

55. Michael Connolly, Interview by author, October 12, 1993.

56. Arthur L. Coe, Letter to California Assemblywoman Sally Tanner, Chairwoman of the California Assembly Environmental and Toxic Materials Committee, February 21, 1991.

57. Arthur L. Coe, Interview by author, October 19, 1993.

58. John Grattan, Interview by author, October 13, 1993.

59. Ralph Frammolino, "Bill Curbing Use of Indian Land Revived," *Los Angeles Times*, August 21, 1990.

60. Michael Smolens, "Senate Panel Switches, OKs Scuttling Campo Dump," *San Diego Union*, August 21, 1990.

61. Daniel C. Carson, "East County Indians Hire Ohio Firm to Build Landfill," *San Diego Union*, September 20, 1990.

62. Michael Smolens, "Governor Vetoes Bill Jeopardizing Reservation Trash Plan," *San Diego Union*, October 1, 1990.

63. Corey Brown, Interview by author, October 19, 1993.

64. John Grattan, Interview by author, October 12, 1993.

65. Daniel C. Carson, "East County Indians Hire Ohio Firm to Build Landfill."

CHAPTER 8. AN ARMED TRUCE

1. Donna Tisdale, Interview by author, October 9, 1993.

2. Corey Brown, Interview by author, October 19, 1993.

3. David Takashima, Interview by author, October 20, 1993.

4. Ralph Goff, Letter to California Assemblywoman Marguarite Archie-Hudson, February 12, 1991.

5. Steve Peace, "Battle Commences to Close Loopholes on Indian Reservations for Garbage and Toxic Wastes," press release, n.d.

6. Jonathan Ross, Letter to Patrick Kenady, Assistant Attorney General for Legislative Affairs, California Attorney General's Office, August 5, 1991.

7. LaDonna Harris, Letter to California Assemblyman Byron Sher, Chairman of the Assembly Committee on Natural Resources, April 25, 1991.

8. Eddie Brown, Letter to California Governor Pete Wilson, May 24, 1991.

9. Bradley Angel, Letter to California Assemblyman Steve Peace, June 12, 1991.

10. Ringe Media, Inc., "Campo: Sharing the Future," Videotape, 1991.

11. John Grattan, Interview by author, October 13, 1993.

12. Daniel C. Carson, "Panel OKs Bill on Waste Sites at Reservations," *San Diego Union*, May 23, 1991.

13. Carson, "Panel OKs Bill on Waste Sites at Reservations"; Ron Roach, "Garbage Dump Limit for Indian Lands Advances in Senate," *San Diego Tribune*, July 6, 1990.

14. Ralph Goff, Letter to California Assemblywoman Doris Allen, June 10, 1991.

15. S. 1687, 102d Congress, 1st Session.

16. Ray Huard, "Indian Dump Dispute's Spillover," *San Diego Tribune*, August 21, 1991; Ralph Frammolino, "U.S. Senator Says Peace Bill on Indian Lands Is Doomed," *Los Angeles Times*, August 21, 1991.

17. Paul Helliker, Interview by author, December 8, 1993.

18. Corey Brown, Interview by author, October 19, 1993.

19. Daniel C. Carson, "Deal Said Near for Dump Site," *San Diego Union*, August 16, 1991.

20. Frammolino, "U.S. Senator Says Peace Bill on Indian Lands Is Doomed."

21. Daniel C. Carson, "Talks to Resume on Indian Lands Bill," *San Diego Union*, August 22, 1991.

22. Ralph Frammolino, "Compromise Reached over Indian Landfills," *Los Angeles Times*, September 11, 1991.

23. Corey Brown, Interview by author, October 19, 1993; State Bar of California, Environmental Law Section, "The Campo Landfill," Panel discussion, Environmental Law Institute, October 21–24, Audiocassette, remarks of Joel Mack.

24. Corey Brown, Interview by author, October 19, 1993; John Grattan, Interview by author, October 13, 1993; Paul Helliker, Interview by author, December 8, 1993.

25. California Statues, Chapter 805 (1991).

26. Taylor Miller, Interview by author, December 7, 1993.

27. Paul Helliker, Interview by author, December 8, 1993.

28. California Environmental Protection Agency, "California Environmental Protection Agency Approves Cooperative Agreement with Campo Environmental Protection Agency," press release, December 10, 1992.

29. Corey Brown, Interview by author, October 19, 1993.

30. State Bar of California, "The Campo Landfill," Panel discussion, remarks of Karen O'Haire.

31. State Bar of California, "The Campo Landfill," Panel discussion, remarks of Taylor Miller.

32. State Bar of California, "The Campo Landfill," Panel discussion, remarks of Joel Mack.

33. Taylor Miller, Interview by author, December 7, 1993.

34. Karen O'Haire, Interview by author, December 8, 1993.

35. Paul Helliker, Interview by author, December 8, 1993.

36. State Bar of California, "The Campo Landfill," Panel discussion, remarks of Joel Mack.

37. Daniel C. Carson, "Governor Signs Tribal Landfill Bill," *San Diego Union*, October 12, 1991.

CHAPTER 9. CONSIDERING THE CONSEQUENCES

1. Associated Press, "Utilities' Merger Plan Hits Setback," *San Francisco Chronicle*, February 2, 1991; Greg Johnson, "Ruling Resurrects Issue of SDG&E's Competitiveness," *Los Angeles Times*, February 5, 1991.

2. Jacqueline Wyland, Chief, Office of Federal Activities, U.S. Environmental Protection Agency, Region 9, Letter to Secretary of the Federal Energy Regulatory Commission, December 26, 1989.

3. Greg Johnson, "Judge Urges U.S. Not to OK Merger of Utilities," *Los Angeles Times*, November 28, 1990; *San Francisco Chronicle*, "State Rejects Huge Utility Merger," May 9, 1991.

4. U.S. Department of Interior, Bureau of Indian Affairs, Sacramento Area Office, *Campo Solid Waste Management Project*, Final Environmental Impact Statement, FES 92–29, vol. 1, November 1992, 1–5.

5. *Colusa (Calif.) Sun Herald*, "BIA Okays Asbestos," July 19, 1988; Jane Ellis, "Indians Protest," *Colusa (Calif.) Sun Herald*, September 23, 1988.

6. Don Knapp, Interview by author, September 3, 1993.

7. Jane Ellis, "Asbestos Dump Defended," *Colusa (Calif.) Sun Herald*, August 11, 1988.

8. Jane Ellis, "Cortina Secretary Claims Illegal Asbestos Moving," *Colusa (Calif.) Sun Herald*, December 6, 1988.

9. Jane Ellis, "Bill, Children Jailed for Asbestos-Related Fracas on Rancheria," *Colusa (Calif.) Sun Herald*, December 7, 1988.

10. Martin Topper, Interview by author, August 31, 1993; Don Knapp, Interview by author, September 3, 1993.

11. *Campo Solid Waste Management Project*, Final EIS, vol. 2, D345–D346.

12. *Campo Solid Waste Management Project*, Final EIS, vol. 2, E5.

13. *Campo Solid Waste Management Project*, Final EIS, vol. 2, E24.

14. *Campo Solid Waste Management Project*, Final EIS, vol. 2, Testimony of Donna Tisdale, F116.

15. U.S. Environmental Protection Agency, Region 9, *Public Hearing: Campo/Cottonwood Creek Sole Source Aquifer Petition*, Transcript of Testimony, Pine Valley, California, July 9, 1992, 136.

16. U.S. Environmental Protection Agency, Region 9, *Sole Source Aquifer Determination: Campo/Cottonwood Creek Aquifer, San Diego County, California*, May 5, 1993.

17. *Rachel's Hazardous Waste News*, "Leachate Collection Systems: The Achilles' Heel of Landfills," no. 119, March 7, 1989.

18. U.S. Congress, Office of Technology Assessment, *Facing America's Trash: What Next for Municipal Solid Waste*, OTA-o-424, October 1989, 86–87.

19. U.S. Department of Interior, Bureau of Indian Affairs, Sacramento Area Office, *Campo Solid Waste Management Project, Record of Decision*, FES 92-29, April 27, 1993, 5; *Campo Solid Waste Management Project*, Final EIS, vol. 1, 2–8.

20. U.S. Congress, Office of Technology Assessment, *Facing America's Trash*, 278, 281, 284.

21. *Rachel's Hazardous Waste News*, "The Catch-22s of Landfill Design," no. 109, December 26, 1988; *Rachel's Hazardous Waste News*, "Analyzing Why All Landfills Leak," no. 116, February 14, 1989; *Rachel's Hazardous Waste News*, "Leachate Collection Systems: The Achilles' Heel of Landfills."

22. David I. Johnson, "Caps: The Long Haul," *Waste Age*, March 1986, 83, 89; *Rachel's Hazardous Waste News*, "The Catch 22s of Landfill Design."

23. *Campo Solid Waste Management Project*, Final EIS, vol. 1, D-3 to D-4.

24. *Campo Solid Waste Management Project*, Final EIS, vol. 1, D-55.

25. *Campo Solid Waste Management Project*, Final EIS, vol. 1, D-11.

26. *Campo Solid Waste Management Project*, Final EIS, vol. 1, S-5 to S-6, 2–4.

27. U.S. Environmental Protection Agency, "Solid Waste Disposal Facility Criteria: Proposed Rule," *Federal Register* 53 (1988): 33,314, 33,366.

28. U.S. Environmental Protection Agency, "Solid Waste Disposal Facility Criteria: Final Rule," *Federal Register* 56 (1991): 50, 978, 51,049.

29. U.S. Department of Health and Human Services, Public Health Service, Agency for Toxic Substances and Disease Registry, "Toxicological Profile for Tetrachloroethylene," ATSDR/TP-88/22, January 1990.

30. U.S. Environmental Protection Agency, Region 9, "Comments on

the Campo Solid Waste Management Project Final Environmental Impact Statement," January 4, 1993.

31. California Integrated Waste Management Board, "Comments on the Campo Solid Waste Management Project Final Environmental Impact Statement," May 4, 1993.

32. U.S. Environmental Protection Agency, Region 9, "Comments on Eagle Mountain Landfill Project Final EIS," September 8, 1992.

33. Phil Duncan, ed., *Politics in America*, 1991, 227–29.

34. Donna Tisdale, Interviews by author, May 7 and October 9, 1993; Michael Connolly, Interview by author, June 13, 1993.

35. Donna Tisdale, Interview by author, October 9, 1993.

36. *Mtn. Empire Press*, "Babbitt to Make Final Decision on Proposed Indian Waste Facility," March 1993.

37. Donna Tisdale, Interviews by author, May 7 and October 9, 1993.

38. Michael Connolly, Interview by author, June 13, 1993.

39. U.S. Department of Interior, "Secretary Babbitt Approves Campo Landfill Lease, Sets Tough Guidelines for New Indian Waste Facility Proposals," press release, April 27, 1993.

40. Donna Tisdale, Interviews by author, May 7 and September 14, 1993.

41. U.S. Department of Interior, "Secretary Babbitt Approves Campo Landfill Lease, Sets Tough Guidelines for New Indian Waste Facility Proposals."

42. U.S. Department of Interior, Bureau of Indian Affairs, Sacramento Area Office, *Campo Solid Waste Management Project, Record of Decision*, FES 92–29, April 27, 1993.

43. Duncan Hunter, "Hunter Says Fight Against Campo Landfill Will Continue," press release, April 28, 1993.

44. Billie Jo Shepherd, "Opponents Say Fight Against Landfill Will Continue," *Alpine (Calif.) Sun*, May 5, 1993.

45. *Half Moon Bay Fishermans' Marketing v. Carlucci*, 857 F.2d 505, 507 (9th Cir. 1988).

46. *Benda v. Grand Lodge of International Association of Machinists, etc.*, 584 F.2d 308, 315 (9th Cir. 1978).

47. *United States v. Odessa Union Warehouse Co-op*, 833 F.2d 172, 174 (9th Cir. 1987).

48. *County of San Diego v. Babbitt*, Order Denying Plaintiff's Motion for Preliminary Injunction, 93-0986-IEG (LSP) (S.D. Cal. Oct. 15, 1993), 6. (Hereafter cited as Order, *San Diego v. Babbitt*.)

49. *Oregon Environmental Council v. Kunzman*, 817 F.2d 484, 492 (9th Cir. 1987).

50. *Robertson v. Methow Valley Citizens Council*, 490 U.S. 332, 346, 350 (1989).

51. *Kleppe v. Sierra Club*, 427 U.S. 390, 410 n.21 (1976).

52. Order. *San Diego v. Babbitt*, 6–7, 9–10.

53. Order, *San Diego v. Babbitt*, 9, 13–14.

54. Order, *San Diego v. Babbitt*, 13–14.

55. Order, *San Diego v. Babbitt*, 14.

56. Michael Connolly, Interview by author, October 12, 1993.

57. Donna Tisdale, Interview by author, January 20, 1994.

58. *Inland Empire Public Lands Council v. Schultze*, 992 F.2d 977, 981 (9th Cir. 1993).

59. Administrative Procedure Act, 5 U.S.C.A., Sec. 706(2)(A).

60. *County of San Diego v. Babbitt*, Order Granting Motions for Summary Judgment, 93-0986-IEG (LSP) (S.D. Cal. Jan. 27, 1994), 16–17.

61. Donna Tisdale, Interview by author, February 7, 1994.

62. Michael Connolly, Interview by author, February 7, 1994.

63. Billie Jo Shepherd, "Opponents Say Fight Against Landfill Will Continue."

CHAPTER 10. THE TIDE OF BATTLE

1. Michael Connolly, Interview by author, October 12, 1993.

2. Billie Jo Shepherd, "CEPA Issues Long-Awaited Construction Permit for Controversial Landfill," *Alpine (Calif.) Sun*, April 13, 1994.

3. U.S. Environmental Protection Agency, Region 9, "U.S. EPA Tentatively Approves Campo Landfill Regulatory Program," press release, May 2, 1994.

4. U.S. Environmental Protection Agency, Region 9, "Campo Band of Mission Indians; Tentative Adequacy Determination of Tribal Municipal Solid Waste Program," April 29, 1994, 5.

5. U.S. EPA, Region 9, "U.S. EPA Tentatively Approves Campo Landfill Regulatory Program."

6. U.S. Environmental Protection Agency, "EPA Policy for the Administration of Environmental Programs on Indian Reservations," William D. Ruckelshaus, November 8, 1984; U.S. EPA, Region 9, "Tentative Adequacy Determination," 6–12.

7. U.S. Environmental Protection Agency, Region 9, "EPA Publishes Tentative Approval of Campo Band's Program and Schedules Public Hearing," Factsheet, June 1994, 1.

8. Jeffrey Zelikson, Letter to Michael Connolly, June 3, 1993.

9. Zelikson to Connolly, June 3, 1994, 1; U.S. EPA, Region 9, "Tentative Adequacy Determination," 25; U.S. EPA, Region 9, "EPA Publishes Tentative Approval," 2.

10. J. Arturo Herrera Solis, Letter to Narendra N. Gunaji, March 25, 1994; Paul Ybarrondo, "Fight On to Stop Campo Landfill," *Daily Californian*, February 19, 1994.

11. Narendra N. Gunaji, Letter to J. Arturo Herrera Solis, May 6, 1994.

12. Robert Ybarra, Interview by author, June 6, 1994.

13. Billie Jo Shepherd, "Border Blockers Protest Landfill," *Alpine (Calif.) Sun*, June 8, 1994.

14. Chet Barfield, "Campo Landfill Foes Gain Allies in Mexico," *San Diego Union-Tribune*, December 2, 1993; Billie Jo Shepherd, "Landfill Issue Goes International," *Alpine (Calif.) Sun*, February 23, 1994.

15. *San Diego Union-Tribune*, "False Alarm: Landfill Opponents Raise Unfounded Fears," Editorial, December 8, 1993.

16. Donna Tisdale, "Water Contamination from Landfill Is Fear of Residents," *San Diego Union-Tribune*, Letter to editor, December 11, 1993.

17. Michael Connolly, Interview by author, June 3, 1994.

18. Donna Tisdale, Letter to Jerry Rindone, Member of City Council, City of Chula Vista, California, September 11, 1993; Duncan Hunter, Letter to Tim Nader, Mayor, City of Chula Vista, California, September 13, 1993; Steve Peace, Letter to Tim Nader, September 21, 1993.

19. *San Diego Union-Tribune*, "Chula Vista Acts to Find Private Disposal Firm," October 21, 1993

20. Donna Tisdale, Letter to Tracy Swanborn, Brown, Vence and Associates, November 30, 1993.

21. City Council, City of Chula Vista, California, Minutes, April 5, 1994; Pauline Repard, "Chula Vista Narrows Field to 3 Trash Haulers," *San Diego Union-Tribune*, April 6, 1994.

22. Gustavo Davilo Rodriguez, Letter to Tim Nader, Mayor, City of Chula Vista, California, April 21, 1994.

23. Stephanie Snyder, Interview by author, June 13, 1994.

24. *Mtn. Empire Press*, "B.A.D. Wants Campo Landfill to Be 'Dumped,'" June 1994.

25. Ron Lietzke, "Despite Debt, Mid-American Sees Future Full of Growth," *Columbus (Ohio) Dispatch*, May 19, 1994.

26. Mid-American Waste Systems, Inc., "Annual Report," 1993, 9.

27. Jeff Bailey, "Mid-American Finds Itself Down in the Dumps," *Wall Street Journal*, June 2, 1994.

28. Lietzke, "Despite Debt, Mid-American Sees Future Full of Growth."

29. David Trossman, Interview by author, June 13, 1994.

30. Vishnu Swarup, Interview by author, June 23, 1994.

31. Donna Tisdale, Interview by author, June 1, 1994.

32. Michael Connolly, Interview by author, June 3, 1994.

CHAPTER 11. WAR AND REBELLION: CAMPO AND LOS COYOTES COMPARED

1. U.S. Department of Interior, Bureau of Indian Affairs, Southern California Agency, "Local Estimates of Resident Indian Population and Labor Force Estimates," January 1991; U.S. Department of Interior, Bureau of Indian Affairs, Southern California Agency, "Tribal Information Directory," n.d.

2. Edwin K. Wiles, Northern Region Manager, Corporate Develop-

ment, Chambers Development Company, Inc., Letter to Banning Taylor, Chairman, Los Coyotes Band of Mission Indians, April 29, 1991.

3. Coalition for Indian Rights, "The Coalition for Indian Rights Speaks Out Against Corporate Exploitation of Tribal Sovereign Rights," press release, n.d.

4. Amy Wallace, "Indians Have a Change of Heart over Dump," *Los Angeles Times*, May 21, 1991.

5. Virgil Townsend, Interview by author, December 10, 1993.

6. Carmen Valencia, "Indians, Firm Differ on Landfill," *San Diego Union*, March 27, 1991; Coalition for Indian Rights, "The Coalition for Indian Rights Speaks Out Against Corporate Exploitation of Tribal Sovereign Rights."

7. Carmen Valencia, "Indians: Activists Are Wary of Landfill Plans," *San Diego Union*, February 15, 1991.

8. Carmen Valencia, "Rugged Valley May Become Landfill," *San Diego Union*, Febuary 20, 1991; Judy Winter Meier, "Landfill Meeting Draws 238 Concerned Citizens," *Borrego (Calif.) Sun*, February 28, 1991; Edwin K. Wiles, Letter to Banning Taylor, April 29, 1991; Susan M. Trager, Letter to Katherine Saubel, Elder, Los Coyotes Band of Mission Indians, March 11, 1991.

9. Martin Wisckol, "Security Cops Protect Workers on Reservation," *Escondido (Calif.) Times Advocate*, March 20, 1991.

10. Valencia, "Indians, Firm Differ on Landfill."

11. Carmen Valencia, "Plans for Reservation Landfill Are in Dispute," *San Diego Union*, April 16, 1991.

12. David Harpster, "Indian Leaders Pull Out of Proposal for Landfill," *San Diego Tribune*, May 21, 1991; Carmen Valencia, "Tribe Rescinds Landfill Agreement," *San Diego Union*, May 21, 1991; Wallace, "Indians Have a Change of Heart over Dump."

13. David Harpster, "Indians Again Vote Not to Allow Dump on Reservation," *San Diego Tribune*, July 1, 1991; Edwin K. Wiles, Letter to Patrick Hemmy, Area Natural Resources Officer, U.S. Department of Interior, Bureau of Indian Affairs, Sacramento Area Office, July 2, 1991.

14. Marina Ortega, "The Off-Again, On-Again Garbage Dump," *Race, Poverty & the Environment* 3, no. 3 (Fall 1992): 13.

15. Virgil Townsend, Interview by author, December 10, 1993.

16. Banning Taylor, Interview by author, December 10, 1993.

17. Gabriella Stern, "Polluted Numbers: Audit Report Shows How Far Chambers Would Go for Profits," *Wall Street Journal*, October 21, 1992.

18. *Campo Solid Waste Management Project*, Final EIS, vol. 1, 3-90; Jana Walker and Kevin Gover, "Commercial Solid and Hazardous Waste Disposal Projects on Indian Lands," in American Bar Association, Section of Natural Resources, Energy, and Environmental Law, Fourth Annual Conference on Natural Resources Management and Environmental Enforcement on Indian Lands, Course Materials, Albuquerque, New Mexico, Feb-

ruary 20–21, 1992, 4-80 to 4-81; Michael Connolly, Interview by author, May 4–5, 1993.

19. Taylor Miller, Interview by author, December 7, 1993.

20. Florence C. Shipek, "Kumeyaay Socio-Political Structure," *Journal of California and Great Basin Anthropology* 4 (1982): 296–303.

21. Walker and Gover, "Commercial . . . Waste Disposal Projects on Indian Lands," 4-81.

22. Walker and Gover, "Commercial . . . Waste Disposal Projects on Indian Lands," 4-81; Connolly, Interview by author, May–5, 1993.

23. Banning Taylor, Interview by author, December 10, 1993.

24. Edwin K. Wiles, Interview by author, December 14, 1993.

25. Banning Taylor, Interview by author, December 10, 1993; Virgil Townsend, Interview by author, December 10, 1993.

26. Virgil Townsend, Interview by author, December 10, 1993.

27. Michael Connolly, Interview by author, May 4 and 5, 1993.

28. Bradley Angel, Interview by author, August 17, 1993.

29. Tom Goldtooth, Interview by author, September 20, 1993.

30. Marina Ortega, Interview by author, September 16, 1993.

31. Marina Ortega, Interview by author, September 16, 1993.

32. Michael Connolly, Interview by author, June 13, 1993.

33. *Campo Solid Waste Management Project*, Final EIS, vol. 2, D360.

34. Margaret Knox, "Their Mother's Keeper," *Sierra*, March–April 1993, 83.

35. Michael Connolly, Interview by author, June 13, 1993.

36. Michael Connolly, Interview by author, June 13, 1993.

37. Marina Ortega, Interview by author, September 16, 1993.

38. Marina Ortega, Interview by author, September 16, 1993.

39. John Anner, "Protecting Mother Earth," *Minority Trendsletter*, Fall 1991, 4, 7.

40. Marina Ortega, Interview by author, October 20, 1993.

41. Marina Ortega, Interview by author, September 16, 1993.

42. Anner, "Protecting Mother Earth," 4, 8.

43. Bradley Angel, Interview by author, August 17, 1993.

44. Donna Tisdale, Interview by author, October 9, 1993.

45. Bradley Angel, Interview by author, August 17, 1993.

CHAPTER 12. SUMMING UP

1. Tom Goldtooth, Interviews by author, September 17 and 20, 1993.

2. U.S. Department of Interior, "Secretary Babbitt Approves Campo Landfill Lease, Sets Tough Guidelines for New Indian Waste Facility," press release, April 27, 1993.

3. U.S. Department of Interior, "Secretary Babbitt Approves Campo Landfill Lease."

4. Donald R. Wharton, "Implementation of EPA's Indian Policy and

Tribal Amendments to Federal Environmental Laws," American Bar Association Conference on Natural Resources Management and Environmental Enforcement on Indian Lands, February 20–21, 1992, 23.

5. Virgil Townsend, Interview by author, December 10, 1993.

6. California Environmental Protection Agency, "California Environmental Protection Agency Approves Cooperative Agreement with Campo Environmental Protection Agency," press release, December 10, 1992.

7. U.S. Environmental Protection Agency, "Campo Municipal Solid Waste Landfill Informational Meeting," Reporter's Transcript of Proceedings, July 1, 1994, 29–30.

8. U.S. Environmental Protection Agency, "Solid Waste Disposal Facility Criteria: Final Rule," 56 *Federal Register* (1991): 50,978, 51,049.

EPILOGUE

1. George Johnson, "Apaches Reject Plan to Store Nuclear Waste," *New York Times*, February 2, 1995; Bureau of National Affairs, "Mescalero Tribe Votes Against Proposal to Build Storage Facility on Reservation," *Environment Reporter: Current Developments*, February 3, 1995, 1876.

2. Robert M. Mussler, Interview by author, February 23, 1995.

3. Keith Schneider, "Utilities Filling Void in Storing Nuclear Waste," *New York Times*, February 15, 1995.

4. *Kelley v. Selin*, 93–1646/93–1710/93–3613/93–3749 (6th Cir. Jan. 11, 1995).

5. Emmet Pierce, "Carlsbad Is County's Latest City to Ship Trash Outside Region," *San Diego Union-Tribune*, October 5, 1994.

6. L. Erik Bratt, "Another City Joins Exodus of Trash," *San Diego Union-Tribune*, February 1, 1995.

7. Emmet Pierce, "Trash Panel Calls a Truce with Cities," *San Diego Union-Tribune*, January 13, 1995.

8. Emmet Pierce, "County Is Urged to Implement Trash Fee," *San Diego Union-Tribune*, November 11, 1994.

9. Emmet Pierce, "Testimony Mostly Goes Against New Fee for Trash," *San Diego Union-Tribune*, November 30, 1994.

10. U.S. Environmental Protection Agency, Region 9, "U.S. EPA Proposes Draft Air Permit for Campo Landfill," press release, May 16, 1994.

11. Matt Haber, Chief, New Source Section, Air and Toxics Division, U.S. Environmental Protection Agency, Region 9, Letter to John M. Lang, Regional Environmental Manager, Mid-American Waste Systems, Inc., December 6, 1994; Matt Haber, Interview by author, February 22, 1995; Steve Ringer, New Source Section, Air and Toxics Division, U.S. Environmental Protection Agency, Region 9, Interviews by author, February 21 and 24, 1995.

12. Felicia Marcus, Letter to Duncan Hunter, n.d.

13. Backcountry Against Dumps, "Comments Opposing EPA's Tentative

Approval of Campo Band's Solid Waste Landfill Regulatory Program," July 28, 1994.

14. Billie Jo Shepherd, "2 Campo Projects Executives Indicted," *Alpine (Calif.) Sun*, January 6, 1993.

15. Michael Connolly, Interview by author, September 6, 1994.

16. Michael Connolly, Interview by author, September 6, 1994.

17. Michael Connolly, Interview by author, September 6, 1994.

BIBLIOGRAPHY

BOOKS AND ARTICLES

Anner, John. "Protecting Mother Earth." *Minority Trendsletter*, Fall 1991.

Austin, Diane E. "Knowledge and Values in the Decision Making Around Hazardous Waste Incineration Facilities: Final Report." School of Natural Resources and Environment, University of Michigan: January 1993.

Bancroft, Hubert Howe. *History of California.* Vol. 7. San Francisco: The History Company, 1890.

———. *The Native Races.* Vol I. San Francisco: The History Company, 1886.

Bean, Lowell John, and Harry W. Lawton. "Some Explanations for the Rise of Cultural Complexity in Native California with Comments on Proto-Agriculture and Agriculture." In *Before the Wilderness: Environmental Management by Native Californians*, ed. by Thomas C. Blackburn and Kat Anderson. Menlo Park, Calif.: Ballena Press, 1993, pp. 27–54.

Bean, Lowell John, and Charles R. Smith. "Cupeño." In *Handbook of North American Indians*, vol. 8, *California*, ed. by Robert F. Heizer. Washington, D.C.: Smithsonian Institution, p. 588.

Bean, Walton. *California: An Interpretive History.* New York: McGraw-Hill, 1968.

Browne, J. Ross. *The Indians of California.* San Francisco: Colt Press, 1944.

Bureau of National Affairs. "Federal Nuclear Waste Negotiator Touts Possible Beneficial Uses of Spent Fuel." *Environment Reporter: Current Developments*, June 17, 1994.

———. "Suit by States Against Energy Department Challenges

Failure to Construct Repository." *Environment Reporter: Current Developments*, June 24, 1994.

———. "Mescalero Tribe Votes Against Proposal to Build Storage Facility on Reservation." *Environment Reporter: Current Developments*, February 3, 1995.

California Environmental Insider. "Solid Waste: Waste Board Issues Report on Remaining State Landfill Capacity," February 29, 1992.

———. "San Diego Cities Begin to Bolt County Waste Program," July 31, 1994.

Carrico, Richard L. *Strangers in a Stolen Land: American Indians in San Diego 1850–1880.* New Castle, Calif.: Sierra Oaks Publishing, 1987.

Castillo, Edward D. "The Impact of Euro-American Exploration and Settlement." In *Handbook of North American Indians*, vol. 8, *California*, ed. by Robert F. Heizer. Washington, D.C.: Smithsonian Institution, 1978, pp. 99–127.

Caughey, John W. *California: History of a Remarkable State.* 4th ed. Englewood Cliffs, N.J.: Prentice-Hall, 1982.

Chase, Alston. *Playing God in Yellowstone: The Destruction of America's First National Park.* San Diego: Harcourt Brace Jovanovich, 1987.

Cohen, Felix S. *Handbook of Federal Indian Law.* Charlottesville, Va.: Michie Company, 1982.

Cook, Sherburne F. *The Conflict Between the California Indian and White Civilization: The American Invasion.* Ibero-Americana, no. 23. Berkeley: University of California Press, 1943.

———. "Historical Demography." In *Handbook of North American Indians*, vol. 8, *California*, ed. by Robert F. Heizer. Washington, D.C.: Smithsonian Institution, 1978, pp. 91–98.

Cox, Isaac. *The Annals of Trinity County.* Eugene, Ore.: John Henry Nash of the University of Oregon, 1940.

D'Angelo, Pamela A. "Waste Management Industry Turns to Indian Reservations as States Close Landfills." *Environment Reporter: Current Developments*, December 28, 1990.

Duncan, Phil, ed. *Politics in America.* Washington, D.C.: Congressional Quarterly, 1991.

Fernandez, Ferdinand. "Except a California Indian: A Study in Legal Discrimination." *Southern California Quarterly* 50 (1968): 161.

Goldberg, Carole E. "Public Law 280: The Limits of State Jurisdiction over Reservation Indians." *U.C.L.A. Law Review* 22 1975: 535.

Goodrich, Chauncey Shafter. "The Legal Status of the California Indian." 14 *California Law Review* 83 (1926).

Green, Stephen, ed. *California Political Almanac, 1991–1992*. Sacramento: California Journal Press, 1991.

Hagan, William T. "Justifying Dispossession of the Indian: The Land Utilization Argument." In *American Indian Environments: Ecological Issues in Native American History*, ed. by Christopher Vecsey and Robert W. Venables. Syracuse, N.Y.: Syracuse University Press, 1980, pp. 65–80.

Hager, Mary. "Dances with Garbage." *Newsweek*, April 29, 1991.

Heizer, Robert F., ed. *The Destruction of California Indians: A Collection of Documents from the Period 1847 to 1865 in Which Are Described Some of the Things That Happened to Some of the Indians of California*. Lincoln: University of Nebraska Press, 1974.

Heizer, Robert F., and Allan F. Almquist. *The Other Californians: Prejudice and Discrimination under Spain, Mexico, and the United States to 1920*. Berkeley: University of California Press, 1971.

Historical Guide to the Back Country: A Self-Guided Tour Through the Rugged Mountains of San Diego's East County. Campo, Calif.: Mountain Empire Historical Society, 1988.

Hurtado, Albert L. *Indian Survival on the California Frontier*. New Haven: Yale University Press, 1988.

Indigenous Environmental Network. "No Nuclear Waste on Indian Lands: Resolution of the Third Annual Indigenous Environmental Network Gathering, Celilo Village, Oregon, June 6, 1992." *Race, Poverty & the Environment* 3, no. 3 (Fall 1992).

Jacques, Terr E. "Serving San Diego County's Southern Indians? Campo Agency Schools." *Journal of San Diego History* 29 (1983): 153–64.

Johnson, David I. "Caps: The Long Haul." *Waste Age*, March 1986.

Kelsey, Harry. "The California Indian Treaty Myth." *Southern California Quarterly* 55 (1973): 225.

Knox, Margaret. "Their Mother's Keeper." *Sierra*, March–April 1993.

Lewis, Henry T. "Matsuka: The Ecology of Indian Fires in Northern Alberta." *Western Canadian Journal of Anthropology* 7 (1977): 15.

Littman, Jonathan. "And the Dealer Stays." *California Lawyer* 13 (1993): 45.

Locke, John. *Two Treatises of Government*. New York: Hafner Publishing, 1947.

Lummis, Charles F. "Three Grains of Corn." *Out West* 22 (1905): 2.

Luomala, Katherine. "Tipai and Ipai." In *Handbook of North Ameri'can Indians*, vol. 8, *California*, ed. by Robert F. Heizer, Washington, D.C.: Smithsonian Institution, 1978, pp. 592–609.

Marsh, John. "Letter of Dr. John Marsh to Hon. Lewis Cass." *California Historical Society Quarterly* 22 (1943): 315.

Ortega, Marina. "The Off-Again, On-Again Garbage Dump." *Race, Poverty & the Environment* 3, no. 3 (Fall 1992).

Pettit, C. L. "Tip Fees Up More than 30% in Annual NSWMA Survey." *Waste Age*, March 1989.

Phillips, George Harwood. *Indians and Intruders in Central California, 1769–1849*. Norman: University of Oklahoma Press, 1993.

Pyne, Stephen J. *Fire in America*. Princeton: Princeton University Press, 1982.

Rachel's Hazardous Waste News. "The Catch-22s of Landfill Design." No. 109: December 26, 1988.

———. "Analyzing Why All Landfills Leak." No. 116: February 14, 1989.

———. "Leachate Collection Systems: The Achilles' Heel of Landfills." No. 119: March 7, 1989.

Rawls, James J. *Indians of California: The Changing Image*. Norman: University of Oklahoma Press, 1984.

Schneider, Paul. "Other People's Trash." *Audubon*, July–August 1991.

Shipek, Florence C. "History of Southern California Mission Indians." In *Handbook of North American Indians*, vol. 8, *California*, ed. by Robert F. Heizer, Washington, D.C.: Smithsonian Institution, 1978, pp. 610–18.

———. "Kumeyaay Socio-Political Structure." *Journal of California and Great Basin Anthropology* 4 (1982): 296–303.

———. "California Indian Reactions to the Franciscans." *The Americas* 41 (1985): 480.

———. *Pushed into the Rocks: Changes in Southern California Indian Land Tenure*. Lincoln: University of Nebraska Press, 1988.

———. "An Example of Intensive Plant Husbandry: The Kumeyaay of Southern California." In *Foraging and Farming: The Evolution of Plant Exploitation*, ed. by David R. Harris and Gordon C. Hillman. London: Unwin Hyman, 1989, pp. 159–70.

———. *The Autobiography of Delfina Cuero*. Interpreted by Rosalie Pinto Robertson. Menlo Park, Calif.: Ballena Press, 1991.

———. "The Shaman: Priest, Doctor, Scientist." In *California In-*

dian Shamanism, ed. by Lowell John Bean. Menlo Park, Calif.: Ballena Press, 1992, pp. 89–96.

―――. "Kumeyaay Plant Husbandry: Fire, Water, and Erosion Control Systems." In *Before the Wilderness: Environmental Management by Native Californians,* ed. by Thomas C. Blackburn and Kat Anderson. Menlo Park, Calif.: Ballena Press, 1993, pp. 379–88.

Timbrook, Jan, John R. Anderson, and David D. Earle. "Vegetation Burning by the Chumash." In *Before the Wilderness: Environmental Management by Native Californians,* ed. by Thomas C. Blackburn and Kat Anderson. Menlo Park, Calif.: Ballena Press, 1993, pp. 117–49.

United Church of Christ. *Toxic Wastes and Race in the United States: A National Report on the Racial and Socio-Economic Characteristics of Communities with Hazardous Waste Sites.* New York: Commission for Racial Justice, United Church of Christ, 1987.

Walker, Jana, and Kevin Gover. "Commercial Solid and Hazardous Waste Disposal Projects on Indian Lands." In American Bar Association, Section of Natural Resources, Energy, and Environmental Law. Fourth Annual Conference on Natural Resources Management and Environmental Enforcement on Indian Lands. Course Materials. Albuquerque, New Mexico. February 20–21, 1992.

Warren, Charles. *The Supreme Court in United States History,* vol 2. Boston: Little, Brown, 1923.

Weinberg, Albert K. *Manifest Destiny.* Baltimore: Johns Hopkins Press, 1935.

Wilson, Darryl. "Five Hundred Years from Now." *News from Native California,* February–April 1991.

Zeiger, Richard. "Rating the Legislators." *California Journal,* March 1990.

―――. "The Capitol's Best." *California Journal,* April 1992.

―――. "California Journal's Third Biennial Survey Spotlights the Legislature's Best." *California Journal,* March 1994.

Zeiger, Richard, and A. G. Block. "The Decline and Fall of Speaker Willie Brown, Jr.?" *California Journal,* April 1988.

NEWSPAPERS

Avila Hernandez, Juan A. "How the Feds Push Nuclear Waste onto Indian Land." *SF Weekly,* September 23, 1992.

Associated Press. "Utilities' Merger Plan Hits Setback." *San Francisco Chronicle*, February 2, 1991.

Bailey, Jeff. "Mid-American Finds Itself Down in the Dumps." *Wall Street Journal*, June 2, 1994.

Barfield, Chet. "Campo Landfill Foes Gain Allies in Mexico." *San Diego Union-Tribune*, December 2, 1993.

———. "Private Landfill Firm Trying to Lure Cities." *San Diego Union-Tribune*, August 7, 1993.

Behrman, John. "Authority OKs New Trash-Fee Schedule." *San Diego Union-Tribune*, August 12, 1994.

Berhman, John. "Oceanside Pullout Won't Kill Plans to Send Trash to Utah." *San Diego Union-Tribune*, August 5, 1994.

Bratt, L. Erik. "Another City Joins Exodus of Trash." *San Diego Union-Tribune*, February 1, 1995.

Brown, Joe. "Area Indian Plight Called 'Intolerable.'" *San Diego Union*, June 9, 1959.

Carson, Daniel C. "East County Indians Hire Ohio Firm to Build Landfill." *San Diego Union*, September 20, 1990.

———. "Panel OKs Bill on Waste Sites at Reservations." *San Diego Union*, May 23, 1991.

———. "Deal Said Near for Dump Site." *San Diego Union*, August 16, 1991.

———. "Talks to Resume on Indian Lands Bill." San Diego Union, August 22, 1991.

———. "Governor Signs Tribal Landfill Bill." *San Diego Union*, October 12, 1991.

Colusa (Calif.) Sun Herald. "BIA Okays Asbestos." July 19, 1989.

Cushman, John H., Jr. "U.S. Weighs Blacks' Complaints about Pollution." *New York Times*, November 9, 1993.

Daschle, Thomas A. "Dances with Garbage." *Christian Science Monitor*, February 14, 1991.

Ellis, Jane. "Asbestos Dump Defended." *Colusa (Calif.) Sun Herald*, August 11, 1988.

———. "Indians Protest." *Colusa (Calif.) Sun Herald*, September 23, 1988.

———. "Cortina Secretary Claims Illegal Asbestos Moving." *Colusa (Calif.) Sun Herald*, December 6, 1988.

———. "Bill, Children Jailed for Asbestos-Related Fracas on Rancheria." *Colusa (Calif.) Sun Herald*, December 7, 1988.

Frammolino, Ralph. "Lawmakers and Indians Wage War over Dump." *Los Angeles Times*, July 5, 1990.

————. "Indian Environmental Bill Clears Hurdle." *Los Angeles Times*, July 6, 1990.

————. "Campo Indians Accuse Peace of Cheap Shots at Landfill Hearing." *Los Angeles Times*, August 14, 1990.

————. "Bill Curbing Use of Indian Land Revived." *Los Angeles Times*, August 21, 1990.

————. "U.S. Senator Says Peace Bill on Indian Lands Is Doomed." *Los Angeles Times*, August 21, 1991.

————. "Compromise Reached over Indian Landfills." *Los Angeles Times*, September 11, 1991.

Gaw, Jonathan. "Dump Profit Gets Slashed." *Los Angeles Times*, July 22, 1993.

Gregory, Dan. "Indian Festival Starts Thursday." *San Diego Union*, July 13, 1959.

Harpster, David. "Indian Leaders Pull Out of Proposal for Landfill." *San Diego Tribune*, May 21, 1991.

————. "Indians Again Vote Not to Allow Dump on Reservation." *San Diego Tribune*, July 1, 1991.

Huard, Ray. "Indian Dump Dispute's Spillover." *San Diego Tribune*, August 21, 1991.

Johnson, George. "Apaches Reject Plan to Store Nuclear Waste." *New York Times*, February 2, 1995.

Johnson, Greg. "Ruling Resurrects Issue of SDG&E's Competitiveness." *Los Angeles Times*, February 5, 1991.

————. "Judge Urges U.S. Not to OK Merger of Utilities." *Los Angeles Times*, November 28, 1990.

Lietzke, Ron. "Despite Debt, Mid-American Sees Future Full of Growth." *Columbus (Ohio) Dispatch*, May 19, 1994.

Mayne, Melvin C. "San Diego Indians May Get Aid." *San Diego Union*, October 2, 1932.

McCutchon, Beverly. "Nuke Storage Protest Now in Mescalero." *Alamagordo Daily News*, August 26, 1992.

MacDonald, Craig. "Boulevard: A Right Turn to Contentment." *San Diego Union*, February 12, 1978.

Meier, Barry. "Casinos Putting Tribes at Odds." *New York Times*, January 13, 1994.

Meier, Judy Winter. "Landfill Meeting Draws 238 Concerned Citizens." *Borrego (Calif.) Sun*, February 28, 1991.

Miller, Ellen. "Indian Lands on Dump List." *Denver Post*, May 15, 1992.

Mtn. Empire Press. "Babbitt to Make Final Decision on Proposed Indian Waste Facility." March 1993.

———. "B.A.D. Wants Campo Landfill to be 'Dumped.'" June 1994.

Pierce, Emmet. "County Tries Price Incentive on Trash." *San Diego Union-Tribune*, May 20, 1994.

———. "350% Hike Studied for Landfill Fee." *San Diego Union-Tribune*, July 15, 1994.

———. "Proposed Fee Increase Stinks, Trash Agency Told." *San Diego Union-Tribune*, August 2, 1994.

———. "Cities Leaving Trash System Warned." *San Diego Union-Tribune*, August 19, 1994.

———. "Carlsbad Is County's Latest City to Ship Trash Outside the Region." *San Diego Union-Tribune*, October 5, 1994.

———. "County Is Urged to Implement Trash Fee." *San Diego Union-Tribune*, November 11, 1994.

———. "Testimony Mostly Goes Against New Fee for Trash." *San Diego Union-Tribune*, November 30, 1994.

———. "Trash Panel Calls a Truce with Cities." *San Diego Union-Tribune*, January 13, 1995.

Reinhold, Robert. "Indians and Neighbors Are at Odds over Proposed Reservation Dump." *New York Times*, January 8, 1990.

Repard, Pauline. "Chula Vista Narrows Field to 3 Trash Haulers." *San Diego Union-Tribune*, April 6, 1994.

Roach, Ron. "Garbage-Dump Limit for Indian Lands Advances in Senate." *San Diego Tribune*, July 6, 1990.

Root, M. S. "Atrocious Cruelty." *San Diego Union*, October 7, 1880.

Rowland, Bob. "El Cajon All But Out of County Trash Net." *San Diego Union-Tribune*, May 19, 1994.

San Diego Union. "On the Eastern Line." February 1, 1880.

San Diego Union. "Our Trip to the Soda Springs." June 17, 1880.

San Diego Union. "Indians Kill White; Fear Campo Riot." July 17, 1927.

San Diego Union. "Campo Indians Rebel; Two Die." July 18, 1927.

San Diego Union. "Deputies Exceeded Authority in Campo Indian Fight, Jury at Coroner's Inquest Finds." July 21, 1927.

San Diego Union. "Bill Aims at Tribe's Dump Plans." March 6, 1990.

San Diego Union-Tribune. "Chula Vista Acts to Find Private Disposal Firm." October 21, 1993.

San Diego Union-Tribune. "False Alarm: Landfill Opponents Raise Unfounded Fears." Editorial. December 8, 1993.

San Francisco Chronicle. "State Rejects Huge Utility Merger." May 9, 1991.

Schneider, Keith. "Utilities Filling Void in Storing Nuclear Waste." *New York Times*, February 15, 1995.

Scott-Blair, Michael. "Cultural Differences Can Breed Tension, Sometimes Hatred." *San Diego Union*, August 6, 1989.

———. "Giving Indian Kids a Boost Up the Educational Ladder." *San Diego Union*, August 6, 1989.

Shaffer, Mark. "Paiutes' Waste-Site Plan Alarms Neighbors." *Arizona Republic*, January 28, 1990.

Shelley, Katherine. "Indians Protest N-Waste Idea." *Gallup Independent*, August 12, 1993.

Shepherd, Billie Jo. "Hunter Suggests Tribe Try Golf Resort," *Alpine (Calif.) Sun*, June 17, 1992.

———. "2 Campo Projects Executives Indicted." *Alpine (Calif.) Sun*, January 6, 1993.

———. "Opponents Say Fight Against Landfill Will Continue." *Alpine (Calif.) Sun*, May 5, 1993.

———. "Landfill Issue Goes International." *Alpine (Calif.) Sun*, February 23, 1994.

———. "CEPA Issues Long-Awaited Construction Permit for Controversial Landfill." *Alpine (Calif.) Sun*, April 13, 1994.

———. "Border Blockers Protest Landfill." *Alpine (Calif.) Sun*, June 8, 1994.

Smolens, Michael. "Senate Panel Switches, OKs Scuttling Campo Dump." *San Diego Union*, August 21, 1990.

———. "Governor Vetoes Bill Jeopardizing Reservation Trash Plan." *San Diego Union*, October 1, 1990.

Stern, Gabriella. "Polluted Numbers: Audit Report Shows How Far Chambers Would Go for Profits." *Wall Street Journal*, October 21, 1992.

Tisdale, Donna. "Water Contamination from Landfill Is Fear of Residents." Letter to Editor. *San Diego Union-Tribune*, December 11, 1993.

Traylor, Susan. "Choctaw Dumping Decision Worries Other Tribes." *Gannett News Service*, April 1, 1991.

Valencia, Carmen. "Indians: Activists Are Wary of Landfill Plans." *San Diego Union*, February 15, 1991.

———. "Rugged Valley May Become Landfill." *San Diego Union*, February 20, 1991.

———. "Indians, Firm Differ on Landfill." *San Diego Union*, March 27, 1991.

———. "Plans for Reservation Landfill Are in Dispute." *San Diego Union*, April 16, 1991.

———. "Tribe Rescinds Landfill Agreement." *San Diego Union*, May 21, 1991.

Wald, Matthew L. "Nuclear Industry Seeks Interim Site to Receive Waste." *New York Times,* August 27, 1993.

———. "Nuclear Storage Divides Apaches and Neighbors." *New York Times,* November 11, 1993.

———. "Nuclear Plant Searches for a Place for Its Waste." *New York Times,* March 28, 1994.

Wallace, Amy. "Unlikely Allies Fight Indian Landfill." *Los Angeles Times,* October 28, 1989.

———. "Indians Have a Change of Heart over Dump." *Los Angeles Times,* May 21, 1991.

Wisckol, Martin. "Security Cops Protect Workers on Reservation. *Escondido (Calif.) Times Advocate,* March 20, 1991.

Ybarrondo, Paul. "Fight On to Stop Campo Landfill." *Daily Californian,* February 19, 1994.

GOVERNMENT DOCUMENTS
United States

Hunter, Duncan. "Hunter Says Fight Against Campo Landfill Will Continue." Press release. April 28, 1993.

U.S. Congress, Office of Technology Assessment. *Facing America's Trash: What Next for Municipal Solid Waste.* OTA-0-424. Washington, D.C.: U.S. Government Printing Office, October 1989.

U.S. Department of Health and Human Services, Public Health Service, Agency for Toxic Substances and Disease Registry. "Toxicological Profile for Tetrachlorethylene." ATSDR/TP-88/22. January 1990.

U.S. Department of Interior, *Annual Reports of the Department of Interior for the Fiscal Year Ending June 30, 1905.*

U.S. Department of Interior. "Secretary Babbitt Approves Campo Landfill Lease, Sets Tough Guidelines for New Indian Waste Facility." Press release. April 27, 1993.

U.S. Department of Interior, Bureau of Indian Affairs. "Indian Service Population and Labor Force Estimates." January 1989.

U.S. Department of Interior, Bureau of Indian Affairs, Sacramento Area Office. *Campo Solid Waste Management Project.* Final Environmental Impact Statement. FES 92–29. Vol. 1. November 1992.

U.S. Department of Interior, Bureau of Indian Affairs, Sacramento Area Office. *Campo Solid Waste Management Project, Record of Decision.* FES 92–29. April 27, 1993.

U.S. Department of Interior, Bureau of Indian Affairs, Sacramento Area Office. *Campo Solid Waste Management Project: Comments and Responses.* Final Environmental Impact Statement. FES 92-29. Vol 2. November 1992.

U.S. Department of Interior, Bureau of Indian Affairs, Southern California Agency. "Local Estimates of Resident Indian Population and Labor Force Estimates." January 1991.

U.S. Department of Interior, Bureau of Indian Affairs, Southern California Agency. "Tribal Information Directory." n.d.

U.S. Department of Interior, Office of Indian Affairs, *Annual Report of the Commissioner of Indian Affairs to the Secretary of the Interior for the Year 1875.*

U.S. Environmental Protection Agency. "EPA Policy for the Administration of Environmental Programs on Indian Reservations." William D. Ruckelshaus. November 8, 1984.

———. "Solid Waste Disposal Facility Criteria: Proposed Rule." 53 *Federal Register* (1988): 33,314.

———. *Decision-Makers Guide to Solid Waste Management.* 1989.

———. "Solid Waste Disposal Facility: Final Rule." 56 *Federal Register* (1991): 50,978, 51,049.

———. *Environmental Equity: Reducing Risk for All Communities, Volume 2: Supporting Document.* Washington, D.C.: U.S. Environmental Protection Agency, June 1992.

U.S. Environmental Protection Agency, Region 9. *Public Hearing: Campo/Cottonwood Creek Sole Aquifer Petition.* Transcript of testimony. Pine Valley, California, July 9, 1992.

———. "Comments on the Eagle Mountain Landfill Project Final Environmental Impact Statement." September 8, 1992.

———. "Comments on the Campo Solid Waste Management Project Final Environmental Impact Statement." January 4, 1993.

———. *Sole Source Aquifer Determination: Campo/Cottonwood Creek Aquifer, San Diego County, California,* May 5, 1993.

———. "Campo Band of Mission Indians; Tentative Adequacy Determination of Tribal Municipal Solid Waste Program," April 29, 1994.

———. "U.S. EPA Tentatively Approves Campo Landfill Regulatory Program." Press release, May 2, 1994.

———. "U.S. EPA Proposes Draft Air Permit for Campo Landfill." Press release, May 16, 1994.

———. "EPA Publishes Tentative Approval of Campo Band's Program and Schedules Public Hearing." Factsheet, June 1994.

U.S. General Accounting Office. *Siting of Hazardous Waste Landfills and Their Correlation with Racial and Economic Status of Surrounding Communities.* Washington, D.C.: U.S. General Accounting Office, 1983.

————. *Nuclear Waste: Operation of Monitored Retrievable Storage Facility Is Unlikely by 1998.* Washington, D.C.: U.S. General Accounting Office, 1991.

U.S. Office of the Nuclear Waste Negotiator. "An Invitation for Dialogue and Participation." Boise, Idaho: 1991.

————. "What Is the Office of the Negotiator?" Boise, Idaho: 1993.

U.S. Senate, Select Committee on Indian Affairs. *Workshop on Solid Waste Disposal on Indian Lands.* 102 Cong., 1st Sess. Committee Print. July 29, 1991.

California

California Environmental Protection Agency. "California Environmental Protection Agency Approves Cooperative Agreement with Campo Environmental Protection Agency." Press release, December 10, 1992.

California Integrated Waste Management Board. "Comments on the Campo Solid Waste Management Project Final Environmental Impact Statement," May 4, 1993.

California Legislature. "Governor's Message." *Journal of the Senate.* 2d sess. January 6, 1851.

California Legislature. "Report of the Special Committee to Inquire into the Treaties Made by the United States Indian Commissioners in California." *Journal of the Assembly.* 3d sess. 1852.

California Legislature. "Report of the Special Committee to Inquire into the Treaties Made by the United States Indian Commissioners in California." *Journal of the Senate.* 3d sess. 1852.

California Statutes, Chapter 805 (1991).

Peace, Steve. "Battle Commences to Close Loopholes on Indian Reservations for Garbage and Toxic Wastes." Press release, n.d.

County of San Diego

County of San Diego. "Comments on the Campo Landfill Final EIS." December 24, 1992.

Ernst & Young. "Management Audit of the Solid Waste Division and Financial Review of the Solid Waste Enterprise Fund." Final Report to the County of San Diego, Executive Summary. December 18, 1992.

San Diego County Grand Jury. "Grand Jury Report No. 3, San Diego County's Tra$h Cri$is." May 21, 1993.

City of Chula Vista, California

City of Chula Vista City Council. Minutes. April 5, 1994.

LEGAL MATERIALS
United States Supreme Court Decisions

Bryan v. Itasca County, 426 U.S. 373 (1976).

California v. Cabazon Band of Mission Indians, 480 U.S. 202 (1987).

Cherokee Nation v. Georgia, 30 U.S. (5 Pet.) 1 (1831).

Kleppe v. Sierra Club, 427 U.S. 390 (1976).

New Mexico v. Mescalero Apache Tribe, 462 U.S. 324 (1983).

Fort Gratiot Sanitary Landfill, Inc. v. Michigan Department of Natural Resources, 112 S.Ct. 2019 (1992).

Rice v. Rehner, 463 U.S. 713 (1983).

Robertson v. Methow Valley Citizens Council, 490 U.S. 332 (1989).

United States v. Wheeler, 435 U.S. 313 (1978).

Washington v. Confederated Tribes of Colville Indian Reservation, 447 U.S. 134 (1980).

Worcester v. Georgia, 31 U.S. (6 Pet.) 515, 561 (1832).

Lower Federal Court Decisions

Benda v. Grand Lodge of International Association of Machinists, etc., 584 F.2d 308 (9th Cir. 1978).

Blue Legs v. United States Environmental Protection Agency, 668 F.Supp. 1329 (D.S.D. 1987), aff'd, *Blue Legs v. U.S. Bureau of Indian Affairs*, 867 F.2d 1094 (8th Cir. 1989).

County of San Diego v. Babbitt, Order Denying Plaintiff's Motion for Preliminary Injunction, 93–0986-IEG (LSP) (S.D. Cal. Oct. 15, 1993).

County of San Diego v. Babbitt, Order Granting Motions for Summary Judgment, 93–0986-IEG (LSP) (S.D. Cal. Jan. 27, 1994).

Half Moon Bay Fishermans' Marketing v. Carlucci, 857 F.2d 505 (9th Cir. 1988).

Inland Empire Public Lands Council v. Schultze, 992 F.2d 977 (9th Cir. 1993).

Kelley v. Selin, 93–1646/93–1710/93–3613/93–3749 (6th Cir. Jan. 11, 1995).

Oregon Environmental Council v. Kunzman, 817 F.2d 484 (9th Cir. 1987).

State of Washington, Dept. of Ecology v. United States Environmental Protection Agency, 752 F.2d 1465 (9th Cir. 1985).

United States v. Odessa Union Warehouse Co-op, 833 F.2d 172 (9th Cir. 1987).

INTERVIEWS BY AUTHOR

Angel, Bradley. August 17, 1993.

Brown, Corey. October 19, 1993.

Coe, Arthur L. October 19, 1993.

Connolly, Michael. May 4–5, 1993.

———. June 13, 1993.

———. October 12, 1993.

———. January 7, 1994.

———. February 7, 1994.

———. June 3, 1994.

———. September 6, 1994.

Corona, Rudy. October 20, 1993.

Goldtooth, Tom. September 17, 1993.

———. September 20, 1993.

Grattan, John. October 12, 1993.

———. October 13, 1993.

Haber, Matt. February 22, 1995.

Helliker, Paul. December 8, 1993.

Knapp, Don. September 3, 1993.

Miller, Taylor. December 7, 1993.

Mussler, Robert M. November 23, 1993.

———. February 23, 1995.

O'Haire, Karen. December 8, 1993.

Ortega, Marina. September 16, 1993.

———. October 20, 1993.

Ringer, Steve. February 21, 1995.

———. February 24, 1995.

Shipek, Florence C. June 12, 1993.

Snyder, Stephanie. June 13, 1994.

Swarup, Vishnu. June 23, 1994.

Takashima, David. October 20, 1993.

Taylor, Banning. December 10, 1993.
Tisdale, Donna. May 7, 1993.
———. September 14, 1993.
———. October 9, 1993.
———. January 6, 1994.
———. January 20, 1994.
———. February 7, 1994.
———. June 1, 1994.
Tisdale, Ed. May 7, 1993.
———. January 6, 1994.
Topper, Martin. August 31, 1993.
Townsend, Virgil. December 10, 1993.
Trossman, David. June 13, 1994.
Wulf, Arol. January 6, 1994.
Wiles, Edwin K. December 14, 1993.
Ybarra, Robert. June 6, 1994.

LETTERS

Angel, Bradley. To Assemblyman Steve Peace, June 12, 1991.
Brown, Eddie. To Governor Pete Wilson, May 24, 1991.
Brown, Corey. To California State Senator Robert Presley, Chairman of the Senate Appropriations Committee, August 16, 1990.
Coe, Arthur L. To Assemblywoman Sally Tanner, Chairwoman of the Assembly Environmental and Toxic Materials Committee, February 21, 1991.
Davilo Rodriguez, Gustavo. To Tim Nader, Mayor, City of Chula Vista, California, April 21, 1994.
Goff, Ralph. To Assemblywoman Doris Allen, June 10, 1991.
———. To Assemblywoman Marguarite Archie-Hudson, February 12, 1991.
Gover, Kevin. To California State Senator Alfred Alquist, Senate Appropriations Committee, August 15, 1990.
Gunaji, Narendra N. To J. Arturo Herrera Solis, May 6, 1994.
Haber, Matt, Chief, New Source Section, Air and Toxics Division, U.S. Environmental Protection Agency, Region 9. To John M. Lang, Regional Environmental Manager, Mid-American Waste Systems, Inc., December 6, 1994.
Harris, LaDonna. To Assemblyman Byron Sher, Chairman of the Assembly Committee on Natural Resources, April 25, 1991.
Herrera Solis, J. Arturo. To Narendra Gunaji, March 25, 1994.

Hunter, Duncan. To Tim Nader, Mayor, City of Chula Vista, California, September 13, 1993.

Marcus, Felicia. To Congressman Duncan Hunter, n.d.

Peace, Steve. To Donna Tisdale, January 12, 1990.

———. To Tim Nader, Mayor, City of Chula Vista, California, September 21, 1993.

Ross, Jonathan. To Patrick Kenady, Assistant Attorney General for Legislative Affairs, California Attorney General's Office, August 5, 1991.

Shipek, Florence C. To author, n.d.

Tisdale, Donna. To Jerry Rindone, Member of City Council, City of Chula Vista, California, September 11, 1993.

———. To Tracy Swanborn, Brown, Vence and Associates, November 30, 1993.

Trager, Susan M. To Katherine Saubel, Elder, Los Coyotes Band of Mission Indians, March 11, 1991.

Wiles, Edwin K. To Banning Taylor, Chairman, Los Coyotes Band of Mission Indians, April 29, 1991.

———. To Patrick Hemmy, Area Natural Resources Officer, U.S. Department of Interior, Bureau of Indian Affairs, Sacramento Area Office, July 2, 1991.

Wyland, Jacqueline, Chief, Office of Federal Activities, U.S. Environmental Protection Agency, Region 9. To Secretary of the Federal Energy Regulatory Commission, December 26, 1989.

Zelikson, Jeffrey. To Michael Connolly. June 3, 1993.

MISCELLANEOUS

Angel, Bradley. "The Toxic Threat to Indian Lands." Greenpeace report, June 1991.

Backcountry Against Dumps. "Addendum to Comments on the Campo Landfill Final EIS." December 30, 1992.

———. "Comments Opposing EPA's Tentative Approval of Campo Band's Solid Waste Landfill Regulatory Program." July 28, 1994.

Coalition for Indian Rights. "The Coalition for Indian Rights Speaks Out Against Corporate Exploitation of Tribal Sovereign Rights." Press release, n.d.

Mid-American Waste Systems, Inc. "Annual Report," 1993. Salzman, Jason. "The Clinton Administration Should Cancel the MRS Program." Boulder, Colo.: Greenpeace, n.d.

Skull Valley Band of Goshutes. "Nuclear Natives: The Proposed

Storage of High Level Nuclear Waste on Native American Reservations." N.d.

Skull Valley Band of Goshutes. "Taa-Pai: Phase IIa Report." N.d.

Southwest Research and Information Center. "Monitored Retrievable Storage—Questions and Answers." n.d.

U. S. Environmental Protection Agency. "Campo Municipal Solid Waste Landfill Informational Meeting." Reporter's Transcript of Proceedings, July 1, 1994.

Vezina, Meredith. "One Hundred Years in Campo Country." Master's thesis, San Diego State University, 1989.

Wharton, Donald R. "Implementation of EPA's Indian Policy and Tribal Amendments to Federal Environmental Laws." American Bar Association Conference on Natural Resources Management and Environmental Enforcement on Indian Lands, February 20–21, 1992.

VIDEO AND AUDIO TAPES

Ringe Media, Inc. "Campo: Sharing the Future." Videotape. Purcerville, Virginia, 1991.

State Bar of California, Environmental Law Section. 1993. "The Campo Landfill." Panel Discussion. Environmental Law Institute, October 21–24. Audiocassette, Versa-Tape Company, P.O. Box 40940, Pasadena, CA 91114.

Tisdale, Donna. Videotape of meeting at Boulevard, California, fire station, October 26, 1989.

———. Videotape of meeting at chamber of commerce in Campo, California, January 16, 1990.

World Monitor, June 5, 1991.

INDEX

AB 240. *See* Assembly Bill 240

AB 3477. *See* Assembly Bill 3477

Act for Government and Protection of Indians (1850), 59–61, 100

Agriculture, 90, 91; burning by Indians, 93–94, 99–100; of California Indians, 93–95; Indians considered incapable of, 67, 68, 75; of Kumeyaay, 71, 95–99; practices of Anglo-American settlers, 64, 76, 100–101; taking of land suitable for, 75, 78–80

Air pollution: control of at landfill, 260–61; in EIS comments, 175

Amas de Casa de Playas de Tijuana, 212

Americans for Indian Opportunity, 150–51

Angel, Bradley: on BAD's strategy, 246–47; on Campo enforcement, 36–38; on environmental risks of project, 238, 247, 256; on targeting of Indian lands, 49; on tribal sovereignty, 37, 151

Anglo-American settlers: avoided by Kumeyaay, 96; of Campo, 76–77; on Indians and agriculture, 90–92, 98–100; land practices of, 64, 76, 100–101

Apprenticeship laws, 60–62

Aquifer, 25; EPA determination as sole source, 176–77; and Los

Coyotes reservation, 225–26; transboundary, 210, 212–13

Asbestos, on Cortina reservation, 172–74

Assembly Bill 240: arguments against, 148, 151–52, 154, 155, 157; arguments for, 148–49, 153, 166; progress of, 147–50, 156–59

Assembly Bill 3477, 37; constitutionality of, 144, 157; federal preemption of, 129, 134, 136; jurisdictional issues raised by, 122–23, 140–43; legislative counsel opinion on, 122–23, 136, 138, 139, 144–46, 157; legislative history, 138–39, 143–44, 146; provisions of, 122; supporters of, 136–38

Audubon Society, 136

Babbitt, Bruce, 195–98, 249–52

Backcountry Against Dumps (BAD): citizens' suit, 192, 210, 256; and cooperative agreement, 162, 166; county-tribal agreement, 142; on economic activity on reservation, 111; EIS comments, 175–77; and elected officials, 15–16; landfill customers, approaches to, 214–15; meetings with Interior secretaries, 194–96; Mexican concerns on rail transport, 212–13; Mexican government, approaches to, 210–14;

power of, 110–11, 205–206; environmental education for, 237–39; harm to in delay of project, 200–201; income of, 105, 107–108; motion for summary judgment, 201–203; original territory of, 21; size of, 53; unemployment rate of, 24, 105; unity of, 53–54, 196, 220, 247; uses for landfill income, 106–107
Carlsbad, Calif., 118, 119
Carter, Jimmy, 39
Casinos. *See* Gaming facilities
Cass, Lewis, 58–59
Cattle grazing, 105, 107, 108
Chambers company: access to Los Coyotes reservation, 224, 227; financial condition of, 230–31; Los Coyotes lease, 223–24, 227–29, 234, 236, 237
Chaparosa, Andrew, 228
Chaparral, 95, 100
Chase, Alston, 92–94
Chase, Richard, 226, 228
Cherokees: Georgia's jurisdiction over, 124–25; seizure of land of, 92
Cheyenne River Sioux, 19
Chino, Wendell, 46–49
Chiricahua Apaches, 46
Choctaws, Mississippi, 30
Chula Vista, Calif., 118, 214–16
Churchill, Frank, 79
Cigarette sales on reservation, 130
Cities, as landfill customers, 116–19, 255, 259–60
Citizens Against Ruining Our Environment (C.A.R.E.), 18
Citizen's Clearinghouse for Hazardous Wastes (CCHW), 12–23
Citizens' suits, and permit to operate, 192, 210, 254
Civil jurisdiction on reservations, 128

Clements, Bill, 91
Coalition for Indian Rights, 138, 225, 242–45
Cochise, Silas, 49
Coe, Art, 142–43
Coling, George, 241
Colville Indian Reservation, Washington v. (1980), 130, 134
Commerce Clause, U.S. Constitution, and bans on imported waste, 118
Common School Act (1860), 87
Composting facility, 106
Congress, U.S., legislation on jurisdiction, 155
Connolly, Michael (Misquish), 22–24; on BAD charges against Goff, 262; on BAD's doggedness and tactics, 203, 262–63; on community relations, 110–12, 205–206; cooperative agreements, 141–43; on county court challenge, 201; credibility of, 209, 237, 239; effectiveness in negotiations, 159; meetings with Interior secretaries, 195, 196; on paternalism, 189–92; on Peace legislation, 18, 144; request for EPA technical assistance, 208–209; on scoping meeting, 10–11; on tribal sovereignty, 241–42; on unity of Campos, 220; on waste board comments, 189
Consultants, technical: education of tribe members, 237–38; funded with development fees, 233, 237; lacking in Los Coyotes project, 234
Contingency fund for remedial action, 35–36
Contracts: of Campos with developer, 34–36; Los Coyotes with developer, 223–24, 230; with waste companies, provisions of, 29